Essays in H(
Wole Soyinka at 80

Edited by
Ivor Agyeman-Duah
and Ogochukwu Promise

ayebia

An Adinkra symbol meaning
Ntesie matemasie
A symbol of knowledge and wisdom

This edition first published in 2014
by the Ayebia Clarke Publishing Limited
7 Syringa Walk
Banbury
Oxfordshire
OX16 1FR
UK
www.ayebia.co.uk
ISBN 978-0-9569307-9-8
Distributed outside Africa, Europe and the United Kingdom and exclusively in the USA by
Lynne Rienner Publishers Inc
1800 30th Street, Suite 314
Boulder, CO 80301
USA
www.rienner.com

Distributed in the UK and Europe by TURNAROUND Publisher Services
at www.turnaround-uk.com

British Library Cataloguing-in-Publication Data

Front cover image of Wole Soyinka © Tunde Owolabi at www.tundeowolabistudios.com
Cover Design by Steve Fleming at Workhaus

Typeset by Avocet Typeset, Somerton, Somerset, TA11 6RT
Printed and bound in the UK by CPI Group (UK) Ltd, Croydon, CR0 4YY

Available from www.ayebia.co.uk or email info@ayebia.co.uk
Distributed in Africa, Europe, UK by TURNAROUND at www.turnaround-uk.com
Distributed in Southern Africa by Book Promotions a subsidiary of Jonathan Ball Publishers in
South Africa. For orders contact: orders@bookpro.co.za

Contents

Editors

Ivor Agyeman-Duah: Director of the Centre for Intellectual Renewal in Ghana is an Advisor to The Lumina Foundation in Lagos, Nigeria, Administrators of the Wole Soyinka Prize for Literature in Africa.

Ogochukwu Promise: Founder of The Lumina Foundation, Administrators of the Wole Soyinka Prize for Literature in Africa and its Chief Executive is an award-winning novelist, poet and painter.

Acknowledgements

This anthology is published as part of memorials and events, both in Africa and internationally to mark the eightieth birthday of Nobel Laureate Wole Soyinka. Conceptualised in late 2012, we set a time-frame and targets towards its realisation. We wanted to move away from previous anthologies which focused largely on his literary work. We also wanted to avoid a collection of purely academic or scholarly articles even as we included some intellectually stimulating essays and memoirs so as to produce a kind of snap portrait of the complete artist that Soyinka is. We will like to thank our contributors for their participation in spite of their busy schedule, which includes other assignments or intellectual projects of their own. We also wish to thank other people who assisted some of our contributors. These include the following: Abby Wolf, Kofi Badu, Rene Boatman, Barbara Caldwell and Miranda Strydom. The UK, European, US and North American editions of this volume will be published by Ayebia Clarke Publishing Limited, the African and Caribbean publishing specialists in Oxfordshire. Bookcraft Nigeria will publish the African edition. We have worked in different capacities with Ayebia Clarke Publishing Limited and are grateful that our paths will cross again for this important publication. Our gratitude to Nana Ayebia Clarke and her husband, David and their production team and Chief Executive Bankole Olayebi of Bookcraft Nigeria and his production team.

We are also grateful to David Owusu-Ansah at James Madison University in the US who read part of the manuscript and Sarah O. Apronti of Asempa Publishers, Accra who read the entire manuscript.

Three people who could be counted among Wole Soyinka's very close and reliable friends are the late Femi Johnson, the insurance broker and businessman who loved theatre and opera, Francesca Yetunde Emanuel (Nee

Pereira), the first female Chief Director of Nigeria's civil service and the younger, Yemi Ogunbiyi, a university lecturer and a media executive. If Johnson were alive he would have been invited to make a contribution so we have taken the liberty of re-producing what he wrote about Soyinka as a man to whom "you can give out your heart for safe keeping (if that was possible), go to Hong Kong, come back and still find the heart pulsating." His essay was originally written under the title; "A Man is Either Master of His Trade or Should Quit the World" was part of the anthology edited by Dapo Adelugba in 1987. Yemi Ogunbiyi's contribution is also from the same source and was originally titled; "Toast to Our Own *WS.*" Ogunbiyi is alive but we did not invite him to make a fresh contribution because we wanted to remind readers of Soyinka's earlier career, sometimes forgotten, hence this re-production. The same reason of uniqueness and address of a particular aspect of Soyinka's life explains the reproduction of Maya Jaggi's "Sooner Death than Indignity" first published in *The Guardian* in 2007 for which she holds the copyright. Francesca Yetunde Emanuel's reflection is written for the occasion. The Nobel Laureate Derek Walcott's brief contribution is a Prelude and comes out in part from the 70th birthday of Soyinka organised at Harvard University which one of us attended. The other is part of a protest letter he wrote with others against Soyinka's harassment by the Abacha regime. We will also want to acknowledge the World Bank Group Staff Art Society, Washington, DC for permission to use the essay, "African Art From Past to Present" by the late Ekpo Eyo which was first published in *The African Art: The World Bank Collection* edited by Alexandre Marc in 2007.

Whatever shortfalls you find in this work are ours.

The Editors

Foreword

Wole Soyinka's place in history is secure. He will go down as one of the great literary figures of our time. In one life he has been many things: the academic always ready to resort to direct action to fight unacceptable reality; a patriot who places the highest premium on the moral health of his nation; a Pan Africanist for whom a threat to liberty on the Limpopo is a threat to liberty on the Niger; an unofficial public prosecutor, accusing on behalf of the past, admonishing on behalf of the future. Wole Soyinka's life has been a blessing and a benefaction. Long may it continue on that course.

Soyinka graduated from University at the dawn of independence of most African countries. The return of independence was the fundamental requirement for Africans to swim back into the mainstream of the human current in their own right and not as colonial subjects of sundry European powers. The extensive work of construction, launched in the wake of independence – the building of schools, roads and hospitals – was characteristic of the first decade of independence. These were the projects that began to change the face of Africa.

With remarkably few exceptions, the turn to one-party systems of government in a number of African countries must be regretted. They did not deliver on any of their promises; they made for neither greater national unity nor accelerated economic and social development. In the final analysis the one-party years in the history of the continent will come to be seen as locust years.

As a generation, the founding of the Organisation of African Unity (OAU) in May 1963 was its greatest collective achievement. With the OAU's Liberation Committee, the continent had a mechanism through which to channel assistance to the liberation movements engaged in armed struggle against the settler minority regimes in Zimbabwe and South Africa, as well as the then Portuguese colonies of Mozambique, Angola and Guinea Bissau. The achievement of a non-racial democracy in South Africa in 1994 was therefore much celebrated by the continent and the wider world.

The role of culture in the recovery of African freedom was an important one. It must never be forgotten that Europe had set out on its colonial adventure by promoting the myth that projected Africans as a people who had stagnated culturally while others had made history. The Europe of the Renaissance had been prepared to accept Chinese and Japanese art and culture at their own valuation. The Europe of the age of imperialism saw African culture (especially its arts and crafts) as no more than the work of a primitive race. Many of the anthropologists, dutifully grinding the axe for the colonial powers, reinforced this perception of African art and culture as was evident from the strenuous efforts by the then white minority regime in Rhodesia to deny the African origin of the great Monomatapa ruins in Zimbabwe.

The literary work of Chinua Achebe and Wole Soyinka, for the first time showed conclusively the depth of the African soul as no one before them had done. Nelson Mandela's testimony that with a volume of Chinua Achebe's novels in his hand the prison walls seemed to fall away, points up neatly the role of culture in Africa's liberation.

I am confident that this book edited by two relatively young award-winning African writers, the Ghanaian Ivor Agyeman-Duah and the Nigerian Ogochukwu Promise will help in confirming the respectable place of Africa and the achievements of Africans in our increasingly globalized world.

Chief Emeka Anyaoku,
Lagos, Nigeria.
October 2013.

Introduction

In ancient traditional societies in Africa, mentees in intellectual spheres showed deep affection for the masters at whose feet they acquired knowledge. Knowledge or wisdom in African folklore is a community experience. Wilks (1996)[1] reminds us of the ancient Muslim Dyula communities of what are now Ghana and neighbouring parts of the west coast of Africa where it was a sign of great appreciation to record names of teachers and mentors as the highest form of appreciation. One such salutation dating five hundred years ago in the form of a graduate's diploma or *isnad* (in Islam) reads: "I, Muhammad son of Sulayman Watara, studied Tafsir al-Jilalayn under Ibrahim son of Ali Kamagate, who studied it under Uthman Tarawi."[2] Such appreciation is also exemplified in the repertoire of the griot's art in both Anglophone and Francophone West Africa where praise poetry as an art form makes historical reference to individual achievements, the revered eldership of professions, community transitions and other epochal events.

Festschrifts or anthological essays in honour of these 'ancient' people whether orally or otherwise, is not new. But we also know that even with this there were, and remain variations in recognizing individual attainments in the art of writing and in literature. We can thus distinguish between the good and the great. In the parlance of a Nigerian theatre lover and businessman: "a man is either a master of his trade or he should quit the world." These words of the late Femi Johnson, the beloved friend of Nobel Laureate, Wole Soyinka, "a large presence in the 'extra-curricular' undertakings of [Wole's] adult existence," summarises what this anthology seeks to do.

Long before he became the first African to win the Nobel Prize for Literature in 1986, he was already a 'thorn in the side' of an oppressive Nigerian political establishment, with his daring critiques of its behaviour towards its

1

citizens as Nigeria and Africa evolved from colonial rule to postcolonial statehood. Soyinka has a diverse and interesting character, which makes him amenable to playing several different roles within society. He is an individual with creative ability in all genres of literature; an actor whose presence dominates a room, a university lecturer, a cultural activist with a notion of an egalitarian sense of life, a collector of art works – especially sculpture, painting and pottery. He is also a musician, a shadow architect who designed his own house, a global traveller, a man with a trademark tunic shirt and able to design his own outfits (if need be), a hunter by night and above all, a wine connoisseur (a certified *Commanderie de la Dive Bouteille* of the Republic of France) who once in 1992, drove through the vineyards of Sienna in the Chianti country-side of Italy in anticipation of a theatre and wine festival for which he had specially written a production, *From Zia with Love*.

This is not the first collection of essays in his honour and will probably not be the last. But this is done to celebrate the longevity and quality of his great output that have been the focus of all these accolades and epithets of his personality.

Another reason is a general salutation to Soyinka's generation as the corpus of their major works is almost a cycle and their physical mortality sometimes create anxiety. It was during the preparation of this anthology in March 2013 that Chinua Achebe passed away as a reminder that we are all mortal. At that time, Soyinka and J. P. Clark stood up for the freedom of the individual and the liberty of African writers. The obituary from the two who (with Achebe) were founders of modern Nigerian literature states:

> Of the pioneer quartet of contemporary Nigerian literature, two voices were silenced-one of the poet Christopher Okigbo and now, the novelist Chinua Achebe. It is perhaps difficult for outsiders of that intimate circle to appreciate this sense of depletion, but we take consolation in the young generation of writers to whom the baton has been passed, those who have already creatively ensured that there is no break in the continuum of the literary vocation...[3]

Faith in the present is indeed reciprocal; for the present were influenced by past generations. Chimamanda Ngozi Adichie, Sefi Atta, Ogochukwu Promise, Nnedi Okorafor, Wale Okediran from Nigeria; Amma Darko, Taiye Selasi and Benjamin Kwakye from Ghana; Monica Arac de Nyeko from Uganda; Nadifa Mohamed from Somalia; Tsitsi Dangarembga and Elizabeth Zandile Tshele with the pen name of NoViolet Bulawayo from Zimbabwe; Sifiso Mzobe and Bridget Pitt from South Africa and Leila Aboulela, half-Egyptian, half-Sudanese constitute a formidable representation that can each point to one or two of Soyinka's generation as a mentor or inspiration for their own writings.

The third reason is Soyinka's attempt at improving humanity universally. The "battlefield" is familiarly Africa but he has fought for the oppressed in the Middle East, in Southeast Asia and in many other parts of the world. Such universality is also reflected in Soyinka's travels globally and in his major body of works – which have been inspired by classical Greek, English and French influences and also by his days at The Royal Court in London. His work has been translated into major languages including Swedish, culminating in the award of the Nobel Prize for Literature.

Critical studies on Soyinka include: *Wole Soyinka* (1971) by Gerald Moore; *Critical Perspectives on Wole Soyinka* (1980) by James Gibbs (editor); *Before Our Very Eyes (1987)*, edited by his long-time friend and former colleague at the Theatre Arts Department of the University of Ibadan Dapo Adelugba; *Who's Afraid of Soyinka?* (1991), and *Wole Soyinka: An Appraisal* (1994) by Adewale Maja-Pearce; *Perspectives on Wole Soyinka: Freedom and Complexity* (2001); *Conversations With Wole Soyinka* (2001) by Biodun Jeyifo; *Wole Soyinka: A Life in Full* (2004) by Bankole Olayebi; *Achebe or Soyinka: A Study in Contrasts* (2009), by Kole Omotoso and others. They show the depth and breadth of his works and the interest this has generated especially among scholars. Some of the essays (if not a large number) delve into Soyinka's own re-interpretation and revision of Yoruba primary sources and philosophies, literary histories in the context of his works. Some people have found it difficult to understand and appreciate portions of this corpus and Soyinka himself often disagrees with interpretations of his work.

The strategy adopted in this volume is to focus on essays from colleagues, public policy makers, leaders, friends, former students and mentees. It is divided into six sections and starts appropriately with Literature, the area through which Soyinka emerged onto the world stage.

The first essay is by Ngũgĩ wa Thiong'o, Soyinka's contemporary and a member of the fraternity that believed they had the capacity to change the course of African history in the 1960s and 70s. Ngugi is a Pan Africanist interested in African language preservation and Soyinka challenged the Negritude Movement led by Leopold Sedar Senghor with his statement that "a tiger does not proclaim its tigritude, it pounces." Both Soyinka and Ngugi have shared honours on Ngugi's return to the University of Leeds in 2004 when he was awarded an honorary doctorate degree when The Wole Soyinka Chair of Drama was inaugurated.

Ngugi's essay is followed by Nadine Gordimer who uses her art to address inequality particularly under Apartheid. Her novel *None to Accompany Me* (1994) expresses concerns with social dislocation in a post-apartheid South Africa… She shares her activism stance alongside Soyinka's but perhaps in a less dramatic form of art for life which was reflected in the award to her of the Nobel Prize for Literature in 1991.

The other contributor in this section represents the younger generation. Sefi Atta is perhaps most remembered for her novel *Everything Good Will Come* not because it won the first Wole Soyinka Prize for Literature in Africa but because it was a marvellous read and further deepened the observation made by Soyinka [later in this collection] that what women writers of the earlier generation suffered from most was suppression of their creative abilities.

Most revealing of Soyinka as a subject of international diplomatic exchanges is Margaret Busby's, "Fragments from a Chest of Memories" and the disclosure that the then British Prime Minister Harold Wilson having to persuade Soyinka to accept the Jock Campbell award of the *New Statesman* through President Yakubu Gowon who had imprisoned him during the Biafra War in 1969. Gowon writes to the Prime Minister ... "His (Soyinka's) detention has nothing whatsoever to do with his literary attributes and he knows it".

A review of Soyinka's work by a former British High Commissioner now the European Union's most senior diplomat for Africa, Nicholas Westcott, has a hidden irony reminiscent of Westcott's predecessor of decades ago, the British District Officer Simon Pilkings in *Death and the King's Horseman*, who has to intervene in the affairs of Nigeria and Africa.

Toni Morrison's contribution ends the first section. She and Soyinka have many things in common: forceful personalities, iconic trademark grey hairs which makes them stand out, published historical memoirs, *Beloved* (a slave narrative fiction; influenced by her growing up in rural Ohio) and *Ake* (a colonial setting of a futuristic Ogun State). Both works are recognized to be among the most read works in literature. Soyinka became the first African to win the Nobel in Literature in 1986 and Morrison the first African American to do so in 1993. Her contribution here and elsewhere is concerned with the tribulations of people and nations and reminds us more than ever of the universality of the arts and a common mission.

Section Two begins with Ama Ata Aidoo's reflections on *Death and the King's Horseman*, (the first of three essays on this play) with intriguing perspectives that marks Soyinka's accomplishments as a playwright. As only she who knows, Aidoo deciphers the nuances of complicated plots of religious and political beliefs and associated rituals for chiefs and kings; the belief in life hereafter common among many African societies (hence the familiarity of the play). Her interpretations are aided by her own Fanti (Akan) background and because she is the daughter of a chief from the coastal region of Ghana. Interestingly Aidoo's *The Dilemma of a Ghost* shares a template with this play of the inevitable contestation of African domestic socio-cultural values and

Euro-American attitudes and regulations of Africa in transition. Parallels can be drawn between the plays in the tensions in marriage in Aidoo's and the obligatory suicide of the king's horseman in Soyinka's which a British colonial administrator equated with a state crime.

The work of literary critics and reviewers often offer insights into the nuances of the setting and the cultural matrix that writers unconsciously conceal in their craft. Soyinka has on the whole had some very useful critics, such as colleagues of his with an understanding of the Yoruba universe that is found in his works. Others, like Adewale Maja-Pearce with *A Peculiar Tragedy* (2010), a critical biography of J.P. Clark have written with a view to sowing discord among Soyinka and some of his colleagues from whatever past disagreements he had had with fellow writers like Clark and Achebe. While these conflicts have been resolved, Maja-Pearce treats them as if they are present concerns.

Henry Louis Gates Jr. is an African American literary scholar of enormous influence and Director of the W. E. B. Du Bois Institute for African and African American Research at Harvard where he has built one of the most respectable institutions in the world. Soyinka supervised Gates' PhD work at Cambridge University where they first met. Gates' resultant work there, *The Signifying Monkey* is heavily informed by Yoruba traditions as seen in his contribution to this collection: "Being, the Will and the Semantics of Death: Wole Soyinka's *Death and the King's Horseman*," the second of the three reflections of Soyinka's play.

Ato Quayson was for several years a Fellow in English at Pembroke College, Cambridge University and a respected scholar in Commonwealth and Postcolonial Studies currently at the University of Toronto. Quayson's work, *Strategic Transformations in Nigerian Writing* (1997) like the one in this collection, " All of the People, Some of the Time… :" The Ethics of Choice in a Soyinkan Action is a reflection on *Death and the King's Horseman*.

Section Three is a direct conversation with Soyinka and explains in part the ultimate award of the Nobel Prize. Though many have written about the contributing factors of that choice, there are new insights here. "A Dramatic Stage in a Dramatist's Life" by Cameron Duodu is a literary history of West Africa in the 1960s and a description of betrayal in adversity when Soyinka was in jail in 1967. Some of his compatriots [writers] based in Accra had sought to justify his incarceration through commentaries in *The Legon Observer*, one of which led to Duodu's rejoinder, "The Literary Critic and Social Reality." The third strand in Duodu's contribution is a conversation with Soyinka weeks after he was awarded the Nobel Prize. He had been touted as a winner several times to no avail but this particular time it was real.

"A Master of His Trade" is a conversation in 1994 with Kwame Anthony

Appiah, the former Princeton University professor and influential philosopher who became friends with Soyinka and Gates at Cambridge University. The ambition to revive the *Transition* magazine as well as complete the *Encyclopaedia Africana* that W.E.B. Du Bois started in Ghana was broached in Cambridge. Appiah has written extensively on Soyinka and conducted interviews with him. They were also together at the Du Bois Institute at Harvard, when Soyinka sought sanctuary from the dictatorship of the Abacha regime in the mid 1990s. Appiah explains what is unique about Soyinka and what went into his selection for the Nobel Prize at a time when it was obvious that there were three candidates from Africa including the late Chinua Achebe and Ngũgĩ wa Thiong'o. Appiah also reflects on that generation and the one that followed particularly focusing on the Nigerian novelist and poet, Ben Okri.

The third part of the conversation with Appiah centres on a major Soyinka interest: slavery. His views go beyond the tragedy of the Trans-Atlantic Slave Trade to issues of evolutionary black identities in the Americas centuries on. The contributions of blacks in the United States to their economy – from the plantations of the Carolinas to the present day as well as in the sphere of socio-cultural enterprise such as the music of Jazz and the import of the writings of Toni Morrison including concepts of Afrocentricism and what it should mean to us all.

Those who know Soyinka also know that he speaks his mind openly and fearlessly to the point of sometimes antagonising others. One such confrontation was with the Kenyan political scientist, Ali Mazrui. It followed the broadcast to global audiences of the latter's television series, *The Africans: A Triple Heritage*. Soyinka found certain aspects of the Series a disservice to the African heritage but in defence of Arabic and Islamic cultures, Mazrui disputed this and had strong exchanges with Soyinka in the revived *Transition*. In San Francisco, US in 1996, there was a conversation with Mazrui about that and his views on African writers in the 1960s and 70s. The cultivated disagreement between the two however seems to have started in their relatively youthful careers in the 1970s. Mazrui in a review of *The Man Died: Prisons Notes of Wole Soyinka* described it as "irrational and … written in anger." It is difficult to be categorical if this was the genesis of it but over the years such mutual criticisms were read until it reached a peak with the TV Series.

The chapter that follows Maya Jaggi's contribution is the making of a documentary film initiated by Wole Soyinka. It took the production team to the Upper East region of Ghana where we were interested in the effects of the Trans-Saharan Slave Trade and how the slaves were transported from there to Mali and parts of the Middle East including Iraq and Saudi Arabia. When this documentary is completed it will be interesting to see if critics and reviewers would do a comparative analysis of it and Mazrui's *The Africans: A Triple*

Heritage. Soyinka, in the third part of this same chapter discusses the expectations of his generation of writers, their disappointments and their leadership deficits.

'Niyi Coker Jr. got his *isnad* studying with Soyinka as a sorcerer's apprentice. As the young always grow, he pays homage by reflection in revered and humorous candour to the master.

Esi Sutherland-Addy and her sister, Amowi Sutherland Phillips saw Soyinka come to see their mother, Efua Sutherland, a Ghanaian playwright and distinguished cultural activist when they were 'little' girls. At that time, Soyinka was a Fellow at the Institute of African Studies at the University of Ghana. He had come out of prison (having been arrested in the precipitous moments just before the Biafra War broke out). Efua Sutherland and Soyinka discussed a lot of issues in the spiralling estate of the Sutherlands in what was probably a forest enclave at the time but now an upper-class setting in Accra. The architectural concept of their home is similar to Soyinka's hidden house in the rocky forest of Abeokuta. The two sisters bring memories of the 1970s.

Section Four opens with what the museum's function should be in a rapidly changing world. The joint essay by two leading curators and eminent museum administrators; Zagba Oyortey and Malcolm McLeod bring to bear their international experiences. Two important variants of Soyinka's artistic personality, art and music follow. Ekpo Eyo, the Nigerian art historian and former Director of its National Commission for Museums and Monuments and John Collins, the British musicologist, guitarist, percussionist and university professor whose fraternity with West African musicians in the1960s led to his biographies of some of the leading musicians at the time including, Fela Anikulapo-Kuti (Soyinka's cousin), and discuss ancient and particularly contemporary trends.

John Maynard Keynes may as well be one of the twentieth century's famous economists but his contribution to the arts goes beyond his support for literary luminaries of the Bloomsbury Group of writers such as Virginia Woolf, E. M. Forster and to strategic investments as his chairmanship of the Committee for the Encouragement of Music and the Arts later called, the Arts Council of England. James D. Wolfensohn his kindred and an investment banker decades after would become the President of the World Bank. He was chairman of Carnegie Hall and the Kennedy Center in Washington, DC. He used his skills to develop these artistic sectors to the admiration of many. But an individual who made her office at the World Bank (as its Managing Director) look like an African museum with West African sculpture and painting collections from the staircase to the boardroom was the Nigerian, Ngozi Okonjo-Iweala. There are also impressive art galleries operated by economists and stockbrokers emerging in many of Africa's capital cities.

Ekpo Eyo's contribution "African Art from Past to Present" details African art and other commodity trading with finance people and businessmen from Phoenicia and Greece who collaborated with African artists centuries before the European experience. And if you enjoy classical music and artistic display of orchestras at leisure at the Kennedy Center or in Pretoria, Harare or Kampala, Collins' contribution of music as a protest tool and a scale for political judgement is another experience. It is made at The Kalakuta Republic in Lagos where Fela was the fearless Afrobeat king of the 1970s. Fela's influence close to two decades after his death has evolved in the new musical forms of Afrobeats of West African sojourners in London, Niger Beat in Nigeria and HipLife in Ghana and the accompanying Azonto dance as well as in fashion. There is a certain level of extended family musicality for Soyinka himself could have been a musician, his famous record, *Unlimited Liability Company* was as popular on radio play time because of its political protestation as Fela's *Zombie*.

Section Five presents Poetry for The Threshold which is intergenerational and mostly for occasions. "Telephone Conversation," "Abiku," and "Live Burial" are famous Soyinka poems but collections such as, *A Shuttle in the Crypt* (1972); *Mandela's Earth and Other Poems* (1988) and his editorship of *Poems of Black Africa* (1975) have extensively projected Anglophone and Francophone African writing. The collection starts with Soyinka's career remembrance by Abena Busia. Atukwei Okai's peculiarly created title *"A Tomboucktouyan Anti-Palaquinity"* which follows a poetic monologue as Soyinka's mother, a long ago resident of the other world watches the exploits of her son and advises him not to hurry to join them because there is much work to be done in Nigeria and Africa. Aderonke Adesola Adesanya and Toyin Falola's epic "The Lion and The Jewel" of "Ogun Abibiman" Literature is a review of the major works of Soyinka from two historians, one of art and the other social and economics with their specialisms very much in evidence. Falola's award-winning memoirs, *A Mouth Sweeter than Salt* may not have the literary intensity of *Ake: The Years of Childhood* or *Ibadan: The Penkelemes Years* and parallel to them in purpose but, they share a common social history of location and geography if even at different times. There is also the poetry of the relatively younger, Ogochukwu Promise who abandons her painting canvas, laptop, sculpture materials and follows Soyinka the hunter into the bush in search of game. There are dangers in hunting at midnight but he is risk adverse and initiated her into the ways and by-ways of it. The last poem is one of true friendship and trust. Francesca Yetunde Emanuel is respected in Nigeria as one of its best public policy experts but she is a creative person and a polyglot whose tribute is a single poetic word: "Legacy."

Leadership, fundamental freedoms of expression and association and their growth in Africa has been a nauseating experience in the larger part of

Soyinka's life. The essays in this last Section are from leaders who admire him and reflect on their varying experiences, expectations and notions of power.

It begins with traditional leadership, the type that Soyinka has shown respect for in some of his major plays. The king of the ancient kingdom of Asante, Ghana, Osei Tutu II writes of what partnerships traditional authorities should forge with elected leaders having himself successfully completed a similar development project with a former President of the World Bank, James Wolfensohn. He casts his mind further afield into Asia to draw on similar lessons and provide evidence of partnerships as a growth model.

This is followed by the thoughts of a sitting president, the President of the Republic of Ghana, John Dramani Mahama, who has been in office since January 2013. In his mid 50s, he had previously served as Vice-President during which period he published his first book, a memoir titled *My First Coup D' Etat*. Mahama has acknowledged the joys of growing up in secondary school reading Soyinka's *The Jero Plays* and lessons of unpleasant truths the author forces us to confront, likening it to a reflection in the mirror. With a literary tendency that connotes an understated combination of public service and writing, perhaps with the imitable aspirations of the Senghors' of earlier times, we were delighted when he agreed to contribute.

The collection appropriately ends with a forecast by Thabo Mbeki, the god-father of post-independent African renaissance construction; a philosopher-king who has devoted his life to South African politics and by extension to Africa's progress. His leadership as Nelson Mandela's Deputy and later as President of Africa's biggest economy, was important not least as one of the architects of the New Partnership for Africa's Development (NEPAD) but as its champion on how intellectual development could push for growth. He has personally paid back to the continent with time and resources, with devotion and understanding, his dues: the resolution of conflicts, including in Ivory Coast and Sudan even after his retirement from formal office. His work in this capacity has attracted some criticism from some quarters. In this last chapter, "Africa's Renaissance and the New Partnership for Development," he outlines what should be done by Africa to claim the twenty-first century, a rhetorical question first posed through a World Bank Report in 2000. An optimist of Africa's bright future, Mbeki thinks that this future would have NEPAD as one of its drivers. He writes, "I am convinced that one of the greatest achievements of the African Continent and its organisation, the OAU and the AU, during the first decade of the 21st century was the acceptance of NEPAD and its partner, the African Peer Review Mechanism, the APRM by the rest of the world..."

There may well be some truth in this with the evidence he gives and the fact that even Soyinka, wary and sometimes doubtful, seems to partly agree

9

(see the chapter, "There is Always Somewhere We Call Home"). His view: "Yes, you can see structures like… not so much the NEPAD as the APRM within the new African Union which is based on the fact that within the leadership there is something seriously wrong…"

Soyinka sees NEPAD and APRM as good instruments of governance created by the African leadership but also explains that when critics like him raised issues of democratic deficiencies, they were not mere criticisms of speaking to power but the absence of such instruments.

Africa is changing and as is the rest of the world. Literary dynamics and production are therefore affected as a result of trade, economic and political policies. Africa's twenty-first century relationship goes beyond the traditional European frontier to include Asia, particularly East Asia with a million Chinese already living in Africa, with the China-Africa Forum, Korea-Africa Trade, Japan's Tokyo International Conference on African Development and together the formation of the Trilateral Policy Consultation on Foreign Policy towards Africa.

Some countries in the Middle East are interested in reviving the ancient trade from Persia of silk products to ornaments of adoration and fashion; establishment of petroleum businesses and commodity trade. Israel has re-established ties with over 40 countries by 2012 (more than before the Yom Kippur war in 1973) and preceded this with its Foreign Minister, Avigdor Lieberman's historic visit to Ethiopia, Kenya, Nigeria, Ghana and Uganda in 2009, some 30 years after a break in diplomatic ties.

The continent's most constructive engagement with South America in its trade, technical assistance, grants and other bilateral agreements is with Brazil, Liberia, Rwanda and Ghana. Others are beneficiaries of technical assistance in housing infrastructure, teaching hospitals and agriculture. With the biggest black population outside of Africa, this engagement with Brazil is unprecedented. Nigeria's first major economic reforms after independence– management of public resources, macroeconomic stability and transparency in fiscal operations under Ngozi Okonjo-Iweala in the early 2000s was partly modelled on Brazil's experience and not, as hitherto on an European model.

Africa's relations with the Caribbean and Pacific countries may not be in very strategic terms economically but certainly of solidarity – common positions on issues of trade, markets and tariffs with the European Union, the World Trade Organisation and multilateral bodies through the fulcrum of the African Caribbean and Pacific Organisation; cultural history is however the most visible in any talk of affinity.

Into the second decade of the century, the interest in Africa has also been engineered by more discoveries of hydro-carbons, enlarging markets, improved technology and telecommunication, leadership in business, middle-class expansion and a reforming political class. The future of the continent would be measured as much by an orderly and agreed to political process as the management of its natural resources – always the source of attraction and in the case of Israel as a trade market for arms and other security infrastructure. The gate-keeping process which will ensure realisation of equitable progress will include, the vigilantism of its writers, novelists, playwrights and poets of the present and the future as their elders did in the past.

It is only in this way that the fortune of Africa would be grander "than the sum of her politics-even of the most progressive tenor."

Ivor Agyeman-Duah
Accra, Ghana.

Between *Ake, Isara* and *Ibadan*: The Penkelemes Years

Ogochukwu Promise

Born on July 13 1934 in Ake in Ogun State, Nigeria, the second of six children to a headmaster of an Anglican primary school, Samuel Ayodele Soyinka and a mother trader and shop owner, Grace Eniola Soyinka, Wole Soyinka's parents were respectively nick-named, "Essay" and "Wild Christian" by their children. The mother was from a distinguished "resistance" family of the Ransome-Kutis' to which the Afrobeat musician, the late Fela Kuti and Human Rights campaigner, Beko Ransome-Kuti (Soyinka's cousin) belonged; a family well-known for opposing both colonial and dictatorial governments from the 1930s.

Soyinka attended the St. Peter's Primary School of his father's in Abeokuta from 1940 and as a ten year old in 1943 acted "The Magician" in the school's operetta. He continued at Abeokuta Grammar School where he was a prodigious collector of literary prizes. Young Soyinka ended up at the elite colonial Government College in Ibadan and enrolled at the University College of Ibadan, then affiliated to the University of London from 1952–54. He however, continued and completed at the University of Leeds studying English Literature (between 1954–57) under the influence of one of the masters at the time, Wilson Knight.

Just before he completed university studies, he started writing and directing plays including for BBC Radio. He returned to Nigeria in 1960 to research on West African drama on a Rockefeller Foundation grant, by which time two of his major plays had been written, *The Swamp Dwellers* in 1958 and *The Lion and the Jewel* in 1959. The beginnings of his theatrical innovation at The Royal Court in London was also on course. It would be the same year that he would establish *The 1960 Masks* and *The Orisun Theatre* groups. Concurrently between 1960–70, he taught and was Chair of the Cathedral of Drama at the University of Ibadan and also engaged in politics, challenging political leadership and sometimes acting as a mediator of dissension. He was arrested just before the outbreak of the Nigeria – Biafra Civil War in 1967 and would be imprisoned for months in solitary confinement on the orders of the Government. The result was the publication, *The Man Died: Prison Notes of Wole Soyinka* and a collection of poems. On release, he went to Accra, Ghana as Guest Lecturer at the Institute of African Studies, University of Ghana, Legon from where he also edited the *Transition* magazine and resigned from the University of Ibadan into voluntary exile in 1971.

From 1975 to 1999, he intermittently worked in Nigeria and abroad including as a Professor of Comparative Literature at the Obafemi Awolowo University, then called the University of Ife. These had been preceded by major works. *A Dance of the Forests* had been written and *The Road* seen at the Theatre Royal, Stratford in 1965 as had *Kongi's Harvest, Camwood on the Leaves, Madmen and Specialists* and the *Jero* plays been performed or published. His interpretation of *The Bacchae of Euripides* had also been commissioned by the National Theatre in London in 1973. As his maturity became meteoric so did his global recognition that had begun earlier with his winning of an Arts Council of England John Whiting Award in 1966/7; and he was an Overseas Fellow at Churchill College, Cambridge between 1973 and 1974. He would write his most famous play, *Death and King's the Horseman* whilst at Cambridge.

By the time he won the Nobel Prize in Literature in 1986 and became the first African to do so, he was already a master playwright, director, poet, novelist and distinguished university professor. That same year, he was awarded the Agip Prize for the Humanities, received an Honorary Membership of the American Academy and Institute of Arts and Letters but before then, an Anisfied-Wolf Book award in the US. Nigeria's national honour, Commander of the Federal Republic was bestowed as well as a Fellowship of the Society for the Humanities at Cornell University. He had been a professor of African Studies and Theatre (at Cornell) whilst also serving as President of The International Theatre Institute in Paris. The Pan African Writers Association with its Secretariat in Accra would name its forecourt, Wole Soyinka and Naguib Mahfouz Court. More honours would follow – Commander Order of Merit by the Italian Government and the George Benson Medal of the Royal Society for Literature respectively. UNESCO would appoint him Ambassador for the Promotion of African Culture, Human Rights and Freedom of Expression and Harvard University would present him with an honorary doctorate degree three years after.

In 1993, he would go into exile in the United States after escaping from Nigeria where the dictator, Sani Abacha put a price on his head, dead or alive! Soyinka spent the exile years first as a Fellow of the W.E.B. Du Bois Institute for African and African American Research at Harvard University from 1994 later joining the Faculty at Emory University in Atlanta as a Robert W. Woodruff Professor of the Arts. He returned to Nigeria in 1998. It would be in 2004 when his old University of Leeds would establish The Wole Soyinka Chair in Drama. He was also presented with the Obafemi Awolowo Leadership in Nigeria and other chieftaincy titles.

Soyinka was appointed the First Elias Ghanem Chair in Creative Writing at the University of Nevada in Las Vegas to serve as Director of Literary Arts, International Institute of Modern Letters in 2002 and also the President's Marymount Institute Professor-in-Residence at Loyola Marymount University, Los Angeles. He divides his time between California, Lagos and Abeokuta from which stations he also honours his international engagements around the world.

Apart from being a BBC World Service Reith Lecturer, he was also a Visiting Fellow, Writer and Guest Lecturer at Yale, Oxford, University of London and universities across Europe, the Americas, Asia, the Middle East and the Caribbean.

By the middle of 2000, he had published over 30 titles in all genres of literature including the following:

NON-FICTION
The Man Died: Prison Notes of Wole Soyinka
Ake: The Years of Childhood
The Open Sore of a Continent: A Personal Narrative of the Nigerian Crisis
The Burden of Memory: the Muse of Forgiveness
Myth, Literature and the African World
Art, Dialogue and Outrage
Isara: A Voyage Around Essay
Ibadan: The Penkelemes Years
Climate of Fear
Interventions (Series)
You Must Set Forth at Dawn
Harmattan Haze On An African Spring

NOVELS
The Interpreters
Season of Anomy

DRAMA
The Swamp Dwellers
The Lion and the Jewel
The Trials of Brother Jero
Jero's Metamorphosis

A Dance of the Forests
Kongi's Harvest
Madmen and Specialists
The Strong Breed
The Road
Death and the King's Horseman
The Bacchae of Euripides
Opera Wonyosi
A Play of Giants
Requiem for a Futurologist
The Beatification of Area Boy: A Lagosian Kaleidoscope
From Zia with Love
King Baabu

POETRY

Idanre and Other Poems
Poems from Prison
A Shuttle in the Crypt
Ogun Abibiman
Mandela's Earth and Other Poems
Samarkand and Other Markets I Have Known

These works have not only reflected on internal stages of Nigeria's over half a century journey of nationhood – the politics of dispute, military interventions and resultant deaths and social disaffection, but non equitable wealth creation and distribution. Environmental hazards have been experienced in the Niger Delta and victims who had justifiably resisted destruction of these natural gifts were made martyrs as prophetically dealt with in *The Swamp Dwellers*. Many of these works are popular because they are familiar with the constraints and characteristics of the continent's diverse cultures and situations. But it has not been totally ugly portraits. Africa has been defended and her civilisations projected too as he recently did in *Harmattan Haze On An African Spring*.

Henry Louis Gates Jr. one of the contributors to this collection has rightly said in another context – a *New York Times* review that, "If the spirit of African democracy has a voice and a face, they belong to Wole Soyinka."

As his journey into the 80s begins, may this spirit be a guiding angel as The Lumina Foundation established as a road-map for literary excellence and enlightenment walks on the dignified path he has shown and into a century in which so much is expected of Africans and Africa.

Lagos, Nigeria.

Section I

Salutatory Musings
for the Master's Taste

Chapter One
The Conscience of Africa
Ngũgĩ wa Thiong'o

Even before his arrival at the now famous 1962 Conference of Writers of English Expression held at Makerere University in Kampala, Uganda, his fame as a guitar-playing poet and playwright and member of the nascent *Mbari* Writers club had preceded him through the oral narratives of Gerald Moore – one of the organizers of the conference. Gerald Moore was then Director of the Extramural Department at Makerere and also a friend of Ulli Beier, with whom he would a year later put together *The Penguin Book of Modern African Poetry,* which would include works by all Nigerian poets at the conference: J. P. Clark and Christopher Okigbo. There were other writers, the late Chinua Achebe, for instance and a large contingent of South African writers in exile among them Es'kia Mphahlele, Lewis Nkosi and Bloke Modisane. While I don't recall a single of Soyinka's text dominating the conference the way Achebe's text *Things Fall Apart* did; or his remarks sparking fire the way Okigbo's quip that he wrote his poetry for poets did, he was a big presence at the Conference.

For example, he had already written and published a considerable body of work including the plays, *The Swamp Dwellers, A Dance of the Forests* and *The Lion and the Jewel*. He had shown the literary versatility and output that later in 1986 would earn him the Nobel Prize in Literature. But at the conference he was just a writer among other writers whose sensibilities were shaped by their experience of colonialism, apartheid and anti-colonial nationalism. These writers were also united by a vision of the possibilities of a different future for Africa. Ever the realist, Soyinka had already punched holes in any starry-eyed vision of the future with his play, *A Dance of the Forests* and elsewhere, he had coined the cautionary line, "a tiger does not pronounce its tigritude, it pounces," in response to tendencies in some Negritude poetry to typify the African past as glorious and conflict-free. Because of the stories preceding him,

I expected him to stand up and recite "Telephone Conversation," the poem that Gerald Moore would always talk about, or play the guitar the way Moore had described it. He did neither. But I did see him once at a Top Life Nightclub, the most famous nightspot in Kampala at the time, dancing cha cha cha, and even some of the other dancing pairs paused to enjoy his moves.

I was then a second year student of English at Makerere, author of a few short stories published locally. Having never set foot on any lands beyond Kenya and Uganda, to me, the Soyinka world of Ibadan, Leeds and the Royal Court in London, sounded far away. If we had never met again, I would have still carried the image of a dancing Soyinka on the floor, an image of the exuberant life that was Makerere and Kampala, a life of creative tolerance and acceptance of difference that a few years later would be shattered by the rise of Idi Amin.

But our paths would cross again and again, at conferences mainly, in the real places of Africa, Europe, America, but also in symbolic spaces of prison and exile. Even at the time of the Makerere encounter, though without my knowing it, we had already met, well, in history. In London 1959, he took a stand on the Hola Camp Massacre in Kenya at which eleven members of the Mau Mau liberation movement were bludgeoned to death under the supervision of British officers; my cousin, Gicini Ngugi, one of the Mau Mau hardcores, as those who refused to cooperate were called, was in Hola at the time, and my brother was in a similar concentration camp in Manyani. In his Nobel lecture years later, Wole Soyinka referred to the massacre, or the little matter of eleven men dead. But the little matter was a turning point in the Kenyan anti-colonial struggle. The whole world now knew. At the event at the Royal Court Theatre, the empire was on trial. Thus the writer at Makerere was already part of the Kenyan anti-colonial struggle.

Our next encounter after Makerere was in 1967 at the Afro-Scandinavian Writers Conference held in Uppsala, Sweden, organized by Per Wastberg. Dan Jacobson, Wole Soyinka and I were supposed to present our memories of childhood. For some reason, I could not find anything really to say about my childhood and I presented an excerpt from my novel *A Grain of Wheat*, in progress at the time. But Jacobson and Soyinka did: what would later become *Ake* that may well have been born at Uppsala. It was not Soyinka's memories of childhood that dominated the conference but rather the question of the gun and the pen in social struggle, triggered by the now well-known 1964 incident in which Soyinka allegedly held a radio station at gun point to substitute Akintola's official victory address with Soyinka's own critical statement.

His brief arrest was forerunner of things to come with his eventual imprisonment for striving for peace in a conflict that would plunge Nigeria into a civil war over the Biafran secession, an experience which led to his prison memoir, *The Man Died*. The book came out in 1972, but little did I then know that *The Man Died* would visit me in Kenya Kamiti Maximum Security prison, five years later. I was put in Kamiti Maximum for my activities with the Kamirithu Community Theatre, principally because of my play *I Will Marry When I Want*, co-authored with Ngũgĩ wa Mĩriĩ. I joined a group of political prisoners already there but we lived in solitary confinement, one man one cell. We were not allowed pen and paper and certainly no books except the Bible and the Quran. But suddenly one day, a package of my books was allowed through. Any material that had the words colonialism had been censored: No works with politics in them were allowed through. Amazingly, Soyinka's *The Man Died* was among the religious and apparently innocuous texts allowed to reach me. I have always wondered whether they thought it a religious text or some kind of metaphysics of death. After all, my block was between that for those condemned to die and others thought to be mentally deranged. Soyinka's book, *The Man Died*, was read by every political prisoner, as a testament of hope, not a treatise on death. I have narrated this in my own prison memoir, *Detained: A Writer's Prison Diary*. To this day I still find the lines, "the man dies in all who keep silent in the face of tyranny," inspiring.

I came out of Maximum in December 1978, following the death of the authoritarian Big Man Jomo Kenyatta and the accession to power of Dictator Big Man Daniel Arap Moi. My daughter, Njoki, born when I was in prison, was now among the family members that welcomed me home. In an act of solidarity, Soyinka had named her Ayerubo, a name she still carries to this day.

Can it get closer home than that? We have met in other places sharing the common experience of writers in exile, the most memorable being Leeds in April 2004 when Soyinka robed me for my honorary Doctorate, an honour he himself had received in 1972. The occasion reminded me that Leeds was our common *alma mater*. I went to Leeds in 1965 after Makerere to find echoes of Soyinka who had been there before me. The Leeds of my time had brought together students from all over the world. I still recall two students from Iraq who had been condemned to death in absentia by the Ba'athist leadership that took power in 1963, for their alleged membership of the banned Iraqi Communist Party. To me they were marked men but they did not seem to be overly concerned. When, in 1994, I read that Soyinka was condemned to death in absentia by Dictator Sani Abacha, I recalled the images of the two Iraqi students on the grounds of Leeds. As Soyinka was putting the ceremonial hood on me, the experience of the two students and his own merged in my mind.

There's the irony of current residence in Southern California. Our two roads from the Makerere of 1962 to different parts of the world had finally led us to the city of angels. Soyinka along with Derrida was on the board of directors of the International Centre for Writing and Translation of the University of California Irvine, which lured me from New York University in 2002 to become Distinguished Professor of English and Comparative Literature and run the Centre. Irvine is only half an hour away from Loyola Marymount University where Soyinka was Professor-in-Residence.

We last shared a platform in 2010 at Loyola Marymount University. We both read from our memoirs; he, from *Ake,* and I from *Dreams in a Time of War*. We had not planned it so, but we both read sections that dealt with our childhood experience of growing up during the Second World War. I could not help but recall the 1967 Afro-Scandinavian Writers conference where we were expected to deliver on memories of childhood.

To celebrate Wole Soyinka's 80th birthday is to cerebrate an extra-ordinary journey of a remarkable man of letters, action and conscience. He is the Byronic hero, or even better, a renaissance figure, dashing, defiant and daring. His writings – plays, poems, memoirs, and novels – carry one common banner: the man dies in him who keeps silent in the face of tyranny. As a writer and public intellectual who has voiced his concerns over major happenings in different parts of the continent over the last fifty years and more, he has become the moral and democratic conscience of Africa.

Chapter Two
For Art and Life
Nadine Gordimer

How I remember him?

I had the joyous honour of celebrating in his home country, our home continent, the award of the Nobel Prize for Literature to Wole Soyinka. It was and is my privilege to be a personal friend of the laureate and to witness the ultimate recognition of this great writer.

Albert Camus once wrote: "One either serves the whole of man or one does not serve him at all. And if man needs bread and justice and what must be done to serve this need, he also needs pure beauty which is the bread of the heart."

As for serving the need for justice, Wole Soyinka went further than words. He publicly denounced the post-independence civil war in his country, literally with his own body, when he attempted to take over the broadcasting station and was imprisoned. Then he stored in his memory, drew on toilet paper, his experiences and those of other prisoners. His book published later as *The Man Died* is a victory of art over all forces of injustice, hatred and cruelty whether committed by colonialism or the present home-grown variety.

During his visits to my part of the continent we share most vivid memories of his personality, but as I read his books I am again and again aware in the present of his outstanding way, among all our different ways to capture as writers the whole of life in places and situations; wherever.

I'm celebrating his 80 years of achievement for art and life.

Chapter Three
Hallo Sefi
Sefi Atta

Soyinka answers email. He answers them promptly and briefly. He begins them with a "Hallo" and ends with his initials WS, or his pen name, Wole Soyinka, SOYINKA in capitals. At least that is how he answered mine.

The first time I received an email from him, I thought perhaps he was showing me special favour as a cousin of my late father-in-law, Professor Olikoye Ransome-Kuti, but having spoken to other Nigerian writers I have come to realize that Soyinka is just accessible in that way. I call him Professor Soyinka but to my husband's family he is Uncle Wole. I was at their house when the news broke that Uncle Wole had been awarded the Nobel Prize for Literature in 1986. I was not writing then, nor did I have any intention to. In fact, I was a banker and thought I would always be one.

When I was a girl I had made up plays. I say "made up" because I don't remember writing them. They were mostly collaborations with my siblings and I was territorial about how to produce them. I knew when our plays didn't work and would get thoroughly embarrassed, even when our parents praised us. I remember a particularly dubious play we performed for them and their friends, about a bully, played by my brother. I came up with the last line, "Only cowards fight girls." I was not yet ten years old and don't remember being aware of gender discrepancies, except that I was a skinny wimp compared to my brother, whom I looked up to because he wasn't afraid to get into playground fights at school.

Much later, as a secondary student at Queen's College, I joined the drama society. I am still not sure why theatre appealed to me. I suspect that had I been shapelier or more coordinated I would have been interested in beauty pageants or sports. My plays were about imaginary kingdoms, with kings, queens, princes, princesses, chiefs and witches. I often starred in them and cast myself as kings. *Village Headmaster*, a television drama I had watched as a child, was an inspiration. So was Shakespeare's *Macbeth*, which I studied for English literature. I had not yet read a Soyinka play, but I had studied "Telephone Conversation" in an English literature class, the theme of racism going over my head. If every Nigerian who studied Soyinka's works in school had a moment when they decided he was incomprehensible, reading "Telephone Conversation" was mine. Also at Queen's College, a friend of mine told me about *The Man Died*. She asked if I'd heard of the book and I said, "No," taking the title literally and wondering what the man died of. She quoted the line, "The man dies in all who keep silent in the face of tyranny," which sounded so impressive I asked her to repeat it.

I had grown up in a house where books were considered important and writers mattered. As a child I'd heard the story of poet Christopher Okigbo, who was killed while fighting for Biafra. For me, it was a family story. Christopher Okigbo was my aunt Sefi's husband and my cousin Obi's father. I was eight years old when my own father, Abdul-Aziz Atta, who was secretary to the federal military government, died in 1972, after the civil war. He was Igbirra, but I grew up more familiar with my mother's culture, Yoruba. I didn't speak Yoruba well and was never really considered a Yoruba girl at Queen's College, but I was more enthusiastic about Yoruba art, music and folklore than most of my Yoruba-speaking classmates. At home, Strauss and Sunny Ade were on par, so were Picasso and Buraimoh. Nigerian and Western cultures were equal.

In 1978, I left Queen's College to attend Millfield School in England and I stopped writing plays because I no longer felt they were significant to my experiences overseas. Millfield had an array of international students, a significant number of whom were Nigerian. Millfieldians were fairly well-travelled, but it bothered me that I had studied Shakespeare and they had not studied Soyinka. I read English and French literature for A-Levels, but while I enjoyed those subjects, I also took an anthropology class with a teacher who had lived in Nigeria. He was regarded as an oddball, but he knew about Wole Soyinka and Christopher Okigbo. I would talk to him, not even about Nigerian literature, but about his experiences in Eastern Nigeria before the civil war. I was impatient whenever I had to explain my Nigerian experiences to my classmates and if they provoked me, such as the time when a boy joked that he could picture me in Lagos riding down the highway on a donkey, I would retaliate "Telephone Conversation" style.

I am ashamed to say that I did not become acquainted with Soyinka's other works until I started writing in the United States in my early thirties. I was working as an accountant and writing part-time. I could blame my lack of familiarity with Soyinka's works on my childhood impression that he was incomprehensible, but it was more due to laziness. I had to make a special effort to buy Soyinka's books, books by any African writer for that matter, because before the Internet they usually had to be ordered and took weeks to arrive.

I had actually met Soyinka a few years before I read his other works. He came to the night party on my wedding day, which was held at my in-law's house. My father-in-law jokingly asked if I knew who he was and I laughed and said, "Of course I do." The next time I met Soyinka was again at my in-law's house, while I was reading *The Man Died*. I don't remember if I told him I was reading the book, but my mother-in-law mentioned I was a writer and I promptly said, "No, I'm not," to which Soyinka replied, "Whether or not you are, it's nice to meet you."

I had stopped working as an accountant and was writing full-time, but I had not yet come out as a writer. If people asked what I was doing, I would only say I was writing a novel. The reason I started writing the novel was that I had things to say about being a Nigerian girl and woman, but I didn't think my novel had enough gravitas.

A question I find difficult to answer about my development as a writer is this: "Who were your literary influences?" For a start, it is hard to say how a writer has influenced my works and for another, I have never wanted to emulate any writer. I admire great writers like Soyinka – who has his fair share of clones and protégés on the Nigerian literary scene – but I believe great writers should simply be admired. They certainly shouldn't be imitated. There is no point. Their greatness is characterized by a singleness of purpose from youth, an uncommon assuredness about their craft and an idiosyncratic vision well ahead of its time, which can result in a biography like Soyinka's. You can't learn how to be a great writer, but you can learn a little from them. Reading Soyinka's works only influenced me to develop my own literary style and what I have learned from him goes beyond the craft of writing.

The Man Died taught me to be more courageous as a writer. The book gave me permission to be blatantly honest and unapologetically angry in a first draft. I don't write nonfiction and shy away from autobiography, but when I write fiction, I am fearless. I am not politically active and often write about characters who are indifferent to politics, but *The Man Died* also validated my childhood dislike for bullies. As an adult, I have never been too afraid to confront bullies and have sometimes been ostracized for being that way inclined; consequently, I've had a few moments when I have secretly wished I were not. Of course, these issues are not the stuff of *The Man Died*, but the book reminded me that it was all right to have an instinct to speak out against people who abuse power. On the back of the book is a quote by Soyinka, which reads, "I believe that from the moment that power is deemed culpable in any way, each family should, in place of, or after its regulation morning prayers, make a ritual of throwing their breakfast slop at a pinned-up photograph of the symbol of power before going out to earn a living under an insupportable system. Every morning religiously…"

Soyinka's advice is easy to justify if the symbol of power is a military dictator, but if he were a husband or a father, things might be less clear cut. That was the case I was trying to make in my debut novel *Everything Good Will Come*. The conceit of all my works is power play in the family: who has it and who does not; how it is gained and lost; and how it is used and abused. I return to it time and time again in my writings and I don't worry that this is repetitive because Soyinka set a precedence of possibility. His life's work is the study of power on a national scale and as if his works are not enough, he himself steps in to redress power imbalances, which, to my mind, is the noblest form of artistic expression.

In 2005, when *Everything Good Will Come* was published, a well-meaning relative made several attempts to reach Soyinka. There was a phone call to his son and a chance meeting with Soyinka himself. I wasn't sure about the details and didn't want to find out because the hardcover edition had so many typos I would rather he didn't read it. But a copy of the novel was handed to Soyinka nonetheless, after which I got my first "Hallo." I couldn't decide if I was nervous or excited when I saw his email. He said he had read my novel. I replied asking what he thought of it and he said it read like an autobiography. I said I had done that deliberately. That was pretty much the extent of our email exchange. I assumed therefore that Soyinka did not enjoy my novel and concluded as much a year later when I read an article on him in *Poets & Writers*, which said he did not care for autobiographies. I found that strange because my favourite Soyinka book was *Ake: The Years of Childhood* and some of his other books I would later read, such as *The Open Sore of a Continent*, were undoubtedly autobiographical.

Regardless of Soyinka's opinion about my novel, I had always answered emails on time, but after my first "Hallo" from him, it became important to me. To this day, I even answer emails from students who ask me to help them with their essays – to tell them I can't. It is a small gesture of courtesy, but if a writer of Soyinka's stature can answer emails, then so can I.

Part of becoming public as a writer is that you have to deal with the consequences of what you write publicly, which might be as severe as state persecution for a writer like Soyinka or as tedious as disapproving readers for the rest of us. From the feedback I received on *Everything Good Will Come*, the novel was seen by some readers as anti-men. I remember a reader who accused me of embellishing about Nigerian fathers having children out of wedlock. I held my tongue because he was an elder, but I would have liked to tell him that

I'd been fair to Nigerian fathers in the novel, more than fair, because it wasn't my experience growing up with a deceased father. However, most of my friends in Ikoyi, Lagos, where I was raised, discovered in their teens that they had siblings they weren't aware of.

After I read *The Man Died*, I read *When the Man Died*, a compilation of reviews on the book and was quite surprised to learn, in an interview with Soyinka in the book, that he had been hurt by a review that deemed the book anti-Hausa. I was also relieved to read Soyinka's response because I'd never believed writers who claimed to be immune to unfair criticisms. I couldn't even understand why writers accepted negative criticisms with grace. I would gladly have thrown my breakfast slop at one or two critics of *Everything Good Will Come* until I decided to stop reading reviews altogether.

In my private life, I can be quite belligerent when defending other people and my opinions, but I am not always when it comes to defending myself. I need to be pushed to the limit. I become all airy-fairy and trust that karma or whatever forces in the universe will take care of me, if I so deserve. For a while, after *Everything Good Will Come* was published, I thought I might deal with critics the same way until I learnt another lesson from Soyinka. Soyinka answers critics. He doesn't accept unfair criticisms with grace. He has no qualms about getting into literary scraps and fighting to the end, publicly, grandly, with page after page of highbrow argument and the occasional underhanded insult. Soyinka might disagree that he has a penchant for autobiography, but if telling someone their life history, as we say in Nigeria, is telling them off, then Soyinka writes biography beautifully.

The second time I got a "Hallo" from him I was in Lagos for Christmas with my family in 2009. He invited me to an event, *An Evening with Wole Soyinka*, to be held in Accra in 2010. I thanked him and told him I would be there. In 2006, when *Everything Good Will Come* won the Wole Soyinka Prize for Literature in Africa, I had missed the ceremony. The shortlist was announced a couple of days before and even if I had taken the next flight out from Mississippi, where I lived, I would have arrived in Lagos too late. I was thrilled to have an opportunity to visit Ghana.

My father's family had a history there. He and his siblings were educated at Achimota School and a few of them had married Ghanaians. I had cousins who lived in Accra, I had been there for readings when *Everything Good Will Come* was published and I looked forward to going back.

As usual I was reticent when I met Soyinka in Accra a few months later – I didn't want to say something foolish for which I would be remembered. "It's Sefi," I said to remind him. "Gboyega Ransome-Kuti's wife." I would say the same again that year when I met him at the state governor's house in Port Harcourt with other Nigerian writers who were invited to *The Garden City*

Literary Festival. In Accra, I was without my peers, so I met up with my cousin who lived there and spent time with her after we had greeted Soyinka.

The evening with Soyinka itself was one of those odd situations in which I find myself as a writer, during which I wonder, "What am I doing here?" I was at a table with a Nobel laureate, a head of state of a Caribbean country and the Vice-President of Ghana. The highlight for me was meeting Ama Ata Aidoo, who initially didn't know who I was. The most memorable part had occurred at the beginning, when I made several attempts to sit at the table with Soyinka and others and was barred by security officers who mistook me for an uninvited groupie. I warded them off and took my seat. None of the men at the table noticed what had happened.

Sometimes, as a woman writer, I am forced to defend myself against my will. At times like this, in addition to questioning my presence, I have also asked myself what a writer like Soyinka would do. I expect, from reading his books that he would write about his experience. Even as I write this, I credit him with seeing every conflict I've faced as material for future works. I also expect that Soyinka would fight back. One would imagine that I might look to a writer like Ama Ata Aidoo for clues as to how to comport myself, but sometimes sheer machismo is what I need now that the "playground" is my arena of work.

The third time I got a "Hallo" from Soyinka, I was the one who initially reached out to him. I invited him to the premier of a one-act play I had written (and made the mistake of producing). He wasn't sure he would be free to attend. I told him I understood that he was busy, but would be happy to see him. I was discovering the untold story of theatre, which was how much drama occurred off-stage. I had dropped several pounds from the stress of dealing with an over-budget production and taken umbrage with the poster design, which I felt, was distracting. I had attended the premiere of the play and learned just before the play began that one of the two actors in the play wasn't even an actor. Half of the audience showed up late and during the play mobile phones rang. A woman behind me answered a call and had a conversation so loud I couldn't hear what anyone on-stage was saying. A well-meaning relative had organized snacks for the audience, which, I later had to acknowledge, was generous, but they were served halfway through the play.

I was actually in tears when I sent my email to Soyinka detailing some of my experiences and to my delight he seemed amused by them, which helped me to put matters in perspective. Perhaps another playwright would have considered my premiere a calamity, but if Soyinka's concern was the state of the nation, my premiere could be comic relief. He confirmed he would come to the next performance of my play, which he did, with his halo of white hair. Even though the production was not as strong as I would have liked, Soyinka was kind enough to sit through it and commission it for the Lagos Heritage Festival. I could say the experience taught me to see generous acknowledgement as encouragement to earn it, but I'd known that even when I was a girl.

Surely, the measure of the man is the number of stories like mine people can tell about the impact he has had on them and perhaps the lessons I have described here are not of import but they are all I can manage from a playwright, poet, memoirist, activist, academic and icon such as himself. In my forties, I became braver as a writer, more confident to call myself one and more at ease with being one until, well, "Hallo Sefi." A few years ago, I withdrew a novel from a Nigerian publishing house that made unauthorized changes to my manuscript and set up a self-publishing outfit. At a recent book launch in Lagos, I answered friendly critics who formed opinions about my latest novel based on an excerpt I'd read and during the production of my last play in Lagos I defended my script against a director who had cut (and added) lines without my consent, while an actor in the cast supported him, saying he could do as he pleased with my script because and I quote, "What if you were dead?" I didn't even have to think about what Soyinka would do in that instance.

In recognizing Soyinka's greatness I remain purely appreciative of his works. I would not dare attempt to mimic his literary style or trouble him for mentoring, not even to satisfy my curiosity about his writing secrets. If anything, as I approach my fifties, I would love to know his beauty secrets. Absolutely! I wouldn't mind looking as young as he does when I turn eighty. When I last saw him in Accra, he was in his seventies and my cousin and I regarded him from a distance. "So this is *the* Wole Soyinka," she said and a moment later added, "He's not bad." I had to agree. Soyinka was not bad for his age at all.

Chapter Four
Fragments From a Chest of Memories
Margaret Busby

The lodestar that is Wole Soyinka began to loom on my horizon when I was in my early teens – those years when anyone more than a decade one's senior seemed positively ancient, and impossibly wise. It was not merely that Soyinka was deserving of all the proper respect due an elder; it was also that, unknowingly, he validated my lifelong bookish aspirations. Ghana-born and British schooled, I was navigating recklessly between the *English* and English literature that had been the staple of my formal educational curriculum and the new world of writing informed by African sensibilities that I was beginning to sight, like a lost voyager, while trying to avoid becoming beached on the well-charted and respectable shores of Medicine and The Law, ostensibly the only respectable professions to pursue. So to salute Soyinka's 80 years I must confront, albeit with a sense of bathos, some of the lesser milestones in my own life.

Particularly significant was the year 1962, which coincidentally saw the rolling out of Heinemann's African Writer's Series (number 1 being Chinua Achebe's *Things Fall Apart*), but for the more personal reason that it was when I first came upon Soyinka's dramatic work.

Home in Ghana on holiday, I went to a production in Accra of an early Soyinka satire entitled *The Trials of Brother Jero* directed by Joe de Graft at the Drama Studio. My contemporaneous dog-eared diary, which I sparsely and erratically used to note the titles of books read or films watched, tells me that this landmark event took place on Friday, 14 September. More than the story of the play, I recall vividly the sense of excitement and discovery and involvement I felt at what I saw and heard. Thereafter, while I could name a more obvious role model in my fellow Ghanaian Efua Sutherland – founder of the national theatre movement and a pioneering woman writer – it was an awareness of Soyinka that would punctuate every decade of my future literary career, with echoes discernible sometimes only in retrospect.

In Soyinka's extraordinary life, which melds activity of every shape and scope, he has chronicled himself in memoirs, with newspaper headlines periodically providing their own surreal gloss. In 1965, in protest at a Nigerian "electoral robbery" he held up a radio station at gunpoint and broadcast a demand for the cancellation of the Western Nigeria Regional Elections. He was arrested but acquitted on a technicality.

The year 1966 saw me back in London, a new young graduate poised to out myself as an upstart ingénue publisher, while trying my hand at journalism. "Skin deep," my first article – a variation on the theme of political correctness, although that term was yet to be invented – was accepted for publication at the end of that November by the *New Statesman*. I was invited to a party at their office, where the then editor Paul Johnson confessed to checking the dictionary for one word I had nonchalantly used: iatrogenic. A regular weekly column was even mooted, a challenge I never took up, since I had other ambitions in mind, being on the brink of launching a publishing house, unfazed by having zero funds or experience. However, after the *New Statesman* article I was contacted by the BBC African Service to elaborate on the theory of "unprejudice" I had raised. Recording "Good Morning Africa," one December afternoon in Bush House, in some context I made a topical reference to Wole Soyinka (triggering a discussion with the producer about the correct pronunciation of his name). *The Lion and the Jewel* was just opening at the Royal Court Theatre, featuring the Ijinle Theatre Company and incorporating Yoruba song, dance and mime. It was the second Soyinka play I saw and I was again mesmerised. As Professor Martin Banham has pointed out,[1] the Royal Court production was notable both for the cultural responses it elicited and for the committed way the playwright's work was championed by artistic director Bill Gaskill. Gaskill wrote to Oscar Lewenstein (then a council member of the English Stage company and latterly a friend and supporter of Allison & Busby, the publishing company I co-founded):

After *Three Men for Colverton* and *Macbeth*, we want to do Wole Soyinka's *The Lion and the Jewel*. This is the first play that we are going to do as part of a tie-up with a group of African actors called the Ijinle Players, who did a tremendous production of Soyinka's play *The Trials of Brother Jero* at the Hampstead Theatre Club, and was the first play I went to see twice in about the last ten years. It had a vitality and immediacy which very few of our new plays have. Wole is a real Court writer in the true sense of the word. He was one of our script readers and a member of the Writers' Group when I ran it and there has been a great backlog of wonderful work which we have always drawn back from doing because of the lack of actors. This group has solved that particular problem.

However, Soyinka's comedy drew praise that, for all its good intentions, was often patronising. One reviewer summed it up by noting that during the interval he overheard an audience member comment: "Aren't they marvellous – so colourful, such a sense of rhythm. And only one of them forgot his lines…" The inference that it was a wonder for an African playwright to be more than barely literate or for African actors to remember their lines at all was a sign of those times that closely paralleled the examples I gave in my little *New Statesman* essay.

Gaskill's enthusiastic plans for a Royal Court production of *Kongi's Harvest* in July 1967 – "when Wole will come over and direct it himself and bring over some African actors and dancers to perform it" – were scuppered by the fact that Soyinka was arrested at the beginning of the Nigerian Civil War, accused by the government of conspiring with the Biafran secessionists, though never formally charged. He was held without trial, mostly in solitary confinement, from August 1967 to October 1969 – for 27 months, a number that resonates symbolically with Mandela's years of incarceration – a remarkable account of that period, *The Man Died*, is an uncompromising indictment against what he called "this humiliation of tyranny."

Recently I read a thought-provoking guest editorial by A.D. Harvey for *The Journal of Commonwealth Literature* entitled "'Does the Queen know about this?' Wole Soyinka and the British Government 1969–1973." Discussing Whitehall worries about an honorary doctorate from the University of Leeds being conferred on the dissident writer by the Duchess of Kent less than a month before an official visit to London by Nigeria's military Head of State Gowon, Harvey refers to an earlier British dilemma involving Soyinka:

Late in 1968, while he was still in prison, he had been awarded the Jock Campbell–New Statesman literary prize. He had turned the prize down, stating that in view of the accusations against him, "I find my position too ambiguous for the acceptance of literary honours." Paul Johnson, the editor of the *New Statesman*, wrote to Harold Wilson, the then Prime Minister, suggesting that Soyinka had been put under pressure to refuse the prize and that Wilson should obtain from the Nigerian government "a fuller and I trust more convincing, explanation". … [O]n 1 April 1969, Wilson wrote to the Nigerian dictator, opening with "My dear General Gowon" and closing with "my warmest personal regards," and suggesting that the Nigerian government "would have a good deal to gain by adopting a lenient attitude towards Mr Soyinka." Gowon replied on 19 April pointing out, "His detention has nothing whatsoever to do with his literary attributes and he knows it. You will agree that in the present situation in Nigeria the needs of state security cannot be ignored merely because of Mr Soyinka's claims to literary eminence [...] he has access to a library and has recently confirmed in a letter that he was deriving immense benefit from his reading [...] I shall not hesitate to authorise his release as soon as I am personally satisfied that to do so would not be detrimental to the public interest."[2]

II

Meanwhile, my fledgling publishing venture took wing, attracting press coverage that delivered an increasingly familiar, if dubious, message of surprised commendation on a par with Dr Johnson's: "Sir, a woman's preaching is like a dog's walking on his hind legs. It is not done well; but you are surprised to find it done at all." After Allison & Busby published its first titles, three poetry books, in 1967, the headline in one national broadsheet almost reverberated with shock: "The Girl from Ghana Goes Into Publishing"!

The flabbergasted publicity was further compounded when in 1969 A&B followed up by making a success of a political thriller called *The Spook Who Sat By the Door*, after it had been much rejected by other publishers on both sides of the Atlantic. It seems strangely serendipitous that this first novel's author, African American Sam Greenlee, shares with Soyinka a 13 July birthdate (as does another favourite novelist-friend, Trinidadian Earl Lovelace), but also that a key element in its plot uncannily mirrors a strand of Soyinka's actual life. The book's hero, Dan Freeman, hired and trained by the CIA to combat accusations of racial discrimination, eventually resigns and passes on his skills to the members of a Black inner-city Chicago gang called the Cobras. He covertly trains them to become "Freedom Fighters," among whose tactics is the take-over of a radio station and the broadcasting of their own propaganda. Art mimicking life? Perhaps more bizarrely, on 8 February 1974, the London *Evening Standard* reported the kidnapping of heiress Patty Hearst by a group styling themselves the Symbionese Liberation Army under the headline: "The Cobras – at war with society... The SLA symbol is the seven-headed cobra and members are reported to have modelled themselves on a fictional black anti-establishment guerrilla group called The Cobras in the popular novel and film *The Spook Who Sat by the Door*." Or life mimicking art?

During the 1970s I had the good fortune to meet the great man in person in London, at the late-lamented Africa Centre in Covent Garden and elsewhere. This was also the decade when he compiled *Poems of Black Africa* for Heinemann (somewhere along the way I think I presumed – dared – to make a cheeky comment about not enough women being included). When in 1982 I published the authorized biography of Fela Kuti, I knew that he was Soyinka's cousin, though not that Soyinka would soon be able to lay claim to being the only Nobel laureate to have made a record. In the era of the International Book Fair of Radical Black and Third World Books, which flourished between 1982 and 1995, the ranks of those of us in the London-based book world being swelled annually by visiting comrades from every corner of the world. Soyinka was an august participant in discussions on resurgence or barbarism with the likes of C.L.R. James and Ngũgĩ wa Thiong'o and John La Rose. When on 21 March 1985 the 4th Black Book Fair was opened by Soyinka, he spoke on "The Nkomati Era."

> We know whose gun-ship helicopters, whose ubiquitous marines snuffed out the lamp of self-determination in Grenada, but what do we say of the consortium of black leaders who spread out the mat of invitation to Ronald Reagan? Who were those shameless so-called leaders who sent out the SOS that read: "Re-colonise us, PLEASE!" We know whose agency manufactured the dastardly instrument which terminated the career of Walter Rodney, but whose was the face beneath the reactionary mask which nodded in Brigades, signed Rodney's death-warrant and emasculated his workers' movement.

Then came the historic Nobel Prize of 1986 and Soyinka's acceptance speech "The Past Must Address Its Present," dedicated to Nelson Mandela, that spoke directly and personally to those who perpetuated the barbarism of the Apartheid system:

> Take a good look... In your anxiety to prove that this moment is not possible, you have killed, maimed, silenced, tortured, exiled, debased and dehumanised hundreds of thousands encased in this very skin, crowned with such hair, proudly content with their very being...

Three years later, in 1989, I edited with Ian Mayes a special edition of the *Guardian Weekend* magazine on Africa. I went to see Wole, who was in London, begging him for a contribution. He gave me a substantial and eloquent piece about the dumping of poisonous industrial waste on African, Latin American and Caribbean states. But space was tight (the magazine's previous special national edition, on Scotland, which was allocated the same amount as our mighty continent), and in the face of Ian's nervousness about editing a Nobel Prize-winner, the necessary judicious trimming fell to me. It was a useful lesson in holding my nerve that stood me in good stead for more extreme editing of his work yet to come and even reduced to a mere 700 words his point was powerfully made:

When illegal argosies shunt from port to port, looking for terrains on which to discharge their toxic wastes, let no one imagine this is an aberration of a maverick chemical sewage industry. It derives its authority from precedence, from the arrogance of nuclear powers that declared their own terrains sacrosanct, then moved on to negligent or mercenary-ruled 'colonies,' overseas real estate, to detonate their putrid eggs over unsuspecting populaces.

From Haiti to Guinea, from Zaire to Nigeria these cargo boats shunt forwards and backwards, bringing to mind the fable of the Ancient Mariner but with a fatal variant: while some have been caught in the act and compelled to remove their plague-bearing albatross, others have got cleanly away.[3]

Generous always in the struggle for freedom, Soyinka contributed part of his forthcoming book, *Ìsarà: A Voyage Around Essay*, to a unique anthology I was also involved with called *Colours of a New Day: Writing for South Africa*. Two years in the compiling, it was published simultaneously in the UK, the USA and South Africa (and subsequently in other countries), the first anthology whose proceeds would go directly to the African National Congress, and it was just a handful of months away from publication in 1990 when Nelson Mandela was finally released, enabling the volume to be graced with a paragraph by him by way of a Foreword. (With hindsight, I realise that my slight offering "A Season of Disillusion" and, which somewhat embarrassingly immediately follows Wole's extract from his novel-in-progress, coincidentally bears a title that harks back to the 1973 Soyinka novel *Season of Anomy*.)

In 1995, I again took my scissors to Soyinka's work when I abridged for BBC's Radio 4 his wonderful memoir *Ake: The Years of Childhood*, whittling it down to a skeleton to be read and broadcast in 10 parts in September 1995. How could I! The knowledge imparted by my producer that people had been spotted reading the book on the tube the week my abridgement was broadcast salved my conscience. My audacity continued as I presumed to pontificate on his work in book reviews. Despite it all, I was gratified that Wole still deigned to speak to me and at the request of English PEN, even let me engage him in public conversation at Waterstone's in Piccadilly in 2000. And when I saw him, during the 2012 London Olympics, being interviewed by Dotun Adebayo at "Nigeria House" in Stratford East it did not then occur to me that the occasion marked a half-century of marvelling at his work in different guises.

Soyinka is a self-acknowledged by-product of the "*penkelemes*" of Nigerian politics, in possession of "an over-acute, remedial sense of right and wrong, of what is just and unjust." His commitment to freedom and human rights has earned him imprisonment (by Gowon), exile (by Babangida and Abacha), a death sentence in absentia (by Abacha) and silencing (by Obasanjo). Yet, acutely aware of the power of both the gun and the pen, he remains able to laugh at himself.

A final irony. Many of us remember the days when to see another black person in certain parts of Britain was such a rare occurrence that it was unthinkable not to greet them, not necessarily to the extent of embracing like long-lost relatives but at least with a smile of recognition or something equivalent to the tipping of the brim of a hat. Accordingly, for years I exchanged nods with someone with whom I occasionally crossed paths on the streets of my patch of north London, a gentleman with magnificently greying Afro bush and beard, who bore more than a passing resemblance to Wole Soyinka. We had never actually spoken, but I imagined that if we ever found the time and inclination to do so, his voice would rumble out with similar deep tones to those of Soyinka, the sure prelude to profound conversation between us about cabbages and kings and whether pigs have wings. Then one day the illusion was shattered forever: the Soyinka avatar, for the very first time, followed up our customary silent civilities with a cheery and alarmingly high-pitched Cockney "allo!" I knew that now I would have to alter my route just to hold on to the fantasy.

We are privileged ever to interact with those who bear the burden of our admiration.

Chapter Five
Soyinka's Cultural Antiphonies
Nicholas Westcott

As a student of African history in the 1970s, my supervisor, John Iliffe, advised us all that there was one African writer we had to read, "the closest Africa has come to its own Shakespeare." His name was Wole Soyinka.

I have been reading his work, on and off, ever since. Not all of it; not regularly, but always with pleasure, always with thoughts provoked. Given my own background, I have been particularly interested in his exploration of the relationship between his Yoruba heritage and the impact the British presence and Nigeria's creation has had on that.

Two works reflect on this in interesting ways. His play *Death and the King's Horseman* (1975), though put forward primarily as an exploration of his own Yoruba cultural heritage, also exposes the mutual incomprehension of British and Nigerian cultural assumptions. A British District Officer is called upon to quell disorder that breaks out when the old King dies. The colonial law requires that nobody should die to accompany the king on his voyage to the other world and his 'Horseman,' Elesin Oba, is arrested to prevent him killing himself in the funeral ceremonies. But for the king to travel alone would be anathema. There is no right answer. Life and death, takes their course. Elesin's son, Olunde, an educated young man favoured by the colonial rulers, does what his father should have been allowed to do. Alien rulers will never understand the spirit of the land and its people and their actions will have unintended consequences, whatever the intentions.

Yet Soyinka's memoirs of his own youth (*Aké*, 1981), amidst the comforting chaos of his family life in the headmaster's house of a mission school in Yorubaland, illustrate the imperceptible mingling of the purely African and the outside influences of church, education and state. Soyinka's childhood fascination with the magnificent Police marching band and with the mysterious written word draw him into a world and a culture well beyond the town of his birth. He connects with the world outside. He cannot do otherwise – it has come to his doorstep and demanded his attention. But he brings to that world outside his African heritage; and he brings back from it to Africa the means to express its soul-searching in the period when independence resumed after the brief colonial interlude.

Soyinka lived through the end of colonial rule, the advent of independence, the hopes grown, the dreams broken, the trials of military rule and the struggle for democracy. All this he charts in his own individual voice, in his verse, his books and his protests. Finding himself a public figure, he used his status in the cause of principles he held dear, principles that were neither "African" nor "British" nor "western," but universal, in practice as much a part of traditional Yoruba culture as anywhere else. He brought to all this a righteous anger and an ability to articulate it, together with a wry humour that turned even dramatic events, such as his own flight from the country to avoid arrest, into a narrative that is at once exciting, moving and comic.

I never met Wole until many years later, when I was living and working in Accra. He visited for a literary festival and later to receive an award – one of many in his long life, all richly deserved. Only then could I appreciate his mellifluous voice, his deep humanity and his personal charm. Talking to him was a lesson in humility and wit. Perhaps great writers are always more human in the flesh than in their reputation. But Wole is someone you would always seek out, given the chance, to spend time with just talking, discussing, exchanging opinions – and find yourself coming out wiser than you went in. He seemed happy to treat anyone as a friend and to listen to their opinion as much as to give his own. And in all this he remained true to himself: a boy who came from his hometown to travel the world, explore its literature and life and create his own voice while remaining wholly Nigerian and easily of the world. This enables him also to see the British heritage in Nigeria as something to accept, part of what makes modern Nigeria what it is, along with all the other influences, ancient and modern, neither more nor less important but part of the messy whole that each of us, and each of our countries, is.

In his eighty years he has given us much. Long may he continue to do so.

Chapter Six
A Man of Sheer Narrative Power
Toni Morrison

It is difficult to know where to begin or where to focus when describing Wole Soyinka-the man, the work, the international influence.

So I will defer and leave the deeper, broader evaluations to others.

My own admiration for Soyinka began while being in his company at large international conferences and small lunches where his intelligence, dedication and humour delighted us all. That admiration increased when exposed to his work in drama – *Death and the King's Horseman* and intensified when I read his memoir – *You Must Set Forth at Dawn* which I regard as a brilliant achievement. I read it cover to cover at one sitting, amazed by the deft language, the clarity and sheer narrative power of his country's life and his own.

I am permanently grateful for his gifts. Wole Soyinka makes the world intelligible.

Section II

The Canvass is Universal:
Philosophy, Literature
and the Politics of Redemption

Chapter Seven

Death and the King's Horseman:
Ten of One in Ten

Ama Ata Aidoo

Ten Reasons why Wole Soyinka's *Death and the King's Horseman* is on the list of the ten books I'd want with me, should I get marooned on a desert island.

According to Wole Soyinka, *'This play is based on events which took place in Oyo, ancient city of Nigeria, in 1946. That year, the lives of Elesin (Olori Elesin), his son and the Colonial District Officer intertwined with the disastrous results set out in the play.'*

The events 'with the disastrous results' centred around Olori Elesin, the Horseman of the King of Oyo. According to the rigid and time-hallowed rules of state, the Elesin had to commit suicide when the reigning monarch died and earlier than the king's burial. This would ensure that he would ride ahead of his lord to herald the latter's entry into the other world. Simply put, if the Horseman did not kill himself, the king did not get buried! However, the Elesin of Soyinka's play allows himself to be tragically or fortuitously distracted–depending on the operating viewpoint – by the pleasures of the world he should be leaving behind, as well as some unwanted colonial intervention. In the end, he loses both precious time and enthusiasm for the suicide, with consequences that were tragic beyond his personal humiliation and shame. The two people who wittingly play pivotal roles in this tragedy are the Iyaloja and the Colonial District Officer.

I never get tired of reading *Death and the King's Horseman*. In spite of having first read it and then begun teaching it more than three decades ago in a number of university contexts, I still return to read it every now and then. For pleasure. Nor do I need to be reminded that plays are essentially scripts, written for theatre productions and not meant to be read for entertainment or relaxation; as one would a novel, a short story, or a poem. After all, the best plays *are* also novels, short stories and poems. Which is exactly where the argument should end. The fact that the average play is much shorter than the average novel can only recommend it further. Length was never a reliable yardstick for judging any piece of reading material besides student's essays and post-graduate theses! With the exception of poetry, none of the other genres can compete with drama in the elegance of form. From just being an outpouring of words, many a novel has relied on drama for a certain fine touch. With some plays, notably all of Shakespeare's tragedies, it can be even counter-productive to try and determine where drama ends and poetry begins.

As a teacher, my enthusiasm for teaching *Death and the King's Horseman* never waned. Selecting it as a pedagogical tool was born out of the desire to regularly share the play with as many students as possible and with students from as diverse backgrounds as could be available to me. For those fairly modest but also rather ground breaking, if I say so, courses on Modern African Literature or Contemporary African Literature in the English Department of the University of Cape Coast in the late 1970's, selecting it as part of a multi-genred list was a relatively straightforward affair. The play's clarity in characterization, mastery of language and philosophical depth, not to mention some sophistry [!] is amazing. As an instant 'classic,' it was always easy, appropriate and absolutely justifiable to teach *Death and the King's Horseman* alongside other modern African classics like Christopher Okigbo's *Labyrinths,* Tayeb Salih's *A Season of Migration to the North* and Luis Bernardo Honwana's *We Killed Mangy Dog*. Those vanguard courses were followed by others on drama from global Africa or some similar themes which were thinly-veiled excuses to teach drama by African playwrights and playwrights of African descent wherever they lived and wrote. Such was what was designed with *Death and the King's Horseman* in mind, plus a pile that would include Efua Sutherland's *The Marriage of Anansewa,* Douglas Turner Ward's *Day of Absence* and Simone Schwartz-Bart's *Your Handsome Captain*. Over the years in especially US universities and colleges, it fitted well into Postcolonial Literature courses that were cross-listed for multiple departments. The category usually comprised of English, Africana Studies and Theatre Arts Departments.

While trying deftly to avoid an unhappy term like 'English as a second language,' I occasionally found myself designing courses based on post-coloniality and which took in quite a bit of the places where what is now being identified as 'World English' is spoken and written. For instance, on the list of texts for a multi-genred course like Post-Colonialism and Communication in the English-speaking world, *Death and the King's Horseman* would find itself in the company of *Omeros*, the epic poem by Derek Walcott of Saint Lucia, as well as novels like *The Handmaid's Tale* by Canada's Margaret Atwood, *Midnight's Children* by the Mumbai-born Salman Rushdie and *July's People* by

South Africa's Nadine Gordimer. If anybody had wanted to charge me with eclecticism at the time or would want to even now, my reply would have been 'why not?' then, and the same for now. What kind of a diverse world and literary landscapes are we dealing with, anyway?

Arguably in *Death and the King's Horseman,* we encounter one of the most intelligent, self-assured and articulate women in Literature. Actually, the Iyaloja was foreshadowed by earlier Soyinka female characters like the equally intelligent, but more youthful and sprightly Sidi in *The Lion and The Jewel,* and Amope in *The Trials of Brother Jero.* If we considered those three characters together, we would admit that Soyinka is one of the few African male writers who 'do women well': as do Sembene Ousmane of *Gods Bits of Wood* for instance, Njabulo Ndebele of *The Cry of Winnie Mandela,* Nuruddin Farah of *Gifts* and Ngũgĩ wa Thiong'o of *Wizard of the Crow.* However, even in comparison to the admirable female characters from those other fictional worlds, the Iyaloja of Soyinka's *Death and the King's Horseman* comes out as completely peerless, although of all of them, she also makes the briefest appearance.

West African women are supposed to be among the most self-assured anywhere in the world, whether they come from traditionally patri-lineal/patriarchal or matrilineal/matriarchal environments. In any case, they themselves think they are! This is across the board: whether or not they have had any formal education: tertiary, secondary, not much, or none at all. Indeed, it is a known fact that certain sections of functionally illiterate women from this sub-region often ridicule their highly educated sisters. The former accuse the latter of losing their senses, as well as a sense of themselves and their strengths as women 'in those big books you people read.' They think that in some ways, highly-educated women allow themselves to be disempowered by Western education in particular and Western culture in general. On the other hand, a lot more West African women know and are not shy to confess that missing out on formal education was always rather costly for them 'big time.'

The Iyaloja is a perfect example of an unlettered West African woman who is indisputably effective in her own milieu: including that milieu's "world of men." She has incredible poise and articulacy. Furthermore, her understanding of the responsibilities that society's big cats owe to society brooks no argument. She is consistent. Thoroughly uncompromising normally, she is also an astute political animal. Therefore, when she senses that only some terrifying compromise makes sense in a given situation, she yields, but with some really damning clarity. In this case, it is the Elesin's instant, staged and consummated[!] marriage of her own son's intended. This is what she has to confront during the night of Elesin's suicide.

WOMAN:	*But she is betrothed to your own son. Tell him.*
IYALOJA:	*My son's wish is mine. I did the asking for him, the loss can be remedied. Tell him, you say! You wish that I burden him with knowledge that will sour his wish and lay regrets on the last moments of his mind.*

On that desert island, I would have time to look at an individual like Iyaloja closely. I shall thoroughly enjoy interrogating how this presumably illiterate African woman manages not to feel cowed in anyway by the representative of British imperial power. Iyaloja treats Pilkings no better than she does the fallen Elesin. She refers to the Colonial District Officer and his group in beastly and scatological terms. '*Evil-smelling goats... cats... pigeons...jackals,*' are not the worst of her appellations for them. She also insists on characterizing any form of association with them as stepping into faeces and '*eating left-overs.*' When Pilkings baulks at her audacity to compare the choices his visiting prince might be compelled to make with Elesin's ordeal, Iyaloja roundly rebukes him with '*Child, I have not come to help your understanding.*' Her bitterness and contempt are palpable here.

As the youth of Ghana would say in the nation's emerging pidgin, 'Iyaloja doesn't give gaba.' Or she doesn't suffer fools gladly. Which is what in the end, in her reckoning at least, the Elesin Oba has turned out to be. Just an ordinary fool. '*Oh you emptied bark that the world once saluted for a pith-laden being...*' she wails in despair. Then later, '*We called you leader and oh, how you led us on. What we have no intention of eating should not be held to the nose.*' Iyaloja's steely clarity is not just formidable, but also rather awe-inspiring.

By contrast, the male protagonist of *Death and the King's Horseman* comes out shambolic. In fact, if the play had been written by a woman, critics of a certain stripe could have accused the playwright of being a 'man-hating, penis-envying' b-word! Towards the end when it becomes clear that he has missed the opportunity to claim his greatness, Elesin weakly looks around for the Iyaloja to blame. '*You were present at my defeat. You were part of the beginnings. You brought about the renewal of my tie to earth.*' To which Iyaloja clearly, curtly and cruelly replies, '*I gave you warning.*' When she doesn't stop there but goes on with, '*The river which fills up before our eyes does not sweep us away with its flood!,*' she confirms her exasperation with him for behaving like some recalcitrant child. Again in response, Elesin just resorts to pathetic drivel: *What were warnings beside the moist contact of living earth between my fingers?*' He whines. '*What were warnings beside the renewal of famished embers lodged eternally in the heart of man?... I made to utter my spells anew but my tongue merely rattled in my mouth. I fingered hidden charms and contact was damp; there was no spark left to sever the life-strings that should stretch from every finger-tip...*'

As happens in some other notable tragedies, the hero/anti-hero here is set up beautifully at the beginning of the play for his inevitable fall later. We catch Elesin at his preening best in the market as he is being made much of by the Praise-singer and Iyaloja with her bevy of feisty young women. To the Praise-Singer's offer to kill himself should Elesin need him on 'this journey,' Elesin first throws him an emotional bone, *'You're like a jealous wife. Stay close to me, but only on this side. My fame, my honour are legacies to the living; stay behind and let the world sip its honey from your lips.'* Later he boasts openly, *'As Horseman of the King, the juiciest /Fruit on every tree was mine./I saw, I touched, I wooed, rarely was the answer No…/Split an iroko tree /In two, hide a woman's beauty in its heartwood/And seal it up again – Elesin, journeying by,/Would make his camp beside that tree.'*

We can compare the foregoing to Lear at the beginning of *King Lear*: He is obviously at the height of his powers as a human, the munificent monarch and a doting father, distributing his properties among his daughters. And absolutely clueless. When we later see him clued in, it seems he has become: just another rejected and abandoned old man, poor, homeless and utterly pathetic. What we cannot escape from is the fact that Lear is being punished for having acted on what he had clearly thought was a good idea. In the end, he had only been a fool. Whoever first said that the 'road to hell is paved with good intentions,' must have known Shakespeare's King Lear. That it is his own daughters who are meting out the punishment only adds a certain vicious clarity to the show. In the same way, though in a different scenario, time and space, it is when Simon neatly shows his father how to do what ought to be done, that the impact of his fall hits him. If Lear has no one to blame but himself, neither does the Elesin. *The contempt of my own son rescued something of my shame at your hands… He will avenge my shame'* he confesses to Pilkings, with tragic irony and pathos aplenty. He does not know what he is talking about: literally! As with so many of the eponymous and other tragic heroes, in the end, the buck stops with Oba Elesin, Oedipus, Othello, Edufa, Murphy, Anowa, Willy Loman…

There cannot be any meaningful appraisal of Soyinka's *Death and the King's Horseman*, or indeed any of his works without bringing some attention to his use of language. Wole Soyinka works magic with the English language, as in Standard English. However, on those rare occasions his characters resort to it, he does the same with Nigerian pidgin. [*I can even hazard that his Yoruba is equally masterful!*] The only fly in the ointment of any appreciation of Soyinka's fascinating control and special way with the English language though, is that it also throws into focus, the predicament of modern African writers.

We work exceedingly hard to enrich the languages of our conquerors. And for no recognition or credit! 'Apart from the Arabic north, Africa is the only continent where its people do not [formally] use their indigenous language[s]'. Whoever said that made a rather frightening but also very true observation.' They also disturbed all over again, a veritable hornet's nest of a debate which we would wish had gone away, especially in these days of Afro-politanism, Lafa-rism, etc. Unfortunately, the issue is still very much with us and so are a few other very uncomfortable facts. Thanks to the continuing inappropriate and now totally collapsed educational systems, even with pidgin, 'broken' and different creoles thrown in, the majority of our people do not speak these modern European languages.

However, we, or our antecedents rather, had come to these modern European languages through some unspeakably oppressive and humiliating processes. Being the languages of our conquerors was just about the beginning. Using the analogy from Vyvyane Loh, it can be said that our tongues were effectively 'broken.' The Singaporean author's first novel *Breaking the Tongue* is as much about being pressured into using English as an 'official' or a working language and having to operate within a generally Europeanized milieu, as it is about a vulnerable population getting caught between two imperial forces.

Here in Africa, we recall tales of notices on school gates throughout the British Empire and the French overseas territories, advising pupils to leave their mother tongues 'outside'. The written, or otherwise but still well-understood rule was that if you were caught speaking your mother tongue, or any of such mother-tongues, you faced some dire consequences. Those punishments included getting caned; doing the flamingo stand for hours on end; or having a plaque hung around your neck while you were in the classroom, or on the playing field: with words like 'I am a fool' written on it!' Now here we were, with our original tongues broken and replaced with some steel weapons that rather undermined us and our world.

The question though is this. If any African writer or any number of African writers can have that much grasp and control over a modern European language, or languages and with anything remotely like what Soyinka accomplishes with English, then could African writers not find a smidgeon of absolution from having *betrayed* ourselves and our people? I employ 'betray' rather guardedly and painfully here. To begin with, it is not as if we had a choice. Of course, the other side of the argument is that we do not have to feel guilty about having to work with these modern European languages. Not if we take into consideration, the fact that we, or rather earlier generations of Africans purchased these modern European languages dearly with pain and humiliation. That in fact, it is high time we relaxed and used them with a sense of calm entitlement.

By any reckoning, *Death and the King's Horseman* is not only an impressive dramatic poem of the dirge variety, but also a philosophical proposition, a sociological thesis and its antithesis and a paean to a lost world, among a few other literary and academic categories. Indeed, one of the pleasures to look forward to on that desert island should be the endless opportunity to attempt to figure out how many genres this play showcases, not to mention the layers and the nuances, the interlocking of meanings, the symbolisms, the over-laps and so much more that it embodies. In the process of reading and re-reading *Death and the King's Horseman* for the umpteenth time, it is not unusual for us to discover noteworthy ideas, words and phrases that we had hitherto overlooked in earlier readings. Nor is it uncommon with this play that we realise that certain familiar ideas, words and phrases are used in quirkier, more humorous, or some other especially superb Soyinkan way than we had earlier found them. Factually, D*eath and the King's Horseman is* a production script and a distressingly short read, as great literatures go. However, like all significant drama and tragedies especially, it still manages to pack a solid punch for all its brevity. Therefore, any close and careful reading of it inevitably becomes a challenge in meaning mining and other forms of analytical exercises. Meanwhile, *since I would be on a desert island, there should be all the time in the world to indulge...*

Great drama travels well. All those high school theatricals, as well as the more mature and professional theatre productions in Africa of foreign classics have convinced us of that. Shakespeare's *Henry V,* Brecht's *Mother Courage,* Chekov's *The Cherry Orchard* and Ibsen's *A Doll's House*, to name only a few. *Death and the King's Horseman* travels extremely well. So on that desolate island, I shall have all the time in the world to deal with despair and kill boredom by regularly reminding myself of the theatre productions of it I had seen. These should include a moving, awe-inspiring production of an African play in a foreign land, albeit in its original working and quite familiar language. The production had been very modern and in an arty kind of theatre space in Birmingham, England. I could do a minute-by-minute recall of that production of *Death and the King's Horseman,* as well as others I had watched over the years.

Or finally, I would like to confess that instead of feeling apprehensive, the prospect appeals to me in a somewhat perverse way. I refer to the possibility of having to live with a fascinating collection of characters for some extended time on a desert island. There should be endless opportunities to examine them as individuals and also as a group. I would have time to examine the relationships between them, tensions, outright hostilities, and all. It would be extremely rewarding, not just to look at the principal pairs made up of Elesin and Iyaloja, Elesin and Praise-Singer; Elesin and Pilkings, but also a pair like Jane Pilkings and Olunde and the somewhat-implied friendship or understanding between them. Furthermore, a careful, focused and in-depth analysis of the one meeting between Iyaloja and Pilkings should yield some interesting results. After all, even on a rather cursory level the unavoidable animosity in that one and only meeting is apparent. However, there are also glimpses – albeit feint – of genuine friendships, camaraderie and even the promise of romantic and other forms of love in the play.

On that desert island, there would be time to deal with and thoroughly enjoy *Death and the King's Horseman by Wole Soyinka,* all over again, as well as the nine other books I shall have with me.

Chapter Eight

Being, the Will, and the Semantics of Death: Wole Soyinka's *Death and the King's Horseman*

Henry Louis Gates Jr.

> Who would fardels bear,
> To grunt and sweat under a weary life,
> But that the dread of something after death,
> The undiscover'd country, from whose bourn
> No traveller returns, puzzles the will,
> And makes us rather bear those ills we have,
> Than fly to others we know not of?
> Thus conscience does make cowards of us all,
> And thus the native hue of resolution
> Is sicklied over with the pale cast of thought,
> And enterprises of great pitch and moment
> With this regard their currents turn awry,
> And lose the name of actions.
> — *HAMLET, Act III, SCENE I*

Not since the civil war in the Congo has a black African nation been so much in the consciousness of the United States as Nigeria is today. Perhaps it is not accidental that Wole Soyinka's play *Death and the King's Horseman* enjoyed its American premiere in October 1979, at Chicago's Goodman Theatre, in the same week in which Nigeria transformed itself to a representative republic, becoming overnight, after thirteen years of military dictatorship, Africa's largest and most prosperous democracy.

Soyinka's public career as a writer dovetails somewhat ironically with modern Africa's anguished struggle for independence from colonial rule and for a democratically elected government. Indeed, his fourth and most elaborated play, *A Dance of the Forests,* performed at Nigeria's Independence

Day festivities, announced his presence as a major creative writer. Yet, even then, the discordant relationship of Soyinka's art to his nation's image of itself was distinctly evident: the production was staged despite its rejection by the Independence Day Committee, rejected no doubt because of its implicit refutation of a linear, naive, romantic idea of time and human progress. Ironically, the play subsequently won the Encounter Drama Competition sponsored by London's *Observer*.

It is difficult to find exact analogues in the West for Soyinka's public role in Nigeria and throughout Africa. Author of over a dozen plays, two novels and three books of poetry, he is perhaps the most widely read African writer, both within and outside of Africa. In addition to this respect from African and European audiences alike, Soyinka is also perceived as a force in the political arena, embodying in a discreet way the moral authority of a disinterested philosopher with the political authority of the *Times* of London's editorial page. As an author he draws upon the public definition of his role – most recently as Secretary-General of the Union of African Writers – both to protest censorship and imprisonment of writers, especially by the African and Latin American governments and to keep alive the dream of a unified Pan African continent governed by the democratic socialism he holds most dear. He has no counterpart here: he is neither poet-turned-politician like Léopold Sédar Senghor, Aimé Césaire, or the late Agostinho Neto; nor is he the artist-in-exile, demanding the mythical return to a federal never-never land, like Pound and Solzhenitsyn; nor, finally is he, like the mutable Amiri Baraka, artist-becoming-ideologue, determined to diminish that precious distance which irrevocably separates art and shadow from act. On the contrary, Soyinka's stature as an artist depends in part on his remarkable ability to void confusing art and politics; never is he reductive, nor does he attempt to mirror reality in a simple one-to-one relationship. He is a profoundly political writer in that most subtle sense, in which Euripides was, or Lorca. Perhaps it is fair to say that his most admirable characteristic as a writer and activist is the compelling manner in which his art and his political acts have always assumed their unique form-separate somehow, but equal.

Born in 1934 to a middle-class Nigerian family, Akinwande Oluwole Soyinka was educated at University College at Ibadan and at the University of Leeds, where he studied with G. Wilson Knight, the virtual dean of Shakespeare critics and with Arnold Kettle, a major practitioner of Marxist criticism. As a Reader to London's Royal Court Theatre from 1957 to 1959, he produced his one-act play, *The Invention*, a few months after two of his plays *The Lion and the Jewel* and *The Swamp Dwellers* were first performed in a "Soyinka Festival" at University College. A series of stunning artistic successes, commencing with the production of his play on Independence Day in 1960, seemed to guarantee for him an international reputation comparable to that of his fellow Nigerian, Chinua Achebe. As Penelope Gilliatt described his poetic diction in a review of *The Road* in the *Observer* in 1965, "Soyinka has done for our napping language what Brigand dramatists from Ireland have done for centuries: booted it awake, rifled its pockets and scattered the loot into the middle of next week."[1] But it was precisely his status as a writer that compelled him to become the dark and foreboding voice for a certain moral order, much to the annoyance of various Nigerian governments. Soyinka has eschewed the familiar role of spokesman against colonialism and racism for the more difficult and politically dangerous role of spokesman against those forms of tyranny which black people practice against each other. "I knew from childhood," Soyinka says, "that independence in my country was inevitable. Freedom, I felt, should be as normal as breathing or eating and I was interested then in what kind of society we were going to have. When I saw what was happening, I found it difficult to be silent to the point of criminality."[2]

Less than a month after *The Road* took first prize in London's 1965 Commonwealth Festival, Soyinka was imprisoned. On October 15, following the dubious election in what was then Western Nigeria, the purported victor, Chief Akintola, taped a speech in which he announced that his party had officially won the elections. What happened then, said the *Times* of London, "could variously be regarded as a serious crime or a riotous practical joke." Instead of the voice of Chief Akintola, the public heard a broadcast that began, "This is the voice of free Nigeria," and continued, "in uncomplimentary terms, to advise Akintola to leave Nigeria, along with his crew of renegades."[3] Soyinka was incarcerated shortly thereafter. A host of American and British writers, including Lillian Hellman, Robert Lowell, Norman Mailer, Alfred Kazin, Lionel Trilling, William Styron, Norman Podhoretz and Penelope Gilliatt, wired their protests to the Nigerian government. Not until late December was he released, with all charges dismissed.

He was incarcerated yet again in 1967. This occurred one year after he received the drama prize at the First World Festival of the Negro Arts at Dakar, where one critic called him "the most original man of letters in Africa,"[4] and less than one month after receiving, with Tom Stoppard, the John Whiting Drama Award, Soyinka was picked up for interrogation just outside the gates of Ibadan University shortly after returning from a writers' conference in Sweden. There he had wondered aloud about the African writer who felt he "must, for the moment at least (he persuades himself) postpone that unique reflection on experience and events which is what makes, a writer"[5] and substitute a more directly political commitment. Eleven days before being arrested, Soyinka had held a clandestine meeting at Enugu, the capital of Biafra, with the secessionist leader, Lieutenant Colonel Odumegwu Ojukwu, to implore him to reconsider the Ibos' decision to secede from Nigeria.

This time, protest from western writers would have no effect. For the next twenty months, Soyinka languished in prison, where he spent some ten months in solitary confinement, in constant fear of his life under the most unbearable conditions. His cell measured four feet by eight: "sixteen paces by twenty three," as he writes in the prison poem, "Live Burial."[6] A Nigerian military government at war refused hundreds of pleas for Soyinka's release. Deprived of human contact, books, medical care and writing implements, only the last-minute intervention of nameless informers saved him from murder. On the ninth anniversary of Independence and his production of *A Dance of the Forests*, the victorious military government announced that Soyinka would be released in a general amnesty.

In his poignant prison notes, published in 1972 as *The Man Died*, Soyinka details the terror of his confinement, the torture and death, "the inhuman assault on the mind."[7] The book, whose name derives from a cable describing the brutal murder of Segun Sowemimo, a Nigerian journalist, for an imagined slight, has been called an African *J'accuse*. Cast in an artistic idiom which few have mastered, it chronicles the starvation of the human spirit and the poet's struggle to survive through words. When at last he was allowed a few books in prison, including Radin's *Primitive Religion*, he "proceeded to cover the spaces between the lines with [his] own writing."[8] Soyinka survived by writing, secretly and in any manner he could. The only visit allowed his wife was announced with new cloths, a haircut, a radio, a typewriter and paper, pen and pencils, all of which were removed upon her departure. Aware of the coming raid, Soyinka allowed himself to enjoy only the luxury of the typing paper, which he stroked and caressed. Only narrowly did he escape murder; only through an act of enormous will did he remain sane. But Soyinka did not die; rather, he emerged from prison a great writer. As Angus Calder wrote in a review of *The Man Died*, "He seems to have accepted now, more fully even than his limitation let him, the weight of duty which that verdict implies. And I think he is, now a great writer."[9]

"The Man Dies," Soyinka writes, "in all who keep silent in the face of tyranny."[10] Yet in Soyinka's writing, the protest against tyranny is as subtle as certain forms of tyranny. Just as the Caribbean Marxist, C.L.R. James, had written a full-length study of Melville twenty years earlier during an unlawful internment on Ellis Island, so too had Soyinka displaced his critique of tyranny. The play, *Madmen and Specialists*,[11] was rather a return to his earlier, ritual form. According to Mel Gussow in the *New York Times*:

> Because of the genesis of madmen, one might expect a political play, but in solitary confinement Soyinka obviously had more important, timeless

concerns on his mind. The theme, as described by the author, is the corrupting effects of powers on one's natural vocation. The central figure is a young doctor, a specialist who has given up medicine to become a tyrannical political force. The play is not at all topical and only peripherally political. The symbolic, ritualistic, and especially, the religious are of much interest to Soyinka.[12]

We can begin to understand such a complex artist, who refuses to allow his own horrendous prison experience to intrude in an obvious sense upon his play, by understanding something of his idea of tragedy and the nature of the tragedian. Two statements seem especially meaningful here, one excerpted from "The Fourth Stage," an essay written in honour of G. Wilson Knight and published while Soyinka was in prison,[13] the other a critique of the western idea of tragedy, which oddly enough appears in *The Man Died*. Soyinka writes in "The Fourth Stage":

Nothing but the will…rescues being from annihilation within the abyss…Only one who has himself undergone the experience of disintegration, whose spirit has been tested and whose psychic resources laid under stress by the forces most inimical to individual assertion, only he can understand and be the force of fusion between two contradictions. The resulting sensibilities are also the sensibility of the artist and he is a profound artist only to the degree to which he comprehends and expresses this principle of destruction and recreation.[14]

It is human will, "the paradoxical truth of destructiveness and creativity in acting man,"[15] with which Soyinka the artist and Soyinka the activist are both concerned: the integrity of the will and a fundamental belief in its capacity to structure and restructure this world in which we live. Along with Gabriel Garcia Marquez and other politically committed writers, he never declaims this notion, nor becomes didactic. His critique of Western definitions of tragedy, along the lines of Brecht, written after his release from prison and published in *The Man Died* helps to explain why this is so:

History is too full of failed Prometheans bathing their wounded spirits in their tragic stream. Destroy the tragic lure! Tragedy is possible solely because of the limitation of the human spirit. There are levels of despair from which the human spirit should not recover. To plunge to such a level is to be overwhelmed by the debris of all those anti-human barriers that are erected by jealous gods. The power of recovery is close to acquisition of superhuman energies and the stagnation-loving human society must for self-preserving interest divert these colossal energies into relatively quiescent channels, for they constitute a force which, used as part of an individual's equipment in the normal human struggle, cannot be resisted by the normal human weapons. Thus the historic conspiracy, the literal brain-washing, that elevates tragedy far and above a regenerative continuance of the promethean struggle.[16]

It is this regard for the status of the will in the face of terror, combined with the unqualified rejection of the indulgence of pity and a belief in the communality of individual struggle, that most characterizes Soyinka's metaphysics.

In response to the adage of Nietzsche's sage, Silenus, that it is an act of hubris to be born, Soyinka responds that "the answer of the Yorubas to this is just as clear: it is no less an act of hubris to die."[17] Not surprisingly Soyinka's muse is his patron god Ogun, god of creativity and the Yoruba "proto-agonist," he who dared to cross the abyss of transition that separates the world of men from the world of the gods in the primal enactment of individual will.

I first encountered *Death and the King's Horseman* in 1973, two years before it was published. Soyinka, who was supervising my graduate work in English at the University of Cambridge, invited me to listen to the first reading of his new play. For three hours we listened as Oxford accents struggled to bring the metaphysical and lyrical Yoruba text to life. Although by now I had become accustomed to this densely figurative language of Soyinka's plays – indeed I had begun to hear its peculiar music – I was stunned by the action of the play. That the plot was an adaptation of an actual historical event was more stunning. And if the play's structure was classically Greek, the adaptation of a historical action at a royal court was compellingly Shakespearean. This, I thought, was a great tragedy.

Perhaps I should describe in outline the historical events before I recount the plot. In December 1944, Oba Siyenbola Oladigbolu, the Alaafin, or King of Oyo, an ancient Yoruba city in Nigeria, died. He was buried that night. As was the Yoruba tradition, the Horseman of the King, Olokun Esin Jinadu, was to commit ritual suicide and lead his Alaafin's favourite dog through transitional passage to the world of the ancestors. However, the British Colonial District Officer, Capital J.A. MacKenzie, decided that the custom was savage and intervened in January 1945 to prevent Olokun Esin Jinadu from completing his ritual act, the act for which his entire life had been lived. Faced with the anarchy this unconsummated ritual would work upon the order of the Yoruba world, Olokun Esin Jinadu's last-born son, Murana, in an unprecedented act, assumed his hereditary title of Olokun Esin, stood as surrogate for his father and sacrificed his own life. The incident, Soyinka told us following the reading, had intrigued him ever since he had first heard of it. It had, he continued, already inspired a play in Yoruba by Duro Ladipo called *Oba Waja*.[18]

Soyinka adapted the historical event rather liberally in order to emphasize the metaphorical and mythical dimensions, outside of time, again reflecting implicitly the idea that an event is a sign and that a sign adumbrates something other than itself by contiguity as well as by semblance. The relation that a fiction bears to reality is fundamentally related to the means by which that relation and that fiction are represented. For Soyinka, a text mediates the distance between art and life, but in a profoundly ambiguous and metaphorical manner. In that space between the structure of the historical event and the literary event, that is to say, the somehow necessary or probable event, one begins to understand Soyinka's idea of tragedy. The plot of a play, certainly, can indicate what may happen as well as what did happen and this concern with what a protagonist will probably or necessarily do, rather than what he did do, distinguishes Soyinka's universal and poetic art from particular and prosaic Yoruba history. It is this central concern with the philosophical import of human and black experience that so clearly makes him unlike many other black writers. A summary of the play's plot suggests this relation.

The Alaafin of Oyo is dead. To guide the Alaafin's horse through the narrow passage of transition, as tradition demands, the Horseman of the King, Elesin Oba, must on the night of the King's burial commit ritual suicide through the sublime agency of the will. The action of the play occurs on the day of his Death. Death for Elesin is not a final contract; it is rather the rite of passage to the larger world of ancestors, a world linked in the continuous bond of Yoruba metaphysics to that of the living and the unborn. It is a death which the Elesin seems willingly to embrace-but not before he possesses a beautiful market girl, a betrothed virgin whom he encounters as he dances the farewell greeting before the ritual marketplace. Though Iyaloja, the "mother" of the market, protests the Horseman's paradoxical selection, she consents to and arranges this ritualistic union of life with death.

Revolted by the 'barbarity' of the custom, a British colonial Officer, Pilkings, intervenes to prevent the death at the precise moment of the Horseman's intended transition. Notified by his family, Olunde, the Horseman's eldest heir, has returned from medical school in England intending to bury his father. Confronted with his father's failure of will, the son assumes this hereditary title only to become his surrogate in death to complete the cosmic restoration of order. In a splendidly poignant climax to the action, the women of the market, led by Iyaloja, unmask the veiled corpse of the son and watch placidly as the Horseman of the King's breaks his neck with his chains, fulfilling his covenant with tradition and the communal will, alas, too late. Two men have died rather than one.

As adapted by Soyinka, this is no mere drama of individual vacillation. Communal order and communal will are inextricable elements in the Elesin's tragedy, which not only reflect but amplify his own failure of will. In this sense, Soyinka's drama suggests Greek tragedy much more readily than Elizabethan tragedy and is akin to the mythopoetic tragedies of Synge and Brecht and to Lorca's *Blood Wedding*. Nor is this merely a fable of the evils of colonialism or of white unblinking racism. *Death and the King's Horseman* is a classical tragedy, in which structure and metaphysics are inextricably intertwined.

Structurally, the play is divided into five acts and occurs almost exactly over twenty-four hours. Its basis is communal and ritualistic; its medium is richly metaphorical poetry which, accomplished continuously by music and dance and mime, creates an air of mystery and wonder. The cumulative effect defines a cosmos comprised at once of nature, of human society and of the divine. The protagonist's bewilderment and vacillation, his courage and inevitable defeat, signify a crisis, confrontation and transformation of values, transfixed in a time that oscillates perpetually in an antiphonal moment. Finally, the reversal of the *peripeteia* ("situation") and the *anagnorisis* ("recognition") occur at the same time, as they do in *Oedipus Rex*.

The characterisation of Elesin, the protagonist, is also classically Greek. The play records the reciprocal relationship between his character and his fate. Elesin's grand flaw does not stem from vice or depravity, but from hamartia (an error of judgement"), a sign of his weakness of will. Although not eminently good or just, he is loved. His will and his character are neither wholly determined nor wholly free. His character is at once noble and prone to error. The nine-member chorus again and again speaks against Elesin's special hubris, his unregenerate will. His, finally, is the great defeat, but suffered only after the great attempt. The play's action is timeless, as timeless as the child conceived by Elesin on the day of his death. Its plot unfolds in "the seething cauldron of the dark world will and psyche,"[19] where ambiguity and vacillation wreak havoc upon the individual.

Although self-sacrifice is a familiar motif in Soyinka's tragedies, Elesin's intended sacrifice is not meant to suggest the obliteration of an individual soul, but rather is an implicit confirmation of an order in which the self exists with all of its integrity but only as one small part of a large whole. Elesin Oba, after all, is a conferred title, the importance of which derives from its context within the community and from its ritual function. The Elesin's character is determined in the play, not by any obvious material relationships, however, but rather by the plot itself, as the formal dramatic elements of any tragedy are determined by a silent structuring principle. Great tragic plots always determine the tragic characters of their protagonists. To paraphrase Pilking's servant, Joseph, the Elesin exists simply to die; he has no choice in the matter, despite the play's repeated reference to the ambiguity inherent in his role. And Pilkings's intervention, a kind of self-defence, challenges fundamentally the communal defence of self which this ritual embodies.

Elesin's dilemma is both individual and collective, both social and psychic, all at once. In the same way that Faust's hubristic transgression occurs within his consciousness-occurs indeed, because of his deification of mind and will-so too is Elesin's tragic dilemma enacted internally, here within his will. As he suggests ominously early in *Death and the King's Horseman*, "My will has outlept the conscious act" (p.18). His hubris is symbolised by the taking of a bride on the morning of his death in a ritual in which the thanatotic embraces the erotic; he chooses the satisfaction of the self over the exactions of the will. This is his tragic flaw. Elesin's inevitable fall results from a convergence of forces at work within the will and without, which conspire to reinforce those subliminal fears that confront all tragic heroes.

Not only is the westernized Olunde's suicide a rejection of the relief of the resolution afforded by the Western philosophical tradition; it is also the ritual slaying of the father at the crossroads. Olunde's death leaves his father entrapped, penned outside of the rite of passage, for the fleeting moment of transition has passed, making ironic even an act as final as death. Iyaloja, perhaps the most powerful characterisation of a woman in African literature, expresses the paradox: we said, the dew on earth's surface was for you to wash your feet along the slopes of honour. You said No, I shall step in the vomit of cats and the droppings of mice; I shall fight them for the left-overs of the world" (p.68). In the face of his son's slaying, the Elesin is poignantly "left-over." There will be no more Elesins, for the unbroken order of this world has now been rent asunder. As Iyaloja remarks, "he is gone at last into the passage but oh, how late it all is. His son will feast on the meat and throw him bones. The passage is clogged with droppings from the King's stallion; he will arrive all stained in dung" (p.76). To paraphrase the praise singer, the world has finally tilted from its groove (p.10).

The ritual passage of the Horseman had served for centuries to retrace an invisible cultural circle, thereby reaffirming the order of this Yoruba world.

The ritual dress, the metaphorical language, the Praise-Singer's elegy, the Elesin's dance of death-these remain fundamentally unchanged as memory has recast them from generation to generation. The mixed symbols of semen and blood, implied in the hereditary relationship between succession and authority and reiterated in the deflowering of the virgin on the day of death stand as signs of a deeper idea of transition and generation. But the role of the Horseman demands not only the acceptance of ambiguity, but also its embrace.

Although Elesin's is an individual dilemma and a failure of the human will, the dilemma is implicit in his role of the King's Horseman, a communal dilemma of preservation of order in the face of change. During the play, at a crucial moment, a traditional proverb is cited which reveals that doubt and ambiguity are not emotions uncharacteristic of the Elesin: "The elder grimly approaches heaven and you ask him to bear your greeting yonder; do you think he makes the journey willingly?" (p.64). All myth, we know, reconciles two otherwise irreconcilable forces, or tensions, through the mediation of the mythic structure itself. The *Orestia* is a superb example of this. This trick of "structuration," as it were, is the most characteristic aspect of human mythology. Soyinka, in his "Director's Notes," in the Playbill of *Death and the King's Horseman* put the matter this way: "at the heart of the lyric and the dance of transition in Yoruba tragic art, that core of ambivalence is always implanted. This is how society, even on its own, reveals and demonstrates its capacity for change."[20]

We do not need to know, as the Yoruba historian Samuel Johnson tells us, that at one time the reluctance of an Elesin to accompany a dead Alaafin engendered such disgrace that the Horseman's family often strangled him themselves, nor that the reluctance of the Elesins grew as contact with the British increased.[21] We do not need to know these historical facts simply because the Horseman's ambiguity over his choices is rendered apparent throughout Soyinka's text. And from *Hamlet* it is that sense of 'conscience" as defined in the epigraph from Hamlet's soliloquy, implying self-consciousness and introspection, which is also the Horseman's fatal flaw-that which colours "the native hue of resolution… with the pale cast of thought."[22] As Elesin Oba put it, in a splendid confession near the end of the play, he commits "the awful treachery of relief and thinks "the unspeakable blasphemy of seeing the hands of the gods in this alien rupture of his world" (p.69). This ambiguity of action, reflected in the ambiguity of figurative language and of mythic structure, allows this to remain a flexible metaphysical system. Formal and structured, it remains nonetheless fluid and malleable with a sophisticated and subtle internal logic.

Soyinka embodies perfectly the ambiguity of the Elesin's action in the ambiguity of the play's language. A play, among all the verbal arts, is most obviously an act of language. Soyinka allows the metaphorical and tonal Yoruba language to inform his use of English. Western metaphors for the nature of a metaphor, at least since I. A. Richards, are "vehicle" and "tenor" both of which suggest an action of meaning, a transfer through semantic "horse" of words: "If a word is lost, a metaphor or proverb is used to find it."[23] As to tenor and vehicle, the horse metaphor implies a transfer or Carriage of meaning, through intention and extension. It is just this aspect of the metaphorical utterances, searching for the lost or hidden meaning of words and events, serves to suggest music, dance and myth, all aspects of poeisis long ago fragmented in Western tragic art.

In Soyinka's tragedies, languages and act mesh fundamentally. A superb example of this is the Praise-Singer's speech near the climax of the play, in which he denounces in the voice of his former King, the Elesin Oba:

Elesin Oba! I call you by that name only this last time. Remember when I said, if you cannot come, tell my horse. What? I cannot hear you, I said, if you cannot come, whisper in the ears of my horse. Is your tongue severed from the roots Elesin? I can hear no response. I said, if there are boulders you cannot climb, mount my horse's back; this spotless black stallion, he' ll bring you over them. Elesin Oba, once you had a path to me. My memory fails me but I think you replied: My feet have found the path, Alaafin. I said at the last, if an evil hand holds you back, just tell my horse there is weight on the hem of your smock. I dare not wait too long…

…Oh my companion, if you had followed when you should, we would not say that the horse preceded its rider. If you had followed when it was time, we would not say the dog has raced beyond and left his master behind. If you had raised your will to cut the thread of life at the summons of the drums, we would not say your mere shadow fell across the gateway and took its owner's place at the banquet. But the hunter, laden with slain buffalo, stayed to root in the cricket's hole with his toes. What now is left? If there is a dearth of bats, the pigeon must serve us for the offering. Speak the words over your shadow which must now serve in your place. (pp. 74–75)

In this stunning speech, the language of music and the music of language are one. In one sense, the music of the play gives it force, the reciprocal displacement of the language of music with the music of language. The antiphonal structure of Greek tragedy is also perhaps the most fundamental African aesthetic value and is used as the party's internal structuring mechanism. As in music, the use of repetition, such as the *voudoun* ("voodoo") phrase, "Tell my horse," serves to create simultaneity of action. The transitional passage before which the Elesin falters is inherent in all black musical forms. Soyinka's dances are darkly lyrical, uniting with the music of the drums and songs of the chorus to usher the audience into self-contained hermetic world, an affected reality. Soyinka's greatest achievement is just this: the creation of a compelling world through language and of language. He has mastered the power of language to create a reality and not merely to reflect reality. But his mastery of spoken language is necessarily reinforced by mastery of a second language of music and a third of the dance. "Where it is possible to capture through movements instead what words are saying," he says, "then I will use the movement instead of the words."[24] To evoke these languages and to evoke the threnodic celebration of the meanings of death and the reciprocity of passage among the past, the present and that state of being to be, and to escape the naive myths of Africa that persist in this country, Soyinka insists upon directing his tragedies himself, as he did the production at Chicago.

As a critic of silent literary texts, I was struck by the dynamic nature of the Chicago production, ever shifting, ever adapting itself toward an unspoken ideal, in a manner which in a short space and time parallels what happens to a text when studied by a critic, but only over a much longer period. Soyinka, of course, knows what he wants a performance to say and knows what combination of textures will suggest his meaning to an alien audience. Confronting an American audience's usual unease with, or condescension towards an African setting no doubt reinforced whatever tendencies he had to adhere to a strict rendering of the play.

But is Soyinka's Yoruba world so very obscure? Is it any more obscure than the tribal world of the ancient Greeks, than Joyce's voices in *Ulysses* or the private linguistic circle of *Finnegan's Wake*? Footnotes to *The Waste Land*, topographies to Joyce, concordances to Shakespeare: we presume a familiarity with these texts that is made possible only by the academic industry of annotation. The fact of Soyinka's Africanness only makes visible an estranged relation that always stands between any text and its audience. As Shakespeare used Denmark, as Brecht used Chicago, Soyinka uses the Yoruba world as a setting for cosmic conflict and never as an argument for the existence of African culture. Always in the language of his texts are ample clues for the decoding of his silent signs, since the relationship among character, setting, and language is always properly reinforcing. This is no mean achievement: it is the successful invocation of a hermetic universe.

It is for this reason that Soyinka is often compared favourably to his direct antecedents, Euripides and Shakespeare, Yeats and Synge, Brecht and Lorca. Statements such as this sound necessarily hyperbolic, no doubt. But it is impossible not to make such comparisons when one searches for a meaningful comparison of Soyinka's craft with Western writers. For so long, black Americans, especially, have had to claim more for our traditions than tact, restraint and honesty might warrant, precisely to redress those claims that our traditions do not exist. But Soyinka's texts are superbly realized, complex mediations between European dramatic tradition and the equally splendid Yoruba dramatic tradition. This form of verbal expression, uniquely his own, he uses to address the profoundest matters of human moral order and cosmic will.

What does remain obscure, nevertheless, is something else, a set of matters so much more subtle and profound than mere reference can ever be. And these matters involve an understanding of tragedy seemingly related to, yet fundamentally unlike, that notion of the tragedy of the individual first defined by Aristotle and in essence, reiterated by Hegel, Nietzsche and even Brecht. Set against the hubris, harmartia and violent obliteration of a noble individual is Soyinka's evocation of a tragedy of the community, a tragic sense which turns upon a dialectic between retributive and restorative justice and order. The relation between the order of the community and the self-sacrifice of the protagonist, whose role is defined by his own intuition and will to act, forms the centre of Soyinka's protagonists for the community; they stand as embodiments of the communal will, invested in the protagonist of the community's choice. Even the moment of the most distinct individuation must always be a communal moment. He summarises his own conception of this relationship in his art:

> Morality for the Yoruba is that which creates harmony in the cosmos, and reparation for the disjunction within the individual psyche cannot be seen as compensation for the individual accident to that personality. Thus it is that good and evil are not measured in terms of offences against the individual or even the physical community, for... offences even against nature may in fact be part of the exaction by deeper nature from humanity of acts which alone can open up the deeper springs of man and bring about a constant rejuvenation of the human spirit. Nature in turn benefits by such broken taboos, just as the cosmos by the demand made upon its will by man's cosmic affronts. Such acts of the hubris compel the cosmos to delve deeper into its essence to meet the human challenges. Penance and retribution are not therefore aspects of punishment for crime but the first acts of a resumed awareness, an invocation of the principle of cosmic adjustment.[25]

It is this disintegration and subsequent retrieval of the protagonist's will that distinguishes Soyinka's tragic vision from its Western antecedents. His understanding of tragedy at long last gives some sense to what is meant by "the functional" and "the collective" in African aesthetics, two otherwise abused and misapprehended notions. Clearly, he reveals, these are relationships effected by the prototypic agonist, the acting individual will. Rightly, we look first to Soyinka's language to begin to understand his direct relation to Shakespeare's mastery of language. And Soyinka's language, always, is his own. Yet, it is this curious metaphysical structure of the tragic which most obviously remains ideas of Western tragedy. Paradoxically, it is "African" certainly, but it is ultimately a Soyinka construct. Soyinka has invented a tragic form and registered it in his own invented language, a fusion of English and Yoruba.

Surely this is his greatest achievement. For, in the end, *Death and the King's Horseman* itself stands as a mythic structure, as a structure of reconciliation. As he concludes about the nature of tragedy:

> Great tragedy is a cleansing process for the health of the community. Tragic theatre is a literal development of ritual. It is necessary for balancing the aesthetic sensibilities of the community. Tragedy is a community event. It is the acting of the neuroses, the recoveries, within a community. It does not just involve a single individual.[26]

Chapter Nine

"All of the People, Some of the Time": The Ethics of Choice in a Soyinkan Action

Ato Quayson

Sometime in 2003 I had the indescribable pleasure of spending an entire hour-and-a-half in a BBC radio studio interviewing Wole Soyinka. The interview was to commemorate the publication of *Samarkand and Other Markets I Have Known*, his first collection of poems since *The Outsiders* in 1999, which was itself much less known than *Mandela's Earth*, of 1988. *Samarkand* returned Soyinka to the tight lyric verse for which he had become famous in earlier poems such as "Telephone Conversation" and "Abiku," both of which are now staples of the curriculum anywhere African literature is taught. The interview moved leisurely over questions of poetic style, but after a while switched to events in his personal life. I was curious to find out more about his famous personal courage and penchant for getting himself in and out of complicated scrapes. He immediately got more animated and stated quite forcefully that he had never actually been afraid for his own personal safety, but only for that of others. He proceeded to recount the time when, a week or so before the interview, he had made a citizen's arrest in the heart of Russell Square in London. The unfortunate object of his wrath? A hapless taxi driver who had made the ignominious miscalculation of ignoring Soyinka's raised hand hailing him and had instead bypassed him to pick up another fare barely 10 meters away from where Soyinka and his female friend were standing. Without a moment's hesitation the author of *The Lion and the Jewel* bounded forward to where the taxi was standing and proceeded to arrest the cabbie. Just like that! On the spot!! After the initial shock the cabbie apologized profusely, by which time his fare had made good his bewildered escape, a "rapid dialogue with his legs," as Soyinka puts it in another context. The cabbie will not have come away without a profound and hopefully abiding lesson. But the story Soyinka recounted also reminded me of countless other stories I had heard about him while at university and afterwards that made him into a legend in mine and my friends' eyes. The story was told, for example, that at a conference in Accra in the 1970s the much younger Soyinka decided to spend the entire time sitting half-bottomly on the chair the organizers had provided him up on stage. On being asked why he decided to sit so unusually he proclaimed that he was protesting what everyone assumed was the commonsense way of sitting on chairs and thus wanted to signal an assault on commonsense by sitting with only one buttock throughout the proceedings. Some other stories could also be gleaned from his own writing. Thus he tells us in *Ibadan: The Pankemeles Years* that just before the outbreak of war in Biafra he had single-handedly held up the regional office of the Nigerian Broadcasting Corporation and replaced the pre-recorded news bulletin with one of his own lambasting the Western Region government for not being bold to criticize what was going on in the Eastern Nigeria. Nevertheless, for all his famed personal fearlessness that he gave vent to in public, I still see Wole Soyinka as an incredibly private and indeed highly sensitive man. That much can be gleaned from his lyric poetry, which reveals all the markings of intense privacy. It is this combination of extreme personal and political courage and the intimate privacy of his literary persona that I want to explore as one of the legacies he has bequeathed to African letters. The point of the first part of my title, then is to suggest that though he is a man for all the people, this is only so for some of the time, because in that small remainder he cultivates the spirit of paradox and beauteous contradiction that we find expressed in his finest plays, essays, and poems. To go even further, everything Soyinka has done over his several decades of public life has been informed by an ethics of choice, the lineaments of which are also provided in his literary writings.

II

I read *Death and the King's Horseman* for the first time when working on my dissertation on Nigerian literary history many years ago. For reasons that I can't completely remember now the play moved me very deeply at the time, especially the point in the action at which Iyaloja comes to rain bitter insults ("Eater of left overs") on Elesin Oba when she visits him in detention at Mr Pilkings' pleasure. Elesin has failed to complete the suicide for which every ritual preparation has been performed by his community. At some point during the exchanges, hers increasingly bitter, his more muted, she spits out at him: "I wish I could pity you!" To which he replies, plaintively: "I need neither your pity nor the pity of the world. I need understanding. Even I need to understand." This scene moved me so deeply that I immediately shut the book and was not able to return to it for some three days afterwards. I kept reflecting on how subtly Soyinka had managed to capture in that one simple exchange the unbearable weight of longing and loss and coupled it to a finely-balanced moment of supreme existential crisis for both the wider Yoruba culture, represented here by the redoubtable Iyaloja, and the tragic protagonist, Elesin Oba. There are other scenes in African writing that have moved me in the same way and given me pause for wonder. Two that spring up unbidden to perch alongside that from *Death and the King's Horseman* are from Ngũgĩ wa Thiong'o's *A Grain of Wheat* and Chinua Achebe's *Arrow of God*, both at once subtle and intricate. The moment from Ngugi's novel is when Gikonyo finally arrives home from several years in detention in one of the infamous Mau Mau camps the British had set up against the insurgency, only to find that Mumbi, his true love for whom he has drawn his every breath, has borne a child in his absence. Gikonyo has trudged many weary miles to get to his homestead, all the time dreaming of the homecoming. But when he enters their smoky hearth kitchen he finds a little child (four, maybe five?) tugging at Mumbi's cloth. Gikonyo turns his eyes from the blearing sight and unto his mother, who is also in the kitchen at the time and intones, almost inaudibly: "Mother, I have walked a long way and I want to sleep." The death wish he had managed to resist all through detention is now embraced in the moment of tragic misrecognition. It is a misrecognition because Mumbi was victim of a rape, perpetrated by the cynicism of the confused times. But Gikonyo is not to find this out until much later and even when he does he is unable to forgive her.

From *Arrow of God* I recall the moment when Ezeulu, in one of the very rare reminiscences about his childhood, recalls his mother: "Nwayi Okper," as they called her in Umuaro, had been a great singer in her youth, making songs for her village as easily as some people talked. In later life when her madness came on her these old songs and others she might have made forced themselves out in eccentric spurs through the cracks in her mind. Ezeulu in his childhood lived in fear of these moments when his mother's feet were put in stocks, at the new moon." That this account is given us in the voice of the third-person narrator must not obviate the fact that the narrator has remained faithfully aligned to Ezeulu's consciousness for much of the narrative, especially in this section where he wakes up suddenly from a nightmare. That Ezeulu recalls his mother after waking up from a nightmare in which the moon plays a part and that one of his duties as the priest of Ulu requires him to watch the faces of the moon in the night sky so as to be able to perform his ritual functions also means that the staring at the moon that we are shown at different points in the novel is affectively bound in his consciousness to moments of great pain and distress. All the three moments I have mentioned affected me at different points in my life with the terrible beauty of human suffering, the way this beauty cannot be expressed except through faltering language, the intensely-charged symbols that perforce are made to take language's place and the ways in which these incoherent symbols manage to expand outwards to illuminate the complex terms of what it means to be human, be you African or Aborigine, young or old, black or white, man or woman.

III

I want to proceed, then, by tarrying with this sense of terrible beauty as encapsulated in *Death and the King's Horseman* and to tie it to the dialectic of stasis and mobility that is never mentioned in commentaries on the play but which I think is crucial to understanding the dynamic of ethical choice that the dialectic helps to illustrate. This dialectic may also be interpreted as a structural correlative to the relation between the public and private personas that make up Wole Soyinka as we celebrate him. His public life calls up images of incessant movement and epic actions, whilst the private is, as I suggested earlier, crafted from the creative solitude that he is also well known for.

Now, to state that *Death and the King's Horseman* is about stasis is to open oneself to incredulity if not outright derision, for nothing seems more opposite. On the occasions that I have taught the play over the past few years I have borne with me to class a large *djembe* drum, a small wooden xylophone and some pieces of *adinkra, kente,* and tie-and-die cloths. I drape the lectern or table in front of the class with the cloths and play vigorously on the drum, alternating this with gentle notes off the xylophone. I then tell my students to imagine the sonic quality and range of the play's opening scene at the marketplace but to keep the resonances of this soniscape in mind throughout their reading of the play. For indeed drumming retains a presence throughout the dramatic action, either appearing directly on stage, as in Acts 1 and 4, or as a vague yet arresting dimension of the background, as in Scenes 2 and 3. The drumming provides a form of perspectival modulation through the sonic sequences that ensure that a sense of undulating vitality is always kept in play, no matter the nature of the precise action that unfolds before us on stage. Another element that might be taken to defeat the proposition of stasis is the sheer verbal artistry and indeed exuberance that is depicted in *Death and the King's Horseman*. Elesin Oba is a master at this yet has not got a monopoly over the fertile proverbial language that we find in the play. All the Yoruba characters have memorable lines, including Iyaloja (but of course!), the Praise-Singer, and even the Girls that design to "look into" Amusa's baggy shorts in the burlesque mocking of authority in Act 3.

What I am describing as stasis, however, must not be interpreted as synonymous with stillness or motionlessness, even though there is some of that in the play as well, especially in the character of the young Bride, who, despite being in a garrulous dramatic action, is not assigned a single line throughout the play. Rather, stasis must be understood primarily in its dialectical relationship to mobility, a dialectical relationship whose key terms are relayed at different levels of Soyinka's dramaturgy. At the most primary level Soyinka sets up relations of spectatoriality in which there is a subtle process of conversion of the characters in the play to witnesses of an unfolding scenario or drama, and, concomitantly and often in a related sequence, of breaking out of the apparent fixity of witness to take decisions that often bear an ethical charge. In its barest ritual form dramaturgical spectatoriality reaches back to Greek tragedy, where the very nature of the relationship between the chorus and the protagonist produced an inherent structure of witnessing as such. The most pristine example of this relationship is to be seen in Aeschylus's *Prometheus Bound*, where Prometheus, chained to a rock as punishment by Zeus, is the very image of stasis and fixity. Prometheus interacts with a sequence of characters that enter and exit to bear witness to his woeful story. The rebellion against the gods lies in the act of bringing enlightenment to man (the "fire" of common lore) but despite his terrible punishment he remains a god and gives proof of this repeatedly in the dire prognostications he makes about the future time. In the course of the entrances and exits we encounter Io, who, in a diametrically opposed movement to Prometheus's condition of stasis and immobility, has had to traverse expansive geographical regions before arriving ahead of Prometheus. That Io is also afflicted by the madness brought on by Hera's infernal gadfly suggests another contrast between her and Prometheus: to her many questions – (16 in the first 50 lines assigned to her) – is counterpoised his confident answers, to her journeying through a maze of anguish his profound prognostications and to his epic rebelliousness her abject victimhood. The roles are however going to be reversed much later, for she will be the maternal forbear of Hercules, whose labours will in the distant future include the freeing of Prometheus.

Shakespeare also has many of such scenes, the most potent for me being the eavesdropping moment when Iago gets Othello to see the conversation Iago sets up with Cassio to provide Othello with the ultimate verification of Desdemona's infidelity in the handkerchief that will be casually seen in the hands of Cassio. That Othello is only privy to the two other characters' facial gestures and not their words and that each gesture has been pre-interpreted for him by Iago means that Othello is literally trapped between a rock and a tornado. Shakespeare is the master of dramatic spectatoriality and Iago its most fervent exemplar. Yet the choice that emerges out of the satisfaction of Othello's quest for epistemological certainty (the "ocular proof" that he had earlier demanded of Iago) is profoundly tragic precisely because it is gained from an inherent misunderstanding of the fragility of his own judgment, a judgment founded as it was on the unsteady combination of ethical absolutism and febrile uncertainties.

With Soyinka the terms of the dialectic of stasis, mobility and spectatoriality are quite different from those of Aeschylus and Shakespeare, partly because this also entails the exercise of forms of orality that are inherently dramatic in and of themselves, thus adding an extra dimension to the performance of specatoriality. The relationship of spectatoriality is always more complex than merely that of requiring people to revert their attention to a character; as we find in *Death and the King's Horseman* it also means adopting a role other than the one typically assigned to you and requiring that other people pay attention to you in your performance of that new and self-chosen role. Thus we find that in Act 1, Elesin Oba interrupts the Praise-Singer, not once or twice but three different times and each time to convert him and the gathered market women into spectators to his impending epic performance as sacrificial carrier through the superlative exercise of devices of traditional orality. And so it is that in the first interruption, Elesin Oba launches into the lengthy and initially baffling story of the Not-I Bird, replete with dense proverbial language and the enactment of the foibles of each individual character within the story while Praise-Singer, Iyaloja and the market women stand entranced. At the end of the Not-I Bird sequence there is a welcome relaxation of the taut mood as the other characters break out of the relationship of spectaroriality and the Praise-Singer is allowed to continue his drumming and *oríkí* (praise singing) once again. Yet it is in that dramatic interlude that the terms of the dialectic between stasis and mobility are set, for Elesin's listeners have been converted into a captive audience and forced to bear witness to his epic greatness and his absolute lack of fear when being courted by death in the form of the Not-I Bird. This initial spectatorial of a strict fixity for the audience within the play that enjoins only cultural affirmation comes later to bear an ethical inflection that is completely unforeseen by the spectators.

The ethical inflection comes in the very next interruption, when as the Praise-Singer continues the ritual preparation by recounting more *oríkí*, the action is suddenly stopped again by Elesin Oba when he complains to the women that he feels naked in the market place. The momentary and palpable panic that the women express is only broken when they understand that Elesin is only asking them to shower him with material largesse, the primary representation of which is the marketplace itself. This they proceed to do by draping him in the best *alari* cloths available at the market and by joining Praise-Singer to sing Elesin's praise names and *oríkí*. Once Elesin has got all his auditors to move from (a) bearing witness to the performative of his epic grandeur and (b) draping him with the material paraphernalia to such greatness, he has prepared them for (c) the question of ethical choice. In other words the repetitions of spectatoriality are actually the rehearsal for a grander ethical proposition. This third interruption is when Elesin spots the young Bride walking down the passageway to the market place:

ELESIN stands resplendent in rich clothes, cap, shawl, etc. His sash is of a bright red *alari* cloth. The women dance round him. Suddenly, his attentionis caught by an object off-stage).

– – –

(The earlier distraction, a beautiful girl, comes along the passage through which ELESIN first made his entry).

ELESIN:	embrace it. And let me tell you, women –
	I like this farewell that the world designed,
	Unless my eyes deceive me, unless
	We are already parted, the world and I,
	And all that breeds desire is lodged
	Among our tireless ancestors. Tell me friends,
	Am I still earthed in the beloved market
	Of my youth? Or could it be my will
	Has outleapt the conscious act and I have come
	Among the great departed?

PRAISE-SINGER:	Elesin-Oba why do your eyes roll like a bush-rat who sees his fate like his father's spirit, mirrored in the eye of a snake? And all these questions! You're standing on the same earth you've always stood upon. This voice you hear is mine, Olohun-iyo, not that of an acolyte in heaven (18).

Elesin insists that he must have the young girl with him that night of monumental crossing and thus suddenly presents his culture with a large and hitherto unanticipated problem. For it turns out that the young woman has been betrothed to Iyaloja's own son. Her initial hesitation is however overcome by the assertion that since he is standing between the living and the dead his every wish must be obeyed to smoothen the way to the other side:

IYALOJA:	Oh you who fill the home from hearth to threshold with the voices of children, you who now bestride the hidden gulf and pause to draw the right foot across and into the resting-home of the great forebears, it is good that your loins be drained into the earth we know, that your last strength be ploughed back into the womb that gave you being (22).

At heart what this rationalization really means is that Iyaloja and the cultural disposition she represents, is prepared to countenance the suspension of the foundational ethics of familial relationships in favour of the apparently higher ethics of communal security and cultural survival. This turns out to be a terrible mistake.

One of the peculiar features of the character of Elesin Oba is that despite the many praise names that are showered upon him throughout the play, not a single one pertains to military prowess. This is decidedly odd for someone whose position as guardian of the king's stable automatically implied the powerful position of commander of the king's army. If not one *oríkì* is delivered regarding his skills as a military commander, might this not be interpreted as Soyinka's subtle critique of the culture's fixation on the flawed vessel that is their chosen conduit for salvation? For all the culture has is the hedonistic, womanizing and overall haughty Elesin Oba. Thus Iyaloja's mistaken ethical choice marks the larger failure of a cultural praxis whose terms may have been thoroughly compromised through the encounter with colonialism. This is not in the simple terms of colonialism's well-documented attempts at undermining indigenous structures of thought and feeling, but that of making the idiom of hierarchical power infinitely replaceable in the mind of traditional cultural agents. This is what leads Elesin Oba to lament to the vociferous Ijaloja:

ELESIN: What were warnings beside the moist contact of living earth between my fingers? What were warnings beside the renewal of famished embers lodged eternally in the heart of man? But even that, even if it overwhelmed one with a thousand fold temptations to linger a little while, a man could overcome it. It is when the alien hand pollutes the source of will, when a stranger force of violence shatters the mind's calm resolution, this is when a man is made to commit the awful treachery of relief, *commit in his thought the unspeakable blasphemy of seeing the hand of the gods in this alien rupture of his world.* I know it was this thought that killed me, sapped my powers and turned me into an infant in the hands of unnameable strangers. I made to utter my spells anew but my tongue merely rattled in my mouth. I fingered hidden charms and the contact was damp; there was no spark left to sever the life-strings that should stretch from every finger-tip. My will was squelched in the spittle of an alien race, and all because I had committed this blasphemy of thought – that there might be the hand of the gods in a stranger's intervention (69; italics added).

Note the nature of the admission: the real blasphemy was in the concession, for one charged moment, that there might be the hand of his own gods in the white man's intervention. In other words, in the liminal status of the crossing, the categories that had organized his world are warped such that he is able to mistake the white man as one of his own gods and vice versa. This is what made me close the book and talk a long walk.

IV

People often wonder whether Africa can produce other Soyinkas, Achebes and even Mandelas. The question itself is somewhat trite and in fact diversionary for the conditions that produced these great personages will not be replicable in the same ways as they were before. Yet there is something that these and other great Africans all share that can be found in many other contexts. In brief, I want to label this as the capacity to act in the face of History. The historic opportunities presented by decolonization and Independence gave a heady sense of destiny to all the newly-educated elites such as Soyinka and others of his generation. And the sense of epic action was grafted into their every choice and gesture, since they were literally making history in their commentary and participation in politics, in the writing of the new African literatures and generally in their conduct of the private and public lives that were taken as models for the teeming populations looking desperate for guidance. After over 50 years of Independence the choices may be different but no less stark: poverty, the stripping of our natural resources, the irresponsible kleptomania of politicians and the collusion of cynics both inside and beyond Africa. All these show that History is still urgent and to be made. While the younger generation of African writers do not have the same intense activist bent that Soyinka and his generation expressed because of their historical times, they are nevertheless also poised to contribute to re-visioning an Africa better than their parent's generation bequeathed to them. And much of this re-visioning is taking place from within the domain of African letters. It would be invidious to attempt a list of the most interesting African writers re-visioning Africa today since no such list can be exhaustive, but whether we look at the poetical realism of Ben Okri, the clear lines of Chimamanda Ngozi Adichie, the irony-laden prose of Ivan Vladislavic, or the Diasporic cosmopolitanisms of Taiye Selasi and Esi Edugyan we see a variety of African writers, who like Soyinka and others before them, work in the face of History.

Section III

Harvest of Past Seasons:
Memoirs, Conversations and Palavers

Chapter Ten
"I Shall Go Beyond and Rest…"
Femi Johnson

Essentially, he is a personal friend. A bosom friend, I find him very dependable, trustworthy. If there is anybody to whom you can give out your heart for safe keeping (if that was possible), go to Hong Kong, come back and still find the heart pulsating, it is Wole.

I call him AMP-Absent Minded Professor because you feel he is always absent-minded. His mind is ahead of his entire body. He grunts and waffles away but he hasn't said anything. Then you ask him, "what about so and so," and because in his mind which had already raced ahead of you and the topic he has, he says, "I've told you…" He'll go home when he was at Ife, for lunch. He advocated this for me; take a break, midday, one hour, just put your feet up and you'll feel better. So he'll go home, get his left-overs from the day before, put it on the stove, sit down, read the papers and at the end, forgets he hasn't eaten. Once he did that and went back to the office. When he came back, his house was filled with smoke and the pot was like cinders. I can't count how many percolators he's ruined that way. He's got a place in Abeokuta now. One day he couldn't find the way to his house! It took us over an hour to find the place. He said, "I know it once I find the green facia of a house and then we'll zoom down…" I started to laugh and so did the driver, at which he was miffed and the driver's head was an immediate anvil to the hammer of his knuckle. Anyway, we finally found it and he went on to show me his farmland and this beautiful place where he wants to build his house which is envisioned to be discreetly ensconced behind huge tropical trees and foliage.

I first met him many years ago in Lagos. I recall Francesca Yetunde Emanuel (Pereira) was having a birthday party at Olondde Street in Yaba. He was smallish then, almost like an imp. He arrived on a bicycle (this was in the early fifties) and he had on a skull-cap made of straw – the typical *dara* hat. But our paths did not meet again until when he came back from England in 1960, and started the *1960 MASKS*. Those were the days of the great cultural activities in Ibadan. Our first performance was *A Dance of the Forests* in which I had a part, but family commitments at the time, kept me busy and I was unable to journey back and forth between Lagos and Ibadan. In the end, I had to pull out. And he felt I was playing the prima donna. In fact, when the programme came out, he referred to some people as having "amateurish dilettantism." Of course, I knew the finger was pointing at me.

We gravitated towards each other and it's been so ever since. I remember I made some allusion to him when we were opening this place (Broking House, my insurance company), as a multi-faceted man. He taught me wine and I taught him food. He never bothered much about food. When he was at Lagos University, anytime he was coming to Ibadan, he would bring the wine (he had his wine smugglers) and I would get the food ready – food in exchange for wine! He is a very compelling person, someone that you not only wine and dine with; he imparts a lot without being didactic about it. It's amazing what influence he has on people. He has got that compelling, charismatic influence. He would shy away from a crowd but then, in intimate company you get the best of him. At times, we sit down together till about 5am just talking. We share a lot in common. If we didn't, it wouldn't be like this. You know, you can't always judge people by appearances. He is an extremely gifted person; a *bon vivant* too.

I never thought in my whole life that I would handle a gun. Years ago, he brought me into hunting; now we go into the bush at weekends. There was this occasion when we went out hunting with this forest gnome called Asimotu. This guy is so lithe, he oozes, doesn't walk and his style of hunting is such that he treks for almost two hours before he gets to the area where he wants to start hunting and he wears no shoes. We happened on this gnome by chance and he and Wole immediately took to each other. So one day, we arranged a night hunt with Asimotu. We started off at about five in the evening. It took us more than two hours to get to this rockery. We had one bottle of coke and one bottle of fanta between us. After we drank it, our tongues still stuck to our palates. Wole looked around, found a pond somewhere and said, "Omi wanbi "(There's water here). We drank some. I took off my boots, laid my back on the rock and passed out. Meanwhile, Wole at one point had to "go for bush." My gun was defective and accidentally, it discharged and just missed Wole's legs as he was returning from off-loading. And he roared, "You'll kill me one day!"

Asimotu had built a fire and dived into his bag to produce some yam tubers. Thank God we ate some of the yam, as unbeknown to us at the time, we were out for a long trek. After we had eaten, Asimotu suggested we propitiate Ogun for a bountiful hunt. On the fire embers he sprinkled some herbs and powder and proceeded with incantations. Hands over fire to receive the affirmation oozing out with the smoke, we bathed our faces. Incantations yielded, for soon after, hawk-eyed Asimotu spotted an animal in the fading twilight. He called Wole to make the kill, but I don't think either of us (at least, I the less) was as hawk-eyed as Asimotu. Wole fired but found no kill. Asimotu then recharges his carbide lamp, Wole his own battery aided hunting headlamp and I, my improvised lamp carried with the gun. Asimotu then suggested we fan out in three directions. Wole said I should take the right path and I said, "no, I'm not going alone by myself." So I followed Asimotu, while Wole went off on his own. Suddenly, I heard a whistle from Wole and I said to Asimotu, "I think the man is in danger." But Asimotu knew that the paths met. He did not show any anxiety and in about two minutes we found him, his light had packed up. So we went on with two lights, in a single file.

We had planned to be back at base by 11pm. At 11.30, when we had still not made a kill, apart from a small civet cat, we told Asimotu that we had had enough. But he was very desperate and disappointed that we'd found nothing. He declaimed constantly, "bawo l'ati se, ta si lo lo lo, ka ma r'eran pa! (What bad luck, to go on and on without a kill!). Then at about two in the morning – of course at this time we were exhausted, Wole said, "Femi, let's sit down," while Asimotu recharges his carbide. And I said, "If I sit down, I won't get up." My back to a tree, I slid down uncontrollably and could only get up thereafter, with my gun as a prop. Trek resumed with constant inquiries of Asimotu as to how far we were from base. Usual answer was, "just a stone's throw." I gasped to Wole, "this is hard labour." "Hard labour? It's punitive!" Wole answered. We eventually, thankfully, attained base, where we found that my wife had been crying her eyes out, thinking the worst had happened. After all that trouble, nine hours, as we were driving out of the bush, we saw an antelope leaping beautifully across the road. Imagine, what we'd spent nine hours looking for! But of course we could do nothing from inside the vehicle, so we just drove home. Further down, we spotted two rabbits from the headlights of the vehicle. I stopped. Wole leapt out. Two rabbits compensated for the night of punition!

Wole is a very keen hunter, a skilled tracker and a good shot. He could be on his own for hours, just waiting for game. I call him the "king of Aparo," he decimated the *Apro* (Bush fowl) population in Ife campus. Delicious things. He told me of an occasion when he took a book and a bottle of wine and sat under a tree, waiting for these uncanny birds, whose take-off propulsion can put jet to shame. He got about three with a single shot. He said as a child, he used to go into the bush with his father. That's how he started hunting. It is a most exhilarating sport. When you go into the bush the peacefulness! Its total elation when you kill, after you've been trekking for miles. He told me that once he went to a place in Abeokuta, not far from his new farmland and lost his way.

He asked the villagers how far it was to the main road and they said it was about an hour's trek. Then he heard talk about a wild boar that had been menacing them in the area. So he decided to pass the night in the village. In the morning, Wole set out together with many of the villagers – husbands, wives and children, with guns, cutlasses, sticks and clubs, after the animal. They followed its track. Suddenly, something reared from underneath one of those broad coco-yaw leaves, (he said it was like a tanker). Instinctively, he released his gun, boum! And the animal's head was shattered. We had heard all these myths about how you can't kill a boar by hitting its head. Anyway, Wole took one thigh and left the rest of the animal for the villagers.

We are talking of a man of many facets; many, many facets – writer, poet, hunter, humanist, wine connoisseur... and his interaction as a human being is wonderful. For him, the human aspect transcends everything else. He will tell you only what he thinks you should know so that you won't get into trouble. He takes responsibility for anything he does and ensures he doesn't get you involved in it. That's his character. In his famous case in which he was accused of holding up the radio station, I was prosecution witness number one, simply because I happened to have been there, by chance, when he telephoned a mutual friend. When he came to my office, somebody told him I was at the NBC studios and he telephoned there to inquire after me. While I was there and answering this call, the man in charge of outside broadcasts was talking about the Premier's broadcast later that night. Wole and I met later at lunch as appointed and this broadcast must have cropped up in our discussion. However, who went there to substitute another tape, I don't know.

He takes many risks. Once his mind is set on something, you can't stop him. Take the trip to the East just before the civil war broke out, for example. He was as convinced as to the rightness of his mission that he did not think twice before exposing himself to the obvious danger. Of course with hindsight, you can perhaps say it was foolhardy of him, but that's the essence of the man. I am sure that if he had to do it again, he would do it exactly the same way. During the Gun-man trial, I went to see him one evening and I found him pacing up and down the corridor of the police station where he was being held pending judgement, like a caged lion. He said he was fine, except for a slight cold. He wanted some Zorro. So came judgement day and the thought of this man being sent to prison made one contemplate a number of possibilities. When he was held, I went to see him at the station. Of course with a policeman sitting next to him, there wasn't much we could say. After his incarceration in solitary confinement for about two years, in connection with the Nigerian Civil War, we lost physical contact but unexpected letters and poems on toilet roll bridged the gap.

He has very strong views. Take the Road Safety Corps for instance. He was passionately involved in the road safety thing because of the carnage on our roads. There were occasions when we travelled together and a car overtook recklessly. He would bring out his cassette recorder and dictate into it so he won't forget. He would say something like, "car number…OY… mad driver, shouldn't be on the road, lunatic driver. Arrest him." But that's the extent of the man's dedication to anything. I won't say he has a temper, but he can't suffer fools gladly. He cannot conceal his likes or dislikes. We've had several disagreements over one thing or the other, sometimes, violent arguments. He is very considerate though, very kind-hearted and good-natured. He is selfless. I saw him cry for the first time when his mother died. They were very close. He got quite a lot from her; a very strong woman.

I have tremendous respect for him as an artist and as a person. He has a limitless mind. I can't fathom him, I just can't. I tell you the man lives ahead of his time. And he works hard! We went out one night and came back about two in the morning. I went to bed. When I woke up at six, I thought I heard rapid fire from an SMG. He was at the typewriter! Once he worked overnight till eleven am and went off to Abeokuta. He doesn't sleep much, maybe five hours a day. The first production of his, after the *A Dance of the Forests* debacle, in which I participated, was *Kongi 's Harvest*. I was working for an insurance company then. "I've got a part for you, tailored for you," he said. "I hope you can do it." I asked, "when is it for." And he said "Next month." I had the part of the Organising Secretary. Quite a part! There is this scene where the Organising Secretary appears, weary, perspiring, just like the script envisioned, trying to cross the border. At that point, you're finished, flat-out. You're drenched. After the performance, over the customary pints of beer, I said to Wole, "Satisfied?" He took a look at me and said, "Satisfied? Shit! You gave the audience what they wanted, not what I wanted." You can imagine how deflated I felt. When it was time for the second performance of the play at the convocation ceremony of the University of Ibadan, he now took the pains to explain the part to me. Remember I had only a month to prepare for that first production. He analysed the part of Organising Secretary as that of a survivalist. Of course my next performance was far better and I saw the difference.

He is a hard taskmaster, a very capable and effective stage director. When he directs a play, he works hard at it. But it is not as easy as it appears on stage. Imagine reading *Madmen and Specialists* in the raw. It is a fantastic play, far meatier than *Kongi's Harvest*. But it's a play that can defy all but an actor under the most accomplished director. There's this bit where somebody is referred to as a "Gushpillator." In my naivety, I went into the dictionary. I couldn't find the word, but as the play progressed, I began to get the idea of a "Gushpillator." It's onomatopoeic. I once said to him, "It takes a madman to write *Madmen and Specialists*." And he said, "yes, but it also takes a madman to act a madman's part." He created the role of Aafaa for me. I have read all of his plays except *Play of Giants*. I don't think one is necessarily better than the other. I have no "best". They are all powerful plays. Take *Death and the King's Horseman*. Olohun-iyo – that's a part I would enjoy. Unfortunately, much to my chargrin, I've not been able to take a role in these other plays because of my many other obligations. Once I sat at a rehearsal in London, watching him direct *The Bacchae of Euripides*. The words flow, they just flow on and on. I find myself on many occasions before I go to sleep (I have a small library beside my bed), reading his expressive prose and getting inspiration from it.

There could be no greater honour than the Nobel. I first heard the news over the phone, from a Frenchman in Lagos who had met Wole in my house. He had been listening to Radio France and felt compelled to phone and share the joy and excitement. I then got a telephone call from Rex Collings, his publisher and a mutual friend, the following day. He confirmed that Wole was leaving Paris on the noon flight and was heading home as he could no longer cope with the media 'harassment', attendant with world recognition of a Nobel laureate. I felt Wole might be up to one of his "kwicky silver" disappearing stunts and ensconced somewhere else and as a diversionary tactic, let it be known that he was on his way to Nigeria. I was not expecting him until a few days later. I asked Rex to double-check over a telephone number I gave him in Paris. He called back, confirming that he was actually taking that noon flight – airline, flight number, unknown; but we conjectured it had to be a regular flight, if he was coming straight to Lagos. So I sent a car. When he came on Saturday, we sat for hours, wined, dined and talked. After my initial rendition of the song,

> Ogun o loun o j'oba
> Ogun o loun o j'oba
> Jeje I' Ogun se jeje
> Ti ijoye gb'ade Ire
> Wa ba Baba Ode O
> Ogun o Loun j'oba

all I could say was "A Man is either master of his trade or he should quit the world."

> Ogun did not seek the throne
> Ogun did not seek the throne
> Quietly retired, minding his own business
> The nobles brought the crown of Ire
> To the ancestor of all hunters
> Ogun did not seek the throne.

Chapter Eleven
"Let Us Think Again"
Yemi Ogunbiyi

"For me, justice is the first condition of humanity"
Wole Soyinka

Consider the following situation: you are thirty-five-years-old and are speaking to a third year dramatic literature undergraduate class. The day's topic is "Introduction to Soyinka's Dramatic Works." And when you ask the students about the 1962 arrest and subsequent celebrated trial of Wole Soyinka for allegedly holding up a radio station in Ibadan, not one of them knows what you are saying.

You think it is all a joke and then it dawns on you suddenly that they may, after all, be right. For, if as it is often the case these days, the average age in our third-year undergraduate classes is nineteen, then presumably, none of your students had been born in 1962! And even you the teacher was possibly in high school at the time. Suddenly, you realise that we have all come a long, long way; Wole Soyinka, you, the teacher, the country and even your students! Suddenly, it dawns on you that our "young" writer of not long ago, who came back home from London only in 1960 and founded a new theatre company, the *1960 Masks*, is not quite so young anymore! He has come a long way from that day in 1966 when one Yoruba Oba said of him to another Oba: "being a small boy, he could be childish in ideas!"

Writing about Wole Soyinka, even on an occasion like this can be as problematic as it is challenging, especially in a piece that makes no pretention to being an exhaustive or even academic treatise. Not even a mere personal testimony to a meaningful and eventful life from the vantage position of acquaintanceship and comradeship, could ever resolve all the problems posed. The reasons for this are many. Wole Soyinka defies easy categorisation. His many-facetedness, what Stanley Macebuth has called "his renaissance posture," compels us not to limit him to merely being a writer or an activist or even a 'politician.' Soyinka is many things to many people. That Sierra-Leonean scholar of English studies, Eldred Jones, dubbed him "our own WS," a reference to the initials Soyinka shares with that other genius of English literature, William Shakespeare. His many students in Nigeria since *Kongi's Harvest* for mysterious reasons, fondly dubbed him "Kongi," after the not so likeable character of that name. That name has stuck ever since!

The difficulty with categorising the man is not without its irony especially as there is in his works, a somewhat Manichean element in the apprehension of events, one which tends towards almost clear-cut polarisation of forces, of the forces of good and evil, of life and death and represents as sharply as possible the duality of human reality.

There is also the additional problem of his being, in certain respects, a misunderstood man. While this misunderstanding derives in part from his own doing some can be traced to certain seemingly contradictory elements in him. Although his roots are firmly grounded in Yoruba cosmology, he is one of the most internationalist, eclectic and most travelled of our artists. An "Ije-Egba" to the core and yet a man of the world!

Although very much a public, even controversial figure, Soyinka is an intensely private person. His careful cultivation of solitude and silence jars sharply with his intense involvement in national life and talent for society. When his mother passed away in 1983 and his concerned colleagues trooped in to console him, he could not deal with the crowd. He kept a condolence book at his residence and escaped somewhere to contemplate alone, in silence, the loss of the one woman who meant a great deal to him.

And yet, he exudes tremendous warmth and a genuineness of the human spirit that is compellingly absorbing. Although his numerous creative and public activities keep him constantly on the move, he remains, surprisingly, a very organised man. An enemy of rigid conventions, he has a knack for being conventional in some respects. I was astounded to find out when I acted for him as Head of the Drama Unit at the University of Ife that he not only answered virtually all the personal letters he received from just about everywhere, on practically every topic under the sun, but also that these letters were neatly filed away.

The letters range from those written by young persons seeking advice on how to start a writing career, to persons seeking other forms of material and non-material assistance. Once a young clerk wrote: "Dear Professor," he started, "I disagreed with my supervisor last week over the use of the word "welcome." He said that his own version was correct. Which is the correct one, Sir?" Soyinka promptly wrote him a reply.

Those who get the biggest disappointment are those who seek material help and get replies explaining that he is unable to offer substantial help because the money is just not there. Somehow, the erroneous notion that our writers are wealthy people (especially too, one who has been writing for so long!) seems to have percolated somewhat. Soyinka's students believe it. His colleagues swear to it and even close friends are, sometimes not too sure themselves! All that needs to be stated here is that royalties for books in these parts amounts to a paltry sum. Ever so often, he gets a cheque for the equivalent of about $100 from a publisher in some faraway country who wants to reprint his poem, "Telephone Conversation." At other times, they do not even bother to get in touch-they just pirate the material!

It ought to be clear, therefore, that not even the most intelligently condensed piece on his entire career can do justice to its full import. Inevitably, one would have to limit oneself to those areas that interest one. For many, of course, his works provide the point of take-off. But I know of a very close friend of his in Ibadan, an insurance magnate to be precise, who would swear that one of the singular beauties of Soyinka is the sensibility of his palate and nostrils, his uncanny ability to distinguish and deliberate on the subtle and characteristic difference between the mellowness of a full-bodied *Clois du Roi* and the elegance and fine, slightly nutty, flavour of a red Burgundy!

The one thing which is clear and hardly contestable is that he is one of the most accomplished and best-known intellectuals of our time. His abilities as a creative artist, his immense contribution to our literature and the diverse nature of that contribution combine to make him undoubtedly our most prolific writer. Taking the volumes of doctoral dissertations at home and abroad that have been written on his works as a basis for judgement, there is no doubt that his works touch on important and fundamental philosophical questions of our time and society.

Playwright, polemicist, mythopoiest, scholar, connoisseur of rare wine and novelist, Soyinka was born in Abeokuta on July 13 1934 to a school headmaster father and an influential Egba mother. The recollections of his early childhood in Abeokuta, recorded so scintillatingly in his award-winning work, *Ake: The Years of Childhood* testifies to a momentous childhood made more purposeful by the strong presence of an array of extended family relations and personages.

Although his writing career goes back to the early 1950s when he was a very young undergraduate at the University College, Ibadan, he did not embark upon serious writing until he went to the University of Leeds in England. Leeds, through contact with the renowned English scholar of Shakespeare, George Wilson Knight, sharpened his critical and literary sensibilities. By 1956, the year before he graduated from Leeds, he had written his first dramatic sketches and by 1958 he had completed work on what were to be first two major plays, *The Swamp Dwellers* and *The Lion and The Jewel*. The rest of the story is now part of our literary history.

Thereafter, he tried his hands at a variety of jobs; a bouncer, a supply teacher in a London school and a freelance writer. But it was the stint at the Royal Court Theatre in London, when the theatre was a centre of English dramatic revival and the haven of young idealistic playwrights that made the substantial difference in his career. By the time he returned to Nigeria in 1960 to found his own theatre company, he had acquired considerable skill and immense self-confidence in himself as a dramatist. The burst of his creative energy which was set forth in 1960 does not seem to have lost its steam, more than twenty-five years after. Today, he is the author of some twenty full plays, that is, not counting the sketches, numerous radio plays, revues and agit-prop materials. But to see him merely as a playwright will be limiting in our effort to understand the scope of his fertile imagination. For had he not written any plays, had he not done any work for the theatre, his reputation could conveniently rest on his two novels *The Interpreters* and *Season of Anomy,* his numerous poetic works, his scholarly essays, his translations and adaptations such as *A Forest of Thousand Demons* and his non-fictional works *The Man Died* and *Ake*. But even in any reasoned discussion of his works, which almost inevitably becomes all-consuming interest will have to determine choice. One major reaction to a difficult and sometimes, obscure writer who sets out to deliberately mystify, is that one or two of his plays are simply unstageable – he does not write for the average reader. Leftist critics have carried the argument forward, somewhat, by insisting that while Soyinka writes undeniably with compassion for the down-trodden in society, his writings lack "a solid class perspective."

To be sure, Soyinka is not the easiest of writers. Some of his writing is difficult, even infuriatingly difficult in places. He is the first to admit that he tends towards an "elliptic style of writing." He calls it a quirk. But to state that he is difficult in places is not to say that he is difficult and deliberately obscure through and through. To put it that way is to deny important assumptions of the literary vocation, namely that no writer writes evenly from beginning to end and that different situations dictate different approaches even within a given literary genre. Somethings are suitable for some kinds of work while in others, they would not work.

Let me illustrate. Some of Soyinka's best works are hardly obscure as any Nigerian high school boy, who has had to participate in an end of school year performance of *The Trials of Brother Jero* will testify. *The Lion and the Jewel* remains a popular fare. The pungent satirical sketches of *Before the Blackout*, which were written for a specific historical period, played to packed audiences in Ibadan in the 1960s. Ideologically suspect as it is, *Death and the King's Horseman* has the 'sweetest' poetry in Soyinka's drama. Its incantatory lyricism, so superbly close to original Yoruba poetry, is breathtaking.

The position adumbrated above does not suggest that Soyinka is your run-of-the-mill playwright. Soyinka can be difficult, but it is difficulty deriving from his complex concept and use of myth in his poetic dramas. In confronting these works, therefore, the thing to do it seems to me, will be to locate that concept, "to enable" fuller understanding of his works. Soyinka has himself tried to explain this concept in some of his more difficult essays. The thing to bear in mind is that with him language "is a vehicle of mythic meaning" rather than an index of style. For him, the legends of Yoruba gods, especially Ogun and less so, Obatala provide a means for illuminating the complexity of contemporary life. To that extent, therefore, the complexity encountered in some of his poetic drama is an inevitable response to an ethnocentric, complex reality.

Another critic had therefore argued that the chaotic nature of the social behaviours of our time might well be Soyinka's justification for meditations on myth. His concern has been to discover "in mythic history certain principles upon which contemporary behaviour might be based and by which it might legitimately be judged." For only in this way can such works as *A Dance, The Road* and *Madmen and Specialists* be fully comprehended.

But for thousands of other admirers, especially in Nigeria, admirers who will never get to read or see a Soyinka play, indeed, who have no need for such luxury, Soyinka remains something of an idol. For, perhaps, more than any other member of his generation, Wole Soyinka has consistently and courageously spoken out against tyranny, brutality and injustice in whatever form. But even more importantly is the fact that he has done so when no one else dares to speak. He has done so, even at great risk to his personal safety.

We all remember the circumstances leading to his arrest and detention by the Gowon administration, after he openly attacked in an article titled, "Let's Think Again" the so-called "police action" against Ojukwu and Biafra as a "disastrous and inglorious war." We remember that at the time he spoke out and called for reason and restraint, a "terrible blood cloud," coupled with a wave of tribal hysteria and hatred, hung over the country. To speak out was to be branded a saboteur. Those were the days of the "Igbos-Must-Go" demonstrations in Lagos, when we all became convinced that Igbos were determined to blow up the city. No other Nigerians dared to speak out against the 'mob' hysteria of those days. None but he, had the courage to remind us that at the end of the day, the bellicose approach we opted for, whether as "police action" or outright civil war was a grim mistake. The spate of attacks that greeted Soyinka's public call for caution and reason indicated the sorry mood of the country. He was promptly arrested and detained for two years, without trial.

We also recall the murder of Adepeju at the University of Ibadan in 1971. And that Soyinka was one of the few people who spoke out on that occasion.

There was the "Ali-Must-Go" crisis during the Obasanjo regime which led to the death of quite a number of students, there was the Bakalori massacre in Sokoto State, there was the murder of Dele Udoh, there were the outbreaks of power rash during the Adewusi years as Inspector General, there were the horrific years of the Shagari administration – in every instance, Soyinka not merely spoke out, but did when it mattered most. There are certainly not many Nigerians like him.

But in this singular quality of his, that of having the courage to speak out, some people have argued lies his biggest weakness. Arguing that Soyinka is given to histrionics and over dramatization, these people insist that Soyinka has a tendency towards being a loner. While recognising Soyinka's acts of courage, they insist further that the way to effect meaningful change in society, especially one like ours, is through collective group action rather than individual acts of courage. There is no doubt that group collective action, especially in situations like our own seems the better option. History teaches us so and plain commonsense dictates it. But while the struggle to build a confluence of progressive forces continues, what role should the Soyinkas in our society play, that is, beyond being a part of the building process? As a scourge of vice and villainy, as a foil for the unbridled corruption which so characterizes our time, as a counter to the despoliation of our country's wealth, do people like Soyinka not make immense difference? Is it not safe to assume that by their exemplary, even if momentary, acts of courage they can and ultimately do provide some direction for a larger group?

Undoubtedly he is committed to the timeless ideals which human kind cherishes, the ideals of freedom, justice and fair play, the example of a man committed to our common humanity, the example of a beautiful human being. And all those who believe in these ideals cannot but join me in wishing him a most deserved happy birthday.

Chapter Twelve
A Dramatic Stage in a Dramatist's Life
Cameron Duodu

In the late 1950s and early 60s, the most stimulating intellectual discussions used to take place at the New Year Schools at the University of Ghana, Legon. Organised by the University's Extra-Mural Studies Department, they consisted of a series of lectures and seminars, some of which were given by distinguished speakers invited from overseas. It was at one of these New Year Schools that I first set eyes on Wole Soyinka.

Sad to say, I do not now remember so much about what he talked about as I do the beauty of a young woman in huge dark glasses who went everywhere with him!

But I do remember that there was a stir about a statement attributed to Wole. Apparently, in a swipe at "Negritude" – a concept which had been transmuted somewhat in Ghana into the "African Personality" and was one of the legs of the high horse on which Dr Kwame Nkrumah was riding into the arena of African affairs – Wole had said that there was not much need for 'Negritude,' inasmuch as "a tiger" did not have to proclaim its "tigritude."

We discussed this idea at our seminar, which was conducted by a Sierra Leonean, William F. Conton, himself the author of a book titled "*The African.*" It was an amazing confluence of Pan African ideas – a Sierra Leonean leading a discussion of a Nigerian's attitude to a concept popularized by a Senegalese (Leopold Senghor) before a Ghanaian audience weaned on 'The African Personality.' And a perfect metaphor for what I think Wole Soyinka stands for above all else: "Get their brain cells working, for God's sake!'" He may not be right all the time; he may be deliberatively provocative at times; he may even be abstruse to the point of exasperation. But he will get them talking – in Africa, in Europe or America, or in Asia. Long before he got the Nobel Prize for Literature, he had locked himself into the African discourse in a manner that defied the charge of his detractors that he was often "dense." If he wasn't understood, then what were all those talking about him going on about?

At the Legon seminar conducted by Willie Conton, I ventured an opinion that I wish Wole had been there to take on. I said that the tiger would not find it necessary to proclaim its 'tigritude' because its power was already so visible and evident. If you didn't believe it, just go near it! The African, on the other hand, had been subjected to a concerted effort – carried out with the most powerful instruments of propaganda available, including books, films, cartoons and posters – by whites to portray him as an inferior being. If he didn't shout "I am," the effects of the propaganda would remain, because much of it had entered people's sub-consciousness and they might not even know it was there unless someone shook or pried it out.

"I've just been reading *Lady Chatterley's Lover* by D. H. Lawrence"! I announced, drawing uneasy titters from the audience. "And do you know what I found? In his vivid reproductions of sex talk, Lawrence somehow manages to find space to make a derogatory remark about blacks. We look 'like mud', he writes! What was the necessity for that?" It was just typical of the casual racism that was taken for granted in what we had been told was "great literature." If someone retorted, "Mr Lawrence, we may look like mud but we ain't got freckles!" would that be engaging in a bout of "tigritude"? I was laughed off my feet.

Wole and I actually had a minor exchange at a conference of African writers held at Kampala, in Uganda, in 1962. I was irritated by the constant use of the word "Bantu" by a white South African speaker to describe the Africans of his country. As editor of the Ghana edition of *Drum* Magazine, which had sprouted its teeth in South Africa, I was sensitized to apartheid phraseology, which appeared to me to use "Bantu" in a sense just once removed from the way the Americans use the "N" word.

So I interrupted the guy loudly: "They are not Bantus! They are Africans!" I said.

He halted in his tracks. It had obviously never occurred to him that the cumulative effect of the "Bantu this" and "Bantu that" legislation in his country – such as the Bantu Education Act and the Bantu Building Workers Act – all of which were discriminatory against Africans, had removed the word "Bantu" from the ethnographic into the political sphere.

Behind me, I heard Wole say in a matter-of-fact fashion, "The Bantus are a whole group of people who populate a huge part of Africa, from the central region right down to the south." I accepted Wole's "scientific" definition, but I retained my own. Anyway, the white South African never used the term "Bantu" again – to my hearing.

Point to note: Wole had made me wonder whether I hadn't been too ready to assign my own understanding of the term "Bantu" to the white guy. Second point to note: None of the black South Africans present had seemed to find it odd to hear themselves being described by their white compatriot as "Bantus"! And they were not lightweight people: Zeke Mphahlele, Lewis Nkosi, Dennis Brutus, Bob Leshoai, Bloke Modisane. Did familiarity breed acceptance?

I had very fond memories of that Kampala conference, and when I heard that the Biafran civil war had broken out in 1967, my first thoughts went to the Nigerian writers I had met there – especially, Chinua Achebe and Christopher Okigbo (on the Biafran side) and Wole Soyinka, Segun Olusola and Mabel Segun on the Federal side. Would they remain safe to pursue their art, or would they succumb to the vicissitudes of war?

My fears were not unfounded. Christopher Okigbo was killed in the first year of the civil war. Wole Soyinka, appalled by the senseless slaughter his country was enduring, began his own secret diplomacy to try and end the war. Courageous as ever (he'd once carried out a "one-man coup" by managing to take over the Broadcasting station at Ibadan, in the Western Region of Nigeria and announcing that the election results being issued from the station by the Western Regional Government were a fraud!) he made the dangerous trip to Enugu to meet the Biafran leader, Colonel Emeka Odumegwu Ojukwu. Of course, the spies of the Federal Government relayed the information back to Lagos and Wole had to go into hiding. But inevitably, he was picked up in September 1967 and spent two years in prison.

When I heard that Wole was in prison in Northern Nigeria, "all the eggs in my stomach burst" (to use an Akan of Ghana phrase that depicts personal disaster). Civil wars bring out the worst in human beings. People who know one another tend to hate each other more than people they do not know, but they bury their hatred in order to be able to live together. When civil war peels away the thin veneer of tolerance and provides an institutional justification for the expression of hatred against those who had once been family, the result can be loathsome.

While we sat in nearby Ghana twiddling our thumbs without knowing what to do, some of Wole's fellow Nigerian writers were going round telling anyone who would listen that Wole had committed treason and was lucky to be alive. They spread rumours that Wole had tried to buy a warplane for the Biafrans! Or that he had tried to get the Midwest to secede and join Biafra. One man doing all that? Ah, but he was "Kongi," you see!

I confronted one of these writers in the house of the Ghanaian dramatist, Joe de Graft and made it clear to him that writing was more important than politics and that he owed it as a duty to his craft to ensure that Wole survived to practise his own craft. We nearly came to blows and I walked away from Joe's house. Another Nigerian writer now a professor used a sort of vigil held in Wole's honour to attack him in *The Legon Observer*. In my riposte , *The Literary Critic and Social Reality (The Legon Observer, March 14 1969)*, I pointed out that it was detestable to accuse a person of unspecified crimes, especially when the person was not available to defend himself. This campaign of vilification by some Nigerian writers led me to suspect that rumours I had myself been hearing – that Wole had in fact been tortured to death – might be true.

I wrote a letter entitled, "IS WOLE SOYINKA DEAD?" and had it published in the Ghana *Daily Graphic*. Despite its normally voluble demeanor, the Nigerian High Commission in Accra did not publish a riposte! I became really worried. Then, as luck would have it, Wole's play, *The Lion and The Jewel*, was staged in Accra. The day after the play opened, I went to the Continental Hotel to indulge in an afternoon sip of cold beer. Who should I find sitting at a table, with two equally pretty friends, an old flame of mine from my Drum days? I joined them and we began to converse. They tore the pants off me laughing at the way I had "put words in the mouth of tins of sardines and bags of flour" in an article I had written in the *Daily Graphic*. I was shocked. So these ladies read? Not only did they read but they remembered what they had read. They quoted whole sections of what I had written!

And then the miracle happened: one of them looked at the way my old flame had been smiling at me and winked at her: "Or did he?"

And they all laughed.

Not to be outdone, the other one also asked, "Or didn't he?"

And again, they laughed uproariously. Then the penny dropped. They were quoting from *The Lion and The Jewel!*

I used their ability to understand the play and be able to apply it to our current situation to posit, in an article, a counterpoint to the oft-articulated criticism that Wole was too difficult to understand. I then narrated the story of Wole's imprisonment, the rumours that he had been tortured to death and the stony silence with which Lagos had greeted the rumours and my fear that they might be true. I circulated this article very widely round the world through a syndication agency called Gemini News. The London *Guardian* published the article under the fetching headline, "Did he... or didn't he?" I believe it made quite a splash in Britain. Anyway, many well-wishers in the British intellectual community also threw in their oar and the Nigerian Federal Government was left in no doubt that Wole would never be allowed to rot in prison, forgotten. Eventually, it saw sense and released him. The book in which he recounted his prison experiences, *The Man Died*, is one of the most harrowing I have ever read.

I was very pleased when, soon after his release in 1969, he told me, at our first meeting: "I have heard of your doings!" I muttered shyly, "It was the least I could do, Prof." On the day he won the Nobel Prize for Literature, I was thoroughly embarrassed: the magazine I was working for *South*, had practically "gone to bed" when the news came. The production editor made it known that there was a window for a 300–word piece to be inserted in one of the late pages. But where was Cameron? Those were the days before mobile telephones and when one disappeared, one disappeared. And disappear one did, when one had managed to write all one's articles to meet the paper's deadline. A lady on the paper who was pretty literate managed to fill in for me and we didn't quite lose out on the story altogether.

It was a very good thing that it was such a short piece that went into the paper. For I was able to use the storm caused by our near-miss to get the editor to commit himself to running a cover story on Wole for the next issue. Would I be able to get an interview for the cover story, everyone asked. I said confidently, "Yes"! Sure enough, I ran him down to ground in Paris. He was as excited as I was, as we spoke on the phone and I rendered the conversation in breathless dramatic form, paying the supreme dramatist the compliment of telling the biggest story of his life in a form that would most please his muse.

But there was the disgust of the *South* Magazine sub-editing desk! What was this? A "report" in dramatic form? No way! They would reduce it to something that was in conformity with the magazine's "house style."

I hit the roof when I saw what they'd done to it. It was the usual soulless report you could have found in any magazine of that sort.

I took the article to the editor, an Argentinean gentleman called Andrew Graham-Yool and said, "You know I am a creative writer as well as a journalist. Look, this is the very best way I can convey Wole Soyinka's artistry to the readers. He is a dramatist. He has won a Prize that nobody expected him to win – least of all himself. So it is a dramatic stage in a dramatist's life. And I have written it up in dramatic form. Of course, it is unusual. But why should every part of a magazine look and read the same? What is a magazine for? The whole meaning?

I hate ultra-conformism and as I was saying this, I'd written my letter of resignation already in my head. Had Andrew Graham-Yool gone with the sub editors, I would have left the magazine. As it was, he calmly asked me to "leave it" with him and I left his office. He didn't say anything to me, but when the advance copy arrived from the printers, not one word had been changed, nor a comma nor a parenthesis nor a stage direction! I shouted, "Dur…" in Hausa and went off to have a celebratory drink.

II

Here are excerpts in the Christmas or December edition of the magazine in 1986:

Wole Soyinka, the 52–year old Nigerian playwright, thought it was a bad joke when someone mentioned the Noble Prize for Literature to him on 16

October. There had been much speculation last year that he would win this most valuable and yet enigmatic prize.

Soyinka had just landed in Paris from New York, where he had put the finishing touches to the production of one of his plays, *Death and the King's Horseman*. The long flight had left him jet-lagged and sleepy. Yet he was due to chair a meeting of the International Theatre Institute (ITI), of which he is President.

Being a regular at such gatherings, he knew that the first session would be unimportant. So he rang the ITI secretary to tell her to start the meeting while he snatched a couple of hours' sleep. The conversation that followed was pure Soyinka in its ironical cross-purpose talk:

Secretary:	It's all right, you wishing to snatch a couple of hours' sleep. But what am I supposed to do with all these journalists?
Soyinka:	Which journalists?
Secretary:	These people who have besieged the office for the last few days… They've camped here and turned the whole place into chaos.
Soyinka:	What for?
Secretary:	Oh, you know what it is.
Soyinka:	I don't know what the hell you're talking about.
Secretary (in disbelief):	You know. The Nobel Prize for Literature.
Soyinka (flaring up):	Not again. You people… what's wrong with you? We had this thing last year and you're letting yourselves fall for it again?
Secretary:	Well, what do I do with them?
Soyinka:	Serve them with drinks and send them on their way. If they won't go, get the security and throw them all out. We've got to have our meeting.
Secretary:	You don't understand. You can't treat it with such levity.
Soyinka:	Well, I'm sorry. Goodnight. Or rather-good morning. I'm going to bed.

Soyinka put down the receiver, only to be hit by a barrage of subsequent calls from European journalists on the trail of the story. Each time, he reacted with scorn at any mention of the Nobel Prize; it was not until a Swedish television journalist came on the line that he realized it was getting serious.

The dialogue – which might have come from a Soyinka play entitled *The*

Laureate and the Ink Hounds – went like this:

Swedish Journalist:	I have instructions to find you and be with you.
Soyinka:	Be with me? I didn't tell you I needed a nurse-maid.
Journalist:	Those are my instructions. I must be with you at 1pm.

Soyinka (remembering from last year that the announcement of the Nobel Prize winner was usually made at 1pm European time):

    Oh, yes – at that time you will hear that some Eskimo writer, some genius there whom all of you didn't even know existed, has won the prize. Then you'll all have the expectation wiped off your faces. It would serve all of you bloody right.

Journalist:	I have instructions to be with you. Absolutely I must.
Soyinka:	I'm sorry, I'm in my cousin's house and I don't invite strangers in there.
Journalist:	You can't hide yourself away like that.
Soyinka:	Hide myself away? From what? You are the ones who spread these rumours.
Journalist:	I'm afraid I don't deal in rumours, Professor Soyinka. I have precise information.
Soyinka (thinking):	Precise information. A Swedish journalist with more than precise information. This is getting very serious… (aloud) Okay, I 'll wait until after the event.
Journalist:	No, No. I must be with you when you hear it. It's the tradition.
Soyinka:	Well, you can't come here…
Journalist:	Okay, let's meet somewhere. Do you know of any cafe nearby?

Neither Soyinka nor the journalist could think of a place known to both of them. So, reluctantly, Soyinka agreed that the man could come to the house. As soon as he arrived, the journalist put on the television. And at 1pm precisely, the programme they were watching was interrupted by a newsflash. "The Nigerian writer Wole Soyinka has been awarded this year's Nobel Prize for Literature."

The drama ends with surprise and delight.

Later on I asked Wole some few more questions two of which were:

Cameron: What of being "frozen into a monument" at 52?

Soyinka: I don't think there is the slightest chance of that. I have not been able to accept the prize on a personal level, you see. I accept it as a tribute to the heritage of African Literature, which is very little known in the West.

I regard it as a statement of respect and acknowledgement of the long years and centuries of denigration and ignorance of the heritage on which all of us have been trying to build. It's on that level that I accept it. As for Wole Soyinka, as I keep saying when I'm asked, its business as usual.

Cameron: What of your own beloved creation?

Soyinka: It's a question that I always find very difficult to answer. I like certain characters which I've enjoyed creating. Brother Jero is one of my favourite characters. He is a rogue, a rascal, a charlatan and so on; his character can be used to make certain statements about society and I enjoyed playing variations on him.

The Professor in *The Road*. I like the character – there's something about him which I've recalled from certain personages I encountered in childhood. So one has selections like that. But to say a work in preference to the others?

In fact, I've received a letter from an American journal which wanted some writers – Baraka (formerly Le Roi Jones) was one of them, myself and a few others. It wants us to choose. It said: "If something happened and all your works were destroyed and there was one section you wanted to be preserved for the year 2500 or something like that, could you send us something?" I find that a most impossible, almost preposterous request. I had to write and apologize and say: "sorry, I can't do that."

III

Since then, I have, of course, followed Wole's own "doings" and I must say I do not know where he gets the energy from to write at such a prolific rate and also to engage, simultaneously, in political activism at the level he does. One day you hear that General Ibrahim Babangida has made him the "Road Safety Czar" of Nigeria. The next, you meet him in the house of Chief M.K.O. Abiola, planning with others to reverse the "annulment" by the self-same General Babangida, of Chief Abiola's election as President of Nigeria.

One of the most dangerous periods he has endured whilst doing politics must, undoubtedly, have been his confrontation with the regime of General Sani Abacha.

One day I heard over the BBC that he had managed to escape from Nigeria – where Abacha had set up a 24-hour surveillance system on him – and had reached Paris. This escape was one of the finest he has ever concocted: he got the guards who kept eyes on him to get used to the idea of his popping into the bush to bag a grasscutter or deer with his hunting gun. His return home got later and later. Then one day, he went never to return – he had arranged a tryst with an "*okada*" (motor-cycle) rider, who took him pinion-riding over bush paths for a whole twelve hours, before depositing him in Cotonou, in neighbouring Benin Republic. The Abacha fellows had seized his passport, and he had to persuade the United Nations Refugee Agency office in Cotonou to issue him with travel papers, before emplaning for Paris. Once there, he gave an interview to the BBC World Service. And that was that.

I saw him shortly after he had made his way to London and he described the struggle he had left behind in Nigeria to me for an article in *The Observer*. In London, he joined the large number of Nigerians whom Abacha had driven into exile, to try and harass the dictator's regime from afar. They set up Radio Kudirat to broadcast clandestinely to Nigeria, and coordinated their efforts with activists at home, through several organisations that operated underground. He told me, at a lunch we had with the former Nigerian Foreign Minister, Prof Bolaji Akinyemi, that he had detected Abacha's secret agents following him in cars around the streets of London. It was only good fortune that saved him from becoming a victim of Abacha's vindictiveness, which saw off Mrs Kudirat Abiola and Mr Alex Ibru, among others.

Then Abacha died in June 1998 and everyone expected that Chief Abiola would be asked to form a Government and make use of all the talent that had been unleashed since the annulment of his election and his own subsequent imprisonment. But alas, that was not to be. Abiola died in mysterious circumstances whilst interacting with an American delegation and many Nigerians' dreams of purposeful, enlightened governance perished with him.

But "Kongi" rules the universe of the logos. And we all know that the pen is an all too mighty weapon! No doubt, one day, Nigeria will be blessed with a Government that is acquainted with Wole Soyinka's ideas about human rights and decent government; an administration that Soyinka would bless, instead of rebelling against. His bushy white hairs proclaim that this must come about very soon, or he will be gathered to his fathers, still longing for the government that his beloved Nigeria deserves.

Chapter Thirteen
A Master of His Trade
Kwame Anthony Appiah

Introduction

In the mid-1970s when Henry Louis Gates Jr. went to Cambridge University for his doctorate degree programme in English literature, people on campus kept asking him whether he had met with Anthony Appiah. He had not but realized that, when white people keep asking a black man such a question, it's most likely the other person is black. He eventually found Anthony Appiah at Clare College where he was initially an undergraduate in medicine before he switched to philosophy and later earning a doctorate. They were in their 20s and became friends, a friendship now into decades. At around that same period in 1973, Wole Soyinka, already an established playwright and poet had completed a two-year solitary confinement in the course of the Biafra war in Nigeria and had before that lived in exile in Accra, where he was affiliated with the University of Ghana. He was in Cambridge to deliver a series of lectures that would later be published as *Myth, Literature and the African World* as part of his two-year lectureship in English at the Faculty. To his surprise, the Faculty did not recognize African literature as a serious area of study within the "English" tripos and was virtually forced to accept an appointment in Social Anthropology. The three became great friends. Soyinka was one of the supervisors of Gates's PhD that would later be published as *The Signifying Monkey*. It was also at Cambridge that they discussed lofty ideals and resurrection of abandoned literary projects. They loved the *Transition* magazine which had been founded in 1961 by Rajat Neogy, an Indian Africanist and at one time edited by Soyinka from Accra as well as the W.E.B. Du Bois's idea of an encyclopaedia, *Africana: the Encyclopaedia of the African, African American Experience* (not the same Du Bois original title though) which had established its office in Accra and for which Kwame Nkrumah had encouraged and invited Du Bois to work on.

Two decades later these dreams were fulfilled. Soyinka had won the Nobel Prize in 1986; Henry Louis Gates Jr. became the Chair of W.E.B. Du Bois Institute at Harvard and one of the leading black scholars in the United States and Anthony Appiah a world philosopher and *New York Times* best-selling author. They also became powerful in diverse ways such that when the Nigerian ruler and dictator, Sani Abacha put a price on Soyinka's head – dead or alive and it was to the W.E. B. Du Bois Institute that he took a sanctuary. On the 8th anniversary of Soyinka's winning of the Nobel in 1994, co-editor, Ivor Agyeman-Duah had a chat with Anthony Appiah in his father's house in Kumasi, Ghana on Soyinka's role in postcolonial literature.

By then also the *Transition* magazine had been resuscitated and Soyinka became Chair of its Editorial Board (as he did with the *Encyclopaedia Africana*). One debate that has stood out in the 'new' *Transition* was ironically between two intellectual leaders: Ali Mazrui and Soyinka. In the chapter that follows this, The Great *Transition* Disagreement is Agyeman-Duah's conversation with Mazrui in San Francisco in November 1996. But first, the one with Anthony Appiah.

II

Q. After Soyinka, we have had two other Nobel laureates in literature from Africa – Nadine Gordimer and Naguib Mahfouz. Why is it that Soyinka is still dominant and seen as very representative?

A. It is partly because he is a public man. Gordimer is someone who because she is a white woman living in South Africa, cannot be a kind of representative. She can represent her situation and she can be on the side of the African National Congress but she cannot, as it were, stand for it.

Mahfouz is a writer whose work has not been so essentially about politics, but about the world in general. Whilst we have some sense of Egyptian politics in his works, we do not think of Egyptian politics as so disastrous as we think of Nigerian politics when we read Soyinka. Most people in Africa think Nigeria has more political problems than Egypt. I am not sure that is true. Egypt has a sort of functionary political system and Nigeria basically does not and so we want to hear people talking about, explaining and criticizing Nigerian politics.

The fundamental thing is simply that Wole is someone who has chosen to become a political actor and to speak for the Nigerian situation in a way that is distinctive. Soyinka is not only a playwright, a novelist and a poet but also author of two great memoirs in English language – *Isara* and *Ake*. He is also an actor and played Patrice Lumumba in *Murderous Angels* (the play on the Congo written by Conor Cruise O' Brien) in Paris in the 1960s. If you put him in front of a crowd and give him the microphone, he can dominate the room.

His role in the Nigerian Civil War was altogether a brave one. His political actions have thus been very significant in the country he lives in.

Q. Some talk of his powerful grammar and his contribution to the English language. Did his style in a way contribute to his selection?

A. It is a very interesting question and one he himself has thought about. I have actually had some discussions with him about this. In his Nobel Prize speech, he was extraordinarily modest. He said, "I am not accepting this for myself... I understand that I am accepting this for Africa..." And l think that was a reflection of the reality. The Swedish Academy knew African writing had been there and that they had not done anything about it. They were waiting for a figure that they thought they could acknowledge and Soyinka was obviously that figure. His politics also helped because one of the reasons why certain people never get the prize is because they have bad politics by the Academy's standards.

There is something that most people do not know. Soyinka's work was very well-known in Sweden already. His poetry was translated into Swedish in the 1960s. So he was someone whom they would have been aware of. But in the end, as Wole himself says, "there is a certain amount of luck." The Academy has to be persuaded – they are in Sweden, they are not in the centre of the world. But at the time Wole was selected, the possibilities were Wole, Achebe and Ngugi.

Q. What is the politics of the Academy and how does it affect some of these writers?

A. Ngugi's politics is perhaps too Marxist for the Academy and too unreconstructed. For instance, Soyinka's early plays were also produced at the Royal Court in London and those days were very important in the development of drama in English. They were at the centre of one of the greatest after New York in terms of high literary drama.

Ngugi's novels are important and I admire them but Soyinka simply created modern African drama – those ways of writing and using the stage are all his inventions.

With Achebe, he has this foreign corpus – I think one of the difficulties for Achebe is that to appreciate what he achieved in *Things Fall Apart*, you have to know the English language very well indeed. What he did in finding ways to express Igbo language in English was to use the language of the Bible, the language of ordinary speech, the language of people translating folklore – all sort of sorts of languages, bring them together in a way that created a new form of language. If you are from Sweden, you would not know that because you cannot get around it.

100

So maybe part of the difficulty for Achebe is simply that the craft of his language is very hard to see – he is such a master that you do not even notice what he is doing. It works without you seeing how it works. And that is not a modernist notion of how to be a great writer. A great writer in the modern scheme of things is not someone like him. Achebe says he is a storyteller and that is true.

Q. So when Achebe said he was happy Africa literature had been recognized with the award to Soyinka in 1986, was he right about his own contribution to it?

A. Absolutely. His work is a large, but by no means unique part of why it had to be recognized. His work is the central corpus but he acknowledges something that is obvious – which is that literary writings exist in the context of other literary works. If you have no other writing you have to be understood in the context of other writings.

If you take together the corpus that include Achebe, Ngugi, Gordimer, Soyinka, Ama Ata Aidoo and others as one, it becomes an enormous, powerful and distinctive corpus of African writing which is very readable by people outside Africa who can appreciate it. It has got to the stage when one can speak of it as having influence.

Q. When we look at the generation that probably followed Soyinka, Achebe and others – Ben Okri, Festus Iyayi, Kojo Laing, how do they compare in style and themes?

A. I guess Okri is the one I have thought about most. I have reviewed his two major novels for American newspapers. Obviously Okri is enormously conscious of Soyinka as a literary figure. There are lots of things in his work, the fact that his novels are about an "Abiku," a child who comes back (Soyinka has a famous poem about that). What is different between their generation and the generation of Ngugi and slightly before that is that, they move in an international sphere where literary writing is more technically complex. Okri's writing is certainly very complex. He does not write in the naturalistic vein like Achebe and to that extent his writings are more international.

The first generation were very pre-occupied with questions of nationalism and independence. Ngugi wrote about the Mau Mau in Kenya, Achebe's novels covered the whole process of colonization and de-colonization and has spoken of trying to give African people a useable past. Again I think contemporary writers are less and less trying to do that. It seems their writing is less about nationalism, especially the nationalism of countries – Ghana, Nigeria and Kenya in the case of Ngugi. Of course that is natural because we are all disillusioned now with national politics and also that is more realistic.

But the fact is, people still use *Things Fall Apart* to teach in schools around Africa especially in English speaking countries. I do not know if they will ever use Okri for that. And that is not a complaint, it is just an observation. One of the things that tends to happen in the reception of African writing of this sort in Europe and America is that it gets seen in a Third World context. So it gets compared with Indian writing and Latin America writing as much as with other African writing.

People have often said that Okri's writing is somehow reminiscent of the magical realist writings of people like Gabriel Garcia Marquez in Latin America. That similarity could be exaggerated. There is some truth to that and we have to remember that the writers who went to College like Soyinka, Achebe, Ngugi and others in the 1940s and 50s were fed on a diet of English and British Literature. Now, even in England, if you read literature, you read literature in English from America, Canada, India, Australia and Africa. You also read translations of Spanish and Portuguese literature and from Latin America. Thus there is more of a sense of an international literary culture if you like.

You can always see this in a writer like Bessie Head who draws on mythology from Europe but also from India and Africa in her writing. A writer should, I believe, feel free to take from whatever stimulates him or her and African writers should feel free to do this.

Q. In *The Famished Road*, Okri seems to have a problem with word economy. Did you observe this in your review and how does it reflect on the works of Soyinka and others?

A. I obviously agree with you. I do not know if you have read the one after – *Songs of Enchantment*. It looks as though it was a little bit taken from the first.

Q. The design, the style looks like *The Famished Road* I noticed?

A. There is nothing gained by the length of it. It is just a continuous repetition and since there is no plot of much substance, you cannot say that it is all necessary. Maybe a good contract.

Q. It means in a sense that famous writers cannot sometimes say No to a publisher?

A. It is absolutely true. Okri is young and he got the Booker Prize for his fist major book. But there is an obvious role model here – Ralph Ellison who wrote the *Invisible Man*, which is arguably one of the most important African

American novels of the century. He never wrote another book. There is supposed to be a manuscript he left when he died which maybe somebody would publish some day. But he died very young and for the forty or so years he lived he just could not produce another. One of the things that happens, this is not what happened to Ellison but I think it might have happened to Okri is that, you can respond in two ways. Ellison responded by saying, "I just can't do it again" and so he never did another. Other people responded by saying, "Oh, I guess I am great so I can do anything I want." And to some extent *Songs of Enchantment* looks as though he just said, "Well, I can do whatever I like because I have the Booker Prize." You cannot do that. You have to continue to exercise discipline. Writing fiction is a very disciplined exercise.

Q. People were surprised that Okri could compete with Achebe who was also shortlisted for the Prize the same year and won?

A. Well, it is like Salman Rushdie winning the award. In things like the Booker Prize, if they pick somebody who is not English, they want someone who is sort of a little bit exotic. Achebe is a very elegant English prose stylist, but he is not stylistically exotic – that is, he writes the way in which Thomas Hardy wrote. He has this lucid way of writing, which putting it simply, is a way of saying Achebe's writing is anti modernist and on the whole literary judges like the kind of writing that is difficult. Achebe was concerned about writing for larger audiences and as it inevitably happened, he was taken less seriously by those literary intellectuals who like things to be difficult.

Okri's work needs explaining. I do not suppose many Nigerians have read Okri's work from beginning to end and if they have, I am sure many of them did not enjoy it. The *Songs of Enchantment* is not addressed to a broad public, certainly not a broad African public. It is addressed to a very literary field. Again, I am not objecting. Writers should write whatever they want to. They should write for whomever they want to write for and I think it is very unreasonable objection to Okri to say "Oh! You should be writing so that the poor masses of Nigerians can read you." This is because there are other people still writing for the poor masses of Nigeria. Cyprian Ekwensi is still writing and people like his writing. We do not want all writing to be the same.

Q. Why do some writers, especially African writers want to make writing difficult even for their kindred? As a philosopher you surprisingly write in simple prose best exemplified in complex issues in, *In My Father's House*.

A. *In My Father's House* could have been more inaccessible but I did not really make it so. I only used the long words when I felt they were necessary. But it is a complicated question and it has something to do with what I called modernism earlier on. I am not against big words and I teach epistemology but you do not need to say it if you are trying to explain Ghanaian politics and when it has nothing to do with it. One of the reasons why I do not like much of the poetry that Anglophone African writers have written is that the language seems simply to be there to demonstrate that they can do it rather than something that the writers are happy with. To me there are a few successful poets in English in Africa contrary to the masters of prose.

III

Q. Initially they were called Niggers, then Negroes and then Afro-Americans. They are now called African Americans. Do you think this sequence of description has changed for the good, the status of African Americans?

A. The change in name is a sign of the change in situation and not a cause of it. The fact that when Jesse Jackson said that black people in America wanted to be called African Americans, people immediately picked it up and said, "Well, if that is what they want to be called, we would call them that," is indicative of this. What we have to remember however is, the first black people in America were called Africans because they came straight from the continent. The question has more to do with how African Americans feel about themselves than what other people feel about them. It is a matter of claiming a connection with Africa despite the fact that in most of American history, Africa has been seen in a negative light.

Q. It was to address this issue of African history being put in the negative that Afrocentricism or Afrocentricity became an issue. Henry Louis Gates Jr. recently cautioned some Afrocentric scholars whom he said knew very little about the history of Egypt but had written about its many virtues. Is it confusing?

A. Afrocentricism in America has come to mean so many things. Some of them are good and some are not so good. One of the things it can mean is the renewed interest in Africa among African Americans. There is a constituency in America that is interested in what America does in Africa and that makes the difference because in America, foreign policy is very much driven by whether there is a group within the US that cares about a place. On the other hand, there is a lot of nonsense in the name of Afrocentricism and a lot of talk about Egypt is by people who don't know much about it by scholarship standards.

Also the whole idea that Egypt is the right place to look is very strange. This is because the cultures that came from Africa to the Americas came from West Africa – from Senegal down to Angola and most of the people who went to the new world – Brazil, the Caribbean, Latin America and North America were Yoruba and Akan and they have very little to do with Egypt 5,000 years ago. There is a lot of hocus-pocus but on the other hand, it has really led to a resurgence of real interest in Africa.

Q. Since some Afrocentric scholars are imparting knowledge, some of which you argue is nonsense, what would be the impact on studies?

A. Many of the people propagating Afrocentricism divert so much from normal scholarly standards that ordinary scholars do not even bother to refute them. If I am a professor of African Studies at my university, I do not spend time refuting something published by somebody in the community about Africa that is not true, I spend my time arguing with other professors who are trying to do serious work on Africa. Scholars should be concerned and make sure that what is said about their subject matter is correct.

The effect of it as I said is complicated; it is a pity because it's a distraction from trying to increase the amount of knowledge about African cultures and about African American cultures, to have to spend your time fighting these battles about something that is somehow irrelevant.

Q. Why do you think some non African Americans also study Afrocentricism and what are their attitudes?

A. Many young white Americans really see the power of African American culture in their popular music. They see it as one of the strengths of American culture so they want to know about it.

Q. Some scholars do not think there is any difference between an Africanist scholar and an Afrocentric one. What, in your view, is it?

A. It depends on which of the many meanings of Afrocentricism you are talking about. If Afrocentric means just centring on Africa, then obviously if you are an Africanist your works centre on Africa so you are an Afrocentric by definition.

Of course the word Afrocentricism was formed to contrast with Eurocentricism and Eurocentricity. Eurocentrism in my view is not just focusing on Europe which is fine if you want to. It has taken Europe to be the centre of the world and everything and it is assuming that anything important about human culture can be understood by understanding European culture or that the European culture provides the highest or best models of cultures.

I do not agree with that but I do not think you should respond to that by saying "no it is not Europe that has the best models and the highest cultures but Africa." I do not think you should turn the prejudice on its head. There are people like Molefi Kete Asante who say that what they mean by Afrocentricism is the view that people of African descent should focus on Africa and those of European descent on Europe and Asians on Asia. This creates two problems – one is, I want to be able to study anything I like. I do not see why because I have ancestry in one place I should only study that place. The other is that you cannot understand the world if you close it up in boxes. You cannot understand Ghanaian history if you forget that we were a colony of Britain for a while; you cannot understand British colonialism if you do not understand how much it affected the Slave Trade and African cultures and now, immigrants.

So if you try and cut the world up in that way, you end up not understanding any of it. This seems to me perfectly sensible but even obvious when you turn to the United States. You cannot understand the United States either just in European or in African or Asian or just American terms. People came and brought significant things with them from all over the world to make the modern United States.

So if Afrocentricism means only focusing on one part of it, then you do not understand the whole picture. One point about the African American for me is that, they are as much typical Americans as anybody else. Their sweat and blood made America; the toil, the labour that went into the creation of the plantation economies of the South; their contribution to American religion – Christianity, even the Christianity practised in the churches, is very shaped by African American contribution.

So is American food very much shaped by African American contributions? The whole business of rice plantations throughout the Carolinas, tell the story. This was because the reason why they took slaves from the Senegal and Gambia was for them to grow rice and work on those plantations. Nobody in Europe knew how to grow rice. They had to get the labour from Africa.

So you have in food, religion and the biggest example – music the overwhelmingly enormous contribution by African Americans. The attempt to practice a kind of cultural apartheid where you say this is black and this is white means you do not understand either.

Q. James Baldwin argues in *The Fire Next Time* that African Americans should forget about Africa as a home because the history of the African Americans is a peculiar history. Some extremists also think they should return home someday.

A. When we had movements like Garveyism in the early part of the century whose slogan was "Back to Africa," only a very small number of people who joined tried to go back to Africa, let alone succeeded in doing so. The association with Africa, I believe is one of interest, perhaps the desire to visit, but it is not at all common for ordinary people (African Americans) to live in Africa. There are always some who may want to, just as there are some Americans who want to live in Europe. The dominant form of interest in Africa is not as a place to go back to because literally most African Americans did not come from Africa – they were born in America.

Baldwin was right to stress the fact that African Americans in America, have the right to be there as anybody else, more right perhaps than some of the people and do not need any territory to claim as home. I do not think (and in fact Baldwin himself did not practice this) that African Americans should or should not be interested in Africa. That is up to people to decide for themselves.

Q. Apart from Baldwin, there has been the other generation of African American writers – Toni Morrison, Maya Angelou and others. To what extent will you say that the cultural background of these writers made them known and to what extent is their success dependent on their own creative abilities rather than their history?

A. In the case of Morrison we have to recognise her as a creative genius. But the imagination always needs something to work on. It cannot work on nothing and all writers draw on their experiences, she herself has so argued. For unlike other important African American writers, she is also a critic and has written about writing. Therefore whilst race and the racial dimensions of her own experiences and experiences of African Americans generally influenced her, she is herself obviously a central figure.

Equally importantly, we should not think of so-called white American writings as having occurred without any awareness of race. Most of the major American writers from Mark Twain to recent writers have racial questions throughout their writings. But the experience of growing up in the case of Morrison in rural Ohio, as a black girl profoundly fits into her writings in the earlier novels. On the other hand, when it comes to a novel like, *Beloved,* her sources are not so much her own experiences as reading slave narratives and also reading about slavery in general.

That part of course is something anybody can do. I do not have any connections with African American slavery in my ancestry but I can read and have read slave narratives and feel I have some understanding of slavery from that. So one of the things that need to be remembered about someone like Morrison is that her deep understanding of slavery is as a result of intellectual labour – study. Nobody is born with the knowledge of slavery. You have to read and understand it and exercise your imagination.

Chapter Fourteen
The Great *Transition* Disagreement
Ali A. Mazrui

Q. *The Africans: A Triple Heritage* TV Series made you more famous than perhaps any other intellectual work you have ever done. Personally is that the case?

A. Well, it is true that it is a different medium and not like what we scholars do which is to write books and articles for academic journals. Journals are very often read by fellow specialists and you have a narrow range of intellectual constituents. The TV was for such international media as the British Broadcasting Corporation (BBC) that has extensive influence. It was watched by millions of people in many different countries and has been translated into different languages. The companion book has also been quite influential and was a bestseller in England and adopted by press clubs in the United States in different ways.

But it also created for me a level of notoriety greater than that which I have been exposed before. I was also on radio which is sometimes not a traditional scholarly approach to disseminating information. But above all, I was the BBC World Service Reith Lecturer in 1979 on *The African Condition*. Those also reached millions.

Q. These have also put you in some controversy especially those aspects of Islam in *A Triple Heritage*. There is this argument you had with Wole Soyinka in the *Transition* for some time. In the last argument you said you wanted a debate with him in any part of the world. Was it a worthy exercise for two elderly African intellectuals?

A. Ideally, it is true we are relatively senior scholars among Africans and the level of discourse was not sometimes adequately detached so that was unfortunate. But Wole Soyinka decided after the showing of my TV series to go around the world not once, not twice, but a number of times describing me as a Muslim fanatic and Islamic fundamentalist. So every time he discussed religious fanaticism, he would include among his examples, the "latter day born-again Ali Mazrui" and his TV series. When I first read about it, I said, "well, Wole will be Wole" so I let it pass. Then I read it again in a speech he gave in Denmark and I became alarmed. He is going around abusing my name this way and I challenged him to cite the chapter and verse where he claimed I was demeaning African culture in favour of Islamic culture. He could not. On the other hand, I cited chapter and verse in different programmes in which I paid homage to the values and traditions of our ancestors. So unfortunately, the argument drifted into a personal vendetta when in fact it could have been at a level of intellectual discourse. But I believe it did serve one purpose: to the best of my knowledge, Wole Soyinka has stopped going around the world describing me as "exhibit A of born-again Islamic fanatic." So it has silenced him on that at least.

Q. On the question of his not watching your TV series but subjecting it to that level of criticism, I am reliably informed that Henry Louis Gates Jr. secured for him the set of nine programmes. In spite of your hot exchanges there were instances of mutual respect though?

A. I have had debates with other scholars which went further down in personality debasement than the one with Wole because, it is true that though in the final analysis the debate with Soyinka was more personal than it should have been, it was still much more civilized than the one I had with a South African scholar who decided to be very vitriolic and abusive which was totally unworthy of a scholar. So you must give it to Wole that in spite of his personality level of attack, he still kept it within bounds. He is definitely a great man. There is no disagreement about that. He is one of our premier playwrights and writers and our generation is fortunate to have watched his works, read his works and interacted with him. He is part of what is positive in the postcolonial generation.

Q. In one of your arguments you accused Soyinka as a censor of articles in favour of Idi Amin when he was editor of *Transition*. You are supposed to be writing a biography of Amin and one of your reasons is that he was a true African. Is this a good enough reason for writing about someone who has done so much damage to Uganda and the image of Africa?

109

A. If the book I am writing will depend on Wole Soyinka to be published, it won't. He will censor it. And that will put an end to that particular exercise. As I said, he has declared that he would not publish anything positive about Idi Amin and that is a nonsensical approach to scholarship. You don't take a position like that and silence people about saying anything about someone like Idi Amin. People shouldn't censor others who found anything positive about Adolf Hitler who was a much worse personality than Idi Amin. So if there is something positive about Hitler and someone is prepared to back it up with evidence, then why should we silence him or her? And it is contradictory in relation to Wole's values which insist on openness. It is true that Idi Amin is a complicated character who did nasty things. If I am writing his biography I wouldn't just write positive things about him. I am not there to write an official biography otherwise, l wouldn't have had to leave Uganda because my life was endangered under him. I was not in Uganda to salute him. Most people thought if I had remained in Uganda longer, he would have killed me. I was fascinated by him as a phenomenon, partly because, he was a rustic, peasant type, unencumbered by imperial culture and pseudo-western sophistication and others and that, I was intrigued by the emergence of a challenge of our monopoly of power and our monopoly of influence.

Q. You previously edited *Transition* as did Wole. What was the editorial and production output in Uganda and then in Accra under him?

A. I was Associate Editor when it was based in Kampala. Of course, it was produced on shoestring budget in terms of technical production. Now in the mid 1990s it is glossy and well produced. On the other hand the Kampala version was scintillating and had a lot of debate on the spur of the moment. The current one is reluctant to have debate. The debate between me and Soyinka is unique in the present format. The problem could also be because it is a quarterly. On the whole, this one will be a better deal once it gets its contents improved towards a sustained spontaneity in the discussion section.

Q. Do you think it is serving Africa well?

A. It is less Africa-oriented than the one that was coming out of Kampala and later Accra. Those were based in Africa, directly edited by Africans living in Africa and so were much more sensitive to the situation than the present one is. On the other hand, this has changed and has redefined Africa to mean global Africa rather than the African continent and the African Diaspora.

Q. Does it have something to do with the background of the editors – Gates and Anthony Appiah?

A. Definitely. With Gates, since he is an African American and is oriented partly towards African American literary studies and his links with the African American establishment. Obviously the magazine reflects that. Though Anthony Appiah is still an important figure in the magazine, it reflects more Henry Gates's than it does Appiah's preferences. Between the two, Anthony Appiah is more Africanist within the configuration. Of course Anthony Appiah has also become a global African living in the western world for so long and now in the United States.

Q. Anthony Appiah told me that when initially you were invited to join the editorial board, you refused. Don't you think your acceptance could have given the magazine the Africanist influence you are talking of?

A. I refused more in indifference to the original editor-Rajat Neogy than because I didn't like the present editors. Neogy regarded himself as betrayed by the revival of the new *Transition*. He said he was not informed of its revival and thought of it as a usurpation. Gates denies this vigorously and I understand Soyinka was quite insulting to Neogy. I didn't want to hurt Neogy by adding my name officially to the board. I joined the board before Neogy died because Gates, a very persuasive person was able to sort things out with him.

Q. You are one of twelve eminent Africans the Organisation of African Unity commissioned to look into reparations for Africa. How feasible is this project for – aren't Africans are too forgetful, too forgiving?

A. You are right that getting Africans to take the course of reparations for enslavement and colonialism seriously is itself an uphill struggle. So we don't take our own martyrdom as a people seriously enough. This is where we can learn from the Jews, they suffered and they used their suffering as a basis for solidarity, for making sure other people don't abuse them again, that other people feel guilty for having made them suffer and have received millions from the Germans as reparation for the holocaust.

You mention to a black audience about reparation for enslavement or colonization and you may get a polite hearing, but the chances are, people feel you are up to something unreal. Sometimes you may even be laughed off the stage as a comedian. So we have to convince each other first about the merits of the case as we go around trying to convince the rest of the world about it. It will be a long drawn-out struggle like the abolition of slavery. So I don't expect this to be given tomorrow or the end of the century. I still regard it as something that requires a sustained crusade.

Q. There are so many forms of reparation; some people talk of it in monetary gains while others see it in different ways. Which type are you looking into?

A. We did allow for the types you mentioned-different forms-transfer of resources or a Marshall Plan for Africa though the one we know was for the reconstruction of the institutions of the World Bank and the International Monetary Fund (IMF) in spite of the fact that Africa has not got the resources to support such increase in representation. Another area will be reparation in the form of skill transfer because both enslavement and colonization were very damaging to the skills and capacities of African people world-wide. So these are the three major ways – capital transfer, power transfer and the transfer of skills.

Q. Some talk of the reparation of artefacts from Europe and America where they are better preserved?

A. Our capacity for preserving things within Africa is still very underdeveloped. The fact that you want to leave your papers with the library in Accra or Lagos and think there will be much left there in ten years time is really a gamble. Our commitment to the culture of archives is very underdeveloped. Even our commitment to preserving those very artefacts that we have is very unreliable. So it is absolutely clear that this is not the generation to be entrusted with Africa's returned treasures. There will be a generation later.

Q. Has your committee targeted itself or have a time-table when this will be done?

A. I think it is good you mentioned this because we should take it into consideration. It will be difficult to have a time-table of when reparation will be paid but we should have a time-table of our work and when it would be better understood in Brazil or taught in schools in Jamaica. We should definitely have a schedule of implementation. So I agree with the recommendation implicit in what you have said.

Chapter Fifteen
Sooner Death than Indignity
Maya Jaggi

When the Nobel Laureate Wole Soyinka visited the Hay Cartagena Festival in Colombia earlier in 2007, in a walled Spanish colonial town on the Caribbean coast, children in the streets instantly thought they recognised the black man with leonine grey hair. But they couldn't decide whether he was Kofi Annan or Don King. They might not have identified the great Nigerian writer, but they were certainly on to something: Soyinka is surely both pugilist and peacemaker.

Soyinka who won the Nobel literature prize in 1986 – the first African so honoured, has for several decades been an abrasive conscience for his country of Nigeria and for a continent. Obsessed with the "oppressive boot and the irrelevance of the colour of the foot that wears it" he has charted the lethal gulf between legitimate authority and the "power that any goon can seize." A scourge of successive Nigerian despots and kleptocrats, he was jailed without trial for 28 months in 1967, most of it spent alone in a tomb-like cell, for trying to head off civil war with breakaway Biafra. The ordeal gave rise to his classic prison memoir written on toilet paper, *The Man Died* (1972) and drove him to self-imposed exile. Thirty years on, he was sentenced to death in absentia for treason under the even more brutal military rule of General Sani Abacha, whose crimes included the hanging of the writer and activist Ken Saro-Wiwa.

We meet in a London pub on his way to give a lecture at the Guardian Hay Festival at the weekend; and his subject is international culpability over what's happening in Darfur. Soyinka presided as chief judge at a mock trial in 2006 when Sudan's President Omar-al Bashir was found guilty in absentia of crimes against humanity in Darfur. For the playwright, poet and novelist, who is also an actor-director, the symbolic court was "play-acting, but of a very serious kind." During the tribunal set up by Genocide Watch, Soyinka heard searing testimony, he says, from "witnesses flown out from southern Sudan, people whose families had been killed, or who had been raped or seen relatives raped or maimed – some broke down. They testified to the war crimes of the Janjaweed (the government's proxy militia) saying they raided villages and killed Nuba at any time.

Tracing the abuses to a vestigial legacy of the Arab Slave Trade that pre-dated the Transatlantic Slavery and likening the Darfur cause to anti-apartheid, when "non-Africans felt aggrieved by the assault heaped on humanity," Soyinka says: "This can't go on. Over 2 million refugees and still raids by Janjaweed, backed by the Sudanese government military, with war spilling into neighbouring countries." Instead of public indictments and sanctions with teeth, "people make token resolutions. It is yet another failure. I don't understand how this can be happening in the 21st century."

He says that all "hidden atrocities" are revealed eventually, even if many years later. "It all comes to light in the end. So why don't these would-be Stalins and Hitlers take a leaf from history instead of burdening us with exposing their crimes? Why does it have to happen again and again?"

The repetitions of history, whether as tragedy or farce, have haunted Soyinka's life and work. I first met him in 1994, when he warned despairingly of impending civil war in Nigeria, after the 1993 elections were annulled, the victorious Moshood Abiola jailed, and power seized by Abacha, the "butcher of Abuja." In his third volume of memoirs, *Ibadan: The Penkelemes Years* (1994), Soyinka reminded fellow citizens of an earlier "electoral robbery" in 1965, when he was arrested for holding up a radio station at gunpoint and broadcasting a pirate protest – but acquitted on a technicality. Within months of our meeting, Soyinka's passport was seized by the Abacha's regime and he made a perilous escape on a 12–hour motorbike ride across the Benin border.

Punctuated by Nigeria's political upheavals, our talks have resumed in varied locations, from his literary compatriot Chinua Achebe's 70th birthday celebrations by New York's Hudson River, to a cous-cous joint in Paris, where he ironically toasted an end to exile after Abacha's unexpected death in 1998. Abiola died mysteriously in prison a month later. While the actor's resonant voice now seems fainter, his convictions remain just as firm.

After Nigeria's interim leader returned his passport "on a gold platter," Soyinka found his welcome overwhelming. There was amazement at what it meant to others, although, within me, I'd never left Nigeria." Unlike his first exile that entailed "an act of internal severance," he threw himself into opposition to Abacha's rule, in which his sons Olaokun and Ilemakin were also active. In *You Must Set Forth at Dawn*, a volume of memoirs published in 2007, Soyinka puts his lifelong belief that "justice is the first condition of humanity" down to an "over-acute, remedial sense of right and wrong."

He has a home in California and affiliations at Harvard and Nevada universities. There is now a Wole Soyinka Chair of Drama at Leeds University, where he studied in the 1950s. Yet Soyinka has restored the house in his birthplace of Abeokuta, outside Lagos, built with the Nobel "windfall' only to be colonised by bats in his absence. It is the place, he says, "Where I recover myself; it's me in every way." His sometimes melancholy new memoir pays tribute to the dead, from Soyinka's parents to his cousin, Afro-beat star Feli Kuti and he says he intends to be buried in a cactus patch in the grounds of his house. He still yearns for the freedom to pursue savoured pastimes, from collecting African art and book browsing, to solitary hunting in the forests ("I take my gun for a walk' for whatever can be eaten, not for trophies").

"Each time I think I've created time for myself," Soyinka says, "along comes a throw-back to disrupt my private space."

The inauguration of Nigeria's President the late Umaru Musa Yar'Adua, was for Soyinka, such a throwback. Along with international observers, he deems the presidential elections "no elections at all," so badly were they rigged. "In some states there were no votes," he says. "We have videos of police commissioners carting off ballot boxes and the police looking on as thugs carted them off." Though the outgoing President, Olusegun Obasanjo, ended military rule in 1999, Soyinka sees his rule as a "civilian dictatorship." He has now "made himself life chairman of the ruling party to dictate policies" he says.

In his memoir he blames Obasanjo – also from Abeokuta, for betraying him in the run-up to the civil war, landing him in jail. Yet far from holding a grudge, Soyinka now wonders if he bent too far backwards not to criticise Obasanjo, "for fear that it might be thought I was still angry. I'm friends with (Yakubu) Gowon (the former military ruler who jailed him). I suspect there's a missionary streak in me as the inheritor of my parents." His schoolteacher father, "Essay," and the mother he called "Wild Christian" are depicted in his early memoirs, *Ake* (1981) and *Isara* (1989).

He initially saw Obasanjo as a "practical stop-gap – a soldier who had been "civilianised" by prison and given a death sentence against which the nation rose on his behalf." Yet once in power, "he built a one-party dictatorship by force majeure." In his second term, after disputed elections in 2003, "he installed a reign of thugs; political assassinations reached a peak never witnessed before. There were crimes and killings. When they realised they had a monster on their hands, he tried to manipulate the constitution to give himself a third term. The money to bribe legislators amounted to billions of naira." Yet for Soyinka, it was a defining moment when "the legislature refused to buckle. It provided a modicum of hope."

Any dictator, secular or theocratic, "merely implants the seeds of eventual rebellion, "he believes. Soyinka belongs to Nigeria United for Democracy, a 'temporary coalition.' As recently as 2004 he was tear-gassed and arrested on a protest march against arbitrary police powers, though he was released within hours. "The police insist they have the authority to decide who walks the streets," he says. "How can they decide whether I can protest against government policy or not? It is unacceptable. If they say I need a police permit, I'll tear it up."

In his 2004 Reith Lectures, published as *Climate of Fear*, Soyinka quoted a Yoruba saying, "Sooner death than indignity," and he sees dignity as simply "another face of freedom". Probing the "psychopathology of the zealot" (" I am right, you are dead"), he says the "lunatic fringe," in both state power and resistance to it, must be watched. In his view, Bush like Obasanjo, believes in a direct hotline to God. "He says, "we don't care about recognition from the world if God approves." It's an extreme fundamentalism of the most dangerous kind – and it has led to Iraq." As for Tony Blair, "It was Blair who spearheaded NATO's involvement in Kosovo on behalf of Muslims battered by the Serb government. Blair acted as a man of principle – to give credit where it is due. Unfortunately, he got carried away by the moral authority he had acquired, failing to recognise George Bush as fundamentalist of a different kind."

Soyinka sees Zimbabwe's President Robert Mugabe as "the latest King Baabu of the African continent" – an allusion to his 2002 play, a satire about a fictional but recognisable tyrannical general called Basha Bash. On Darfur, he hopes that not only will Arab and African countries alike pull their weight but, China will reverse its support for the Sudanese government.

"One's own self-worth is tied to the worth of the community to which one belongs, which is intimately connected to humanity in general," he says. "What happens in Darfur becomes an assault on my own community and on me as an individual. That's what the human family is about."

Chapter Sixteen

There is Always Somewhere We Call Home

Ivor Agyeman-Duah

I will come again to these Shores
I must come again to these Lands

Return once more to AncestralTime
Feel again the last embrace of PrimalJoy
of birth waters lap lap lapping against
these feet grown weary with waywardness.

I have walked the Distant Earth
Flown the Final Sky
Stepped across Horizons
drapped in Sorrows's Somber Hue.

In Wellington once I watched the Maori
dance and sing the loss of Ancestral Lands and Gods
From Medellin of the Distant Dream
to Baranquijia on Colombia's Carib Shores
In Santiago de Cuba of a Troubled Hopeful Time and
in Haitian nightmares of Santo Domingo
I saw I heard I felt I smelt I even tasted
a trail of Blood across our History's Final Sigh.

But now
I must come again to These Lands
I will walk again on These Shores
There is something about The Place You Call Home:

Something about familiar contours of The Land
about the very Taste of Air
that essential Smell of Earth
something about the Very Feel of Things
    the Geography of Lost Landmarks
    the Chemistry of Fond Memories
even about the Nothingness of Time

those Little Joys
wrapped in Mists of Memory
and the Faint Echoes
of Old Laughters

a thing about the MorningSkies
gone wild with ThunderStorms
and the EveningClouds
so restless with RainbowJoys

the third CockCrow
and the early walk to the village stream
daily nuisance of grass still wet with dew

the harmattan wind and its biting touch
midnight hooting of the lonesome owl
shrieking call of seagull's orphan child
the termite eaten fence
where often you stood
on One Leg
trembling holding
your breath for a Lover
now lost to Childhood dreams

In The Place You Call Home
there was this thing about
the haunted house behind the Church

the old graveyard with a new tombstone
where once you sang your last song
for a classmate lost to a lightning flash

In The Place You Call Home

there was a thing about
the old school bell with its nasal twang

the huge presence of the Headmaster
his slender cane with the constant threat
the School Inspector's annual call
and the nervousness of all Teachers

the Class Bully who now is a mere ScareCrow

and ah! That Lead Sports Girl with a Slender Neck
who brought so many trophies home
rewarded your Timid Smiles
with a handkerchief
embroidered with your Secret Name.

The Place We Call Home
defines our sense of Self of Time of Place.

So I must come again to These Shores
I will come again and again to These Lands
Still awash with Primal Memories.

Kofi Anyidoho[1]

It had been a while since we met. We had, thanks to the internet however tracked down the destination of each other's travels. When we last did in 2007, it was in London. I was living there and he was passing through for a few days. He suggested that we go to the School of Oriental and African Studies where Obiageli Okigbo, the daughter of his late friend and poet, Christopher Okigbo was having an exhibition of her father's photos and papers. We walked around and listened to audio recordings of Okigbo's poetry at the Brunei Gallery. Soyinka was crestfallen yet happy at the same time for what a daughter has done to keep alive the memory of a dead father. Christopher, an Igbo had died gallantly for the cause of Biafra in the Nigerian civil war (1967–70) when Obiageli was only two-years-old. Okigbo had dedicated one of his famous collections, *Labyrinths* to Obiageli.

Okigbo was a greatly valued poet of his generation. Ali Mazrui was disturbed about the risks he took and he paid the ultimate price. In a memorial novel, *The Trial of Christopher Okigbo*, he wondered why the poet wasted "his great talent on a conflict of disputable merit… No great artist has a right to carry patriotism to the extent of destroying his creative potential."[2] In a diplomatic distancing from this position, Okigbo's all time friend and fellow Biafran patriot, Chinua Achebe wrote: "for while other poets wrote good poems, Okigbo conjured up for us an amazing, haunting, poetic firmament of a wild and violent beauty. Forty years later I still stand by that assessment."[3]

Soyinka stood between these two conclusions and played a peace-building role of getting the major players in the war to the table. This was misunderstood and sent him, literally and mentally to a Golgotha as a gallows' bird: suspected 'agent' of the Republic of Biafra. The result of the two-year solitary period was the man who died in the face of all who kept silent in tyranny.

Now an architect, Obiageli lived at the time in Brussels, where she also ran the Christopher Okigbo Foundation. Obiageli has said in her contribution to Ato Quayson's book titled *Fathers and Daughters*: "I have no conscious memory of my father... It must have been a traumatic experience for a young child and I am sure that I do have memories but they have been buried, deep down, in the shadowy caves of the subconscious."[4] I have wondered how a two-year old could but here was the poetry of her father speaking through her.

After an hour, Soyinka took us to an Italian restaurant nearby. We settled on red wines of his recommendation whilst waiting for the food. The conversation shifted from his recollection of happy days with Christopher to injustice and political leadership in Nigeria. He was to address a mass protest rally for which he had received mild threats. "Prof, I think you should be careful. You have already done enough for Nigeria in the midst of great risk," Obiageli had said in a sincere and tender voice. "I think you are right," Soyinka responded.

But even as I got him back to his flat after lunch, it was obvious he had been affected by the day's encounters – an old friendship remembered in the agility of Okigbo's daughter.

Since then as I say, we were in touch electronically though infrequently sometimes. We also had lunches and dinners in Lagos and Accra. He introduced me to one of the best Chinese restaurants in central London – New Fortune Cookie. The Chinese owner had been so gracious to him and a group of Sani Abacha dissidents who had nowhere else to hold meetings but at his place.

In early January 2011, I received an email from Soyinka about a TV documentary for which he wanted me to be a production advisor. It is about the Arab Slave Trade and its consequences. Previously, he had initiated me into how he discovered the history of black presence in Iraq partly through this. Of course, the almost conventional wisdom has been that blacks were better treated as slaves if conversion to Islam took place compared to those like Olaudah Equiano who had to buy back their freedom. He had already travelled to parts of the continent to film. There is a lot to do in the Northern Region of Ghana and further, the Upper East that has a rich slave history as far as to Burkina Faso, the neighbouring country.

Ever the meticulous personality, his email messages are still of refined prose and not mere media messages. The one of January 5, 2011 reads:

> "*Ivor*,
> *Greetings for a most successful New Year!*
> *I now have specific dates to propose:*
> *Arrive Accra Monday 17th, fly to Tamale 18th and back in Accra Friday 21st. If we come in early enough for the flight to Tamale, could you tell me when that is? I understand there is only one flight – we could proceed straight to Tamale, then set off by road to the target villages early Tuesday-the Baga Slave Camp in Pikworo, Sandema, Sampa, Jenini, Nalerigu. My idea is that we begin with Pikworo which is furthest North, then return southwards taking in as many spots as we can handle during the three days available… I already have quite a bit of footage from those places. The Feok festival is already over, but even that is well covered in the footage. The main target now – I'd better explain-is to find an old person who has kept the Memory. Or descendant of a family that has preserved the lore of that slaving period. That's the main purpose…"*

The understanding of his studied geography was as impressive as the purpose of the documentary. He emailed again from Boston a week later on January 13th, angry at the abuse of this new technology so useful to us. He wrote:

> "*TAKE NOTE, ONE AND ALL!!!*
> *Former email address has been breached by commercial hackers.*
> *It will be shut down permanently from 12 noon GMT 15th January.*
> *I apologise for an unpredictable period of mild to heavy break in contact.*
> *May the birds dropping dead around the globe prove to be hackers zapped in cyber space – A – a-ase!!!"*

Though we had to reschedule the travel twice for unexpected international engagements, we finally made it and spent almost a week with the crew, Tunde Kelani one of Nigeria's best cameramen and his production manager, "Debo Maduka." Kelani's works I was familiar with but "Maduka" I did not know. It was a bit of an amusement when I kept calling "Maduka" as "Maduka." He politely never said anything. Soyinka jumped in as we were having lunch in Tamale: "but why do you call him Maduka?" To which I replied, "you said that was his name in the email you sent to me." "Ah! I know the problem now" he said, as he filled his wine glass. When he was sending me names for tickets to Tamale, the capital city of the Northern Region he did not know the name of Kelani's assistant who would travel with us so had created a phantom one. The real name is Jamiu Shoyode and I understand Soyinka had also nicknamed him, Alhaji Essential Commodity.

If that was a revelation, the sequel was dramatic. As the evoked laughter of this was dying down, we saw a lady making her way to our table; her eye sockets were bewildered of what she was seeing. As she got closer and surer with her movement, it was bemusement and not so much of bewilderment. She approached the professor.

"Good afternoon sir?"

"Good afternoon."

"I am sure it is professor Wole Soyinka I am seeing?" She inquires with a smile.

"I guess so" Soyinka responds.

"For goodness sake and in the name of God I want you to do me a favour" the passer-by said as she searched the pocket of her blue jeans to take out a mobile phone. All silence.

Her daughter, one of Soyinka's devotees, was studying in Canada and just a day earlier had phoned about the joys of her latest Soyinka reading.

"Will you, professor Soyinka please speak to my daughter so she will know what a wonderful mother I can be in her life?"

We all started laughing. She dialled the number as Soyinka's facial composition was still unsettled at the request. The daughter was asleep but was woken up by the call.

Mother to daughter: "My dear, do you know who I am with at The Gariba Lodge this afternoon as he takes lunch? Wole Soyinka!!"

The daughter thought it a prank until the mother gave Soyinka the phone and on loudspeaker we heard her scream as Soyinka asked, "Young lady, how are you doing? I am under instructions from your mother to speak to you."

After few more pleasantries and elated responses from this young lady, Soyinka wished her good luck with her studies. The mother still enthralled thanked him profusely and apologised for interrupting our lunch.

We finished lunch and continued. We travelled from Tamale further north to Bolgatanga, the capital city of the Upper East region and to surrounding little villages of Pikworo within Paga that has a slave camp and closer to the border with Burkina Faso and Sandema. Our interest was the route of the Trans-Saharan Slave Trade from where they took captives through to Tamale, Burkina Faso, Mali, parts of North Africa and the Arab states. Soyinka was particularly interested in how the captives joined the caravan trail that also had victims from Somalia, Ethiopia, the Sudan and Niger. A number would find themselves in Saudi Arabia, Qatar, Dubai and Iran.

In the rocky hills of what remains of the Pikworo Slave Camp in Paga (Upper East), Soyinka was completely appalled at the degradation of slavery conditions. Our official guide who was overcome with extreme joy was a fellow who had had difficulty understanding *The Lion and the Jewel* as a student but was now the guardian historian of its famous author and in a remote village. He explained the conditions as Soyinka recalls:

> "To ensure that they were reduced, virtually, to the status of beasts, they were denied any semblance of plates and bowls. Instead the captives were made to chisel hollows in the rock surface, using stones… Albeit smoothened by time and weather, the eating holes gouged into those rocks, symbolise the permanent scars of dehumanisation still borne by the indigenes… and their condition as glorified slaves within their own nations."[5]

We watched demonstration of it as Kelani's cameras rolled, as little children with token payment danced to rock music provided for our edification by their elders as the captives did before their horrendous journeys. For Soyinka, a Yoruba man from Abeokuta, the rocky hills and contour caves were nature's gift to be admired. They reminded him of the Stonehenge, the prehistoric rock monuments in the English county of Wiltshire – wonderful in their formation!! It was as we sat on those rocks that he told me his envisaged title for the documentary, *The Amphitheatre of Death*.

We had also journeyed from here to Sandema (still within the Upper East) and recorded the traditional music of the people at the palace – melodies of group and community participation in which lyrics in shrill voices combine with whistling and the sound effects of feet stomping raising the tonal pitch even in a quiet afternoon and at a lesuire time easily a musical turned carnival. We were regaled with the stories of Almami Samori, a famous guerrilla warrior who prevented powerful ethnic groups from dominating others, discouraging slavery and later the French entry into West Africa for colonialism in the 1890s. Though no one could give first-hand information about this famous warrior, the British Historian, Ivor Wilks in the 1950s and 60s met Isaka Dodu (in the region) then an old man who had fought in Samori's army and confirmed this with evidence many of the exploits of the old warrior.

Soyinka hates injustice and still cannot bear the issue of slave trade. He told me, "And so, I, from childhood, could never bring myself to understand absolutist power. What is that?"

It is this lack of understanding that in earlier years took him to the Caribbean as a documentary filmmaker where, as he tells us in, *You Must Set Forth at Dawn:* "In Bekuta: a centuries-wide reunion with my own history sent a tingle down my vertebrae-an encounter with descendants from my own hometown, Abeokuta, on a far-flung Caribbean island, in the hills of a once slave settlement called Jamaica."[6]

It has always between the two 'metaphors' – hills and rocks and where home really is!!

But where really is it for this cosmopolitan entity? Anyidoho's epigraph poem for this essay – of wanderings in the world and the sentimental 'feel' and 'smell' of the history of slavery and the Caribbean as a location tingle the vertebrae of all Africans who visit. Yet Anyidoho returns to a place he calls home and Soyinka wanders and wanders and is still, at 80 on board, witness to the hooting of plane engines like that of an owl at night; a wandering soul of the universe.

II

But besides shooting locations, lunches and dinners, we have also sat quietly to reflect on the past. In an afternoon in Accra in 2007 we discussed fifty years of postcolonial Africa in the context of Ghana's 50th Independence Anniversary; expectations from their generation of intellectuals and what the Yoruba culture has particularly done to his writings.

Q: You saw the decolonisation of Africa after 1957 and the aspirations and hopes of the people. From afar – whether you live in Los Angeles or Lagos or Abuja – do you think these aspirations have been met fifty years on?

A: I'm afraid not. I sometimes refer to my generation as the "wasted generation" and by that I was referring in fact to the aspirations and the achievements. In other words: the vision was there, the enthusiasm was there and in fact the confidence was also there. I sometimes refer to ourselves as the "renaissance people" because we felt there was absolutely no limit to the potential for rebirth of the African continent and in some kind of false mythical, romantic way we felt we were the generation to produce this. I often refer to us as the "wasted generation" because of that disparity between vision, aspiration and achievement.

Q: What went wrong?

A: Leadership was the main problem. Yes, of course a lot of blame must be placed on the shoulders of the former colonial powers who never really left. That's why the term "neo-colonialism" was invented by the analysts of the African situation and the colonial experience, including I believe, Kwame Nkrumah. So that was there, but then collaboration had to take place; from a perspective of very short-term advantages and a determination to build a personality cult around oneself. Kwame Nkrumah was also at fault in this aspect, in which the personality cult became something that existed for itself and could be nurtured by either side of the ideological divide. So there was a failure to carry people along as partners in the enterprise of decolonisation and genuine, total liberation. But of course some were far guiltier than others. You don't compare Nkrumah with Idi Amin. It is a combination of that skewed perspective of leadership ego in contrast to an acceptance of being complete, total, equal partners in the enterprise of true liberation.

Q: Has there been something right about the period within the last fifty years?

A: Certainly some leaders have learned from the errors of the past. I would group among such people Julius Nyerere, who also had a very advanced, progressive ideological orientation, but whose resources and interpretation of the possibilities of the resources in the modern world did not actually match the reality. But you give him credit for remaining faithful to the vision right to the very end. He experimented with *Ujamaa*, which was people-oriented but unfortunately didn't quite work out on account of the resources available and also the somewhat artificial approach to the re-organisation of traditional community development and reproductive strategies.

For me, it was enough that people like these were sufficiently motivated, had a vision, and pursued that vision. And then of course you have the supreme, absolutely unmatchable example of leaders like Nelson Mandela, who mixed both vision and practice in a unique way, which of course was embodied by his own personality and recognised the realities of internal decolonisation, the Apartheid. It was a collective effort – but it was very pragmatic. Leaders like Oliver Tambo, Desmond Tutu and the new generation of activists within the African National Congress (ANC) managed to find a formula that did not blow up. And this was very much on the cards: not to blow up the entirety of South Africa, setting back the self-recovery of the African continent, as would have happened a couple of decades ago. There are other experiments in various areas – Thomas Sankara tried a populist approach in Burkina Faso, but again geared towards the involvement of the people as partners in progress, to use a cliché. The economic experimentation of the Ivory Coast, which worked up to a certain point but failed politically because of the policy of *ivoirité*, which was exclusionist and therefore led to the problems in the Ivory Coast. I'm sorry that each time I try to point to a positive I have to point to a negative, but we have to be practical because we're talking also to the new generation and letting them understand what errors have been committed.

Q: There was definitely a problem with leadership – weaknesses in some sense – and good in others. Do we see elements of this in the contemporary leadership in Africa?

A: Yes, you can see structures like… not so much the New Partnership for Africa's Development (NEPAD) as the peer review structure within the new African Union which is based on the fact that within the leadership there is something seriously wrong. It is no longer the Wole Soyinkas, the Chinua Achebes, the Ngũgĩ wa Thiong'o's saying; it is the leaders themselves who recognise that there is something desperately wrong and so they set up this mechanism. But they have to make this mechanism open. I believe very much not just in accountability but also in openness and transparency. They have to let the people know that this kind of mechanism is serious and it's not just an anodyne, just to paper over the cracks.

You have all over the continent, with all the failures admitted, a recognition of the fact that stepping into the shoes of the departing colonial masters, you're not allowed to dominate your own people and act towards them like internal colonisers. It doesn't work any longer. So that is a shift in thinking. The development also of organisations like the Economic Community of West African States; the former East African Economic Community; the South African Development Committee, the South African partnership with some of the former front-line states – these are efforts at recognising the fact that we cannot continue to blame the past.

Q: One of the fascinating things that took place from the 1960s to the early 1970s – was the Heinemann African Writers Series, which started with Chinua Achebe's *Things Fall Apart*. What was the mission of your generation of writers?

A: I'm glad you mentioned that because, on the cultural field, there has been a real, genuine and sustaining explosion of creativity in all the fields – music, the arts, the plastic arts, but literature most vibrantly. Literature and culture have been at the forefront of the decolonisation and the liberation process and the African Writers Series was able to bring out quite a few remarkable gems of literature which normally would have just atrophied for lack of indigenous publishing enterprise. And that indigenous publishing enterprise, despite its setbacks from time to time, has really brought up quite a number of really inspiring writers in the younger generation.

There have also been economic reverses on the African continent, which affected publication. Writing cannot hope to escape the general economic malaise which has overtaken many of these nations and so we must recognise the fact that, yes, there will be ups and downs in the dissemination of literature on the African continent.

Q: Do you see a transition from that of your generation compared to the current one? If you live in London, New York or Paris, people talk more of black writing as we used to know it.

A: I wouldn't say there has been a period of transition; I think this thing has been on a very normal developmental curve, like everything else. Foreign publishers recognise the fact that African literature is not just a quota system: "Oh, we've spoken of this regional literature for some time, it's about time we speak of African literature." This has been improved by the numerous prizes – regional, Commonwealth, etc. – being received by African writers. You look at the young crop of female writers in particular, especially in the novel; it is really remarkable. And the young generation of writers also stationed outside: Ben Okri, Chris Abani, Ifi Amadiume, Sefi Atta…

Q: What do you think accounts for this, because it wasn't the case in the 60s and 70s? Now, there are a lot of women writing and winning prizes. Sefi Atta, who won the maiden edition of the Wole Soyinka Prize, wrote such a fantastic novel.

A: I don't think it's a shift; it just shows that women constantly get marginalised, whether in politics, social development, or literature, but they have been there all the time; that's what we are all learning. If one looks at the tradition of the Griots, for instance, you'll find that some of those countries where the Griot culture is deeply entrenched, there have also been female Griots, even though the men tended to be more aggressive. I think and I hope I don't exaggerate here, but according to my direct experience, especially when I was doing my research in theatre, which also meant of course the epic, music and so on, the female in our traditional society has always been more or less at par with male productivity. So maybe what we're witnessing is a return to that cycle of equilibrium. I like to think so.

Q: What did the Yoruba culture do to your writing?

A: I would even put it in a different way and say that Yoruba culture has been central and fundamental to my literary perception. Yes, I write in English, but I always like to quote the translator of one of my plays, Akin Isola, when he was asked about *Death and the King's Horseman*, this play which is quite well-known. He was asked, "Didn't you find it very difficult to translate Wole Soyinka into Yoruba?" and he said, "Not in the least, because what I discovered was that I was translating back that play into the language in which it was originally thought." Now, for me this is a very perceptive statement and I think it answers your question adequately.

Q: What elements in the culture have deeper meaning for your works?

A: First of all, I have been absorbed in a very natural way into the Yoruba pantheon, the Yoruba world-view: its mythology; the relationship between mortals and immortals; the concept of a continuum of existence between the world of the living, the unborn and the dead. I had been inducted at an early age into the manifestations of this culture in terms of the *Egungun*, the ancestral masquerade, the *Agemo*, the music, the liturgy of Yoruba religions, even the very musicality of the Yoruba language. In the Diaspora, Yoruba culture went over there with the slaves, integrated or synchronised with Roman Catholic religion to the extent that on altars you have, side by side, Roman Catholic sayings and their equivalents in Yoruba culture. It was the richness of that which, from a very early age, just struck me. Though I was brought up in a Christian environment, I was drawn very early to that not so prominent aspect of the cultural environment in which I lived. And incidents happened in my childhood that also brought me closer, which were interpreted for me in terms of Yoruba culture and deities. Of course, that will make you curious and I got drawn deeper and deeper into it.

Q: Yoruba culture must have political dimensions then. There is a transition in your own writings from the early plays to for instance *Kongi's Harvest* – these are very political things that you write about. Were these also influenced by the politics of the Yoruba culture?

A: Let me give you an instance. Yoruba political culture does not accept the principle of direct succession. There is something very profound about that. In other words: you don't say that you are the son of a reigning king, therefore you will become the next king. It is a kind of democratisation of the principle of succession. The ruling houses meet, they consult also the oracle and so you have a process of elimination, selectiveness, which ensures that the dynastic mentality is completely obviated, so you don't have power constantly concentrated in one household. It is not the ultimate democracy of universal suffrage, but it is a controlling mechanism to ensure that there is participation at so many levels in governance. The king therefore is a kind of constitutional monarch. You have the house of the *Ogbuni* for instance, a very strict executive arm of the monarchy that controls it. And you have a tradition whereby if the king, who is the supreme individual becomes autocratic the chiefs meet, examine his conduct and then hand him a symbolic calabash. They say, "Go into that room and open the calabash." When he goes in there, the symbolism of the items inside – whether a cockatoo feather or whatever – indicates his punishment and he knows he must commit suicide, usually, or maybe escape through the window and never be seen again in that environment. I recognise and understand democracy as checks and balances, distribution of authority or power – in fact substituting for power, authority, which is something you derive from people, not something you arrogate to yourself. I grew up in an environment – as I recounted in my childhood autobiography, *Ake* – where women mobilised and chased out the monarch, who was supported by the European District Officer. A powerful monarch, they chased him out with his tail between his legs. And so I, from childhood, could never bring myself to understand absolutist power. What is that? Who is an individual who wants to exercise absolutist power over a community of more than one? These experiences and tradition have shaped my political attitude, which explains maybe my total rejection of absolutism.

Q: So the Yoruba culture is against dictatorship and, by extension, you are against dictatorship. But has this culture been able to cover you well in your fights against dictatorship in Nigeria and Africa?

A: Nigeria is a conglomerate of many nations. The Yoruba nation is one, the Igbo nation is one and the Hausa nation is one. These are nations that were cobbled together for the convenience of the colonial powers. It is not a homogenous nation and what we've been trying to do has been to make it work. But this does not obliterate the fact that some are coming from a republican culture – the Igbo, who had no history of kings before the arrival of the British – or the democratic monarchism of the Yoruba, or the feudal tradition of the Emirates and the Caliphates of the North, and then the even more scattered and less homogenous minorities you will find in some of the Middle Belt. Many people don't understand the war that went on for a long time.

Q: It makes it very complex. Is it this complexity that makes democracy and other extensions of it difficult to operate in Nigeria?

A: Yes, I agree with you. The complexity is there and it is a question of which ideology wins out because there are sections which are totally feudally oriented… are not prepared to give up that feudalist, absolutist mentality; this condescending patronage system of social organisation in which there is a very small section at the top which then doles out condescending largesse to the masses of the people. This contrasts with those who believe that, from the very beginning, there has to be an agreement on governance, methods of governance, resources and so on.

Q: Not very long ago, I re-read *The Man Died*, your prison notes, and recently *You*

Must Set Forth at Dawn, your major memoir of the last two decades. It looks like nothing has changed in your views and how you construct Nigeria and Africa. Is it you who has not changed or is it the situation in Nigeria that has not changed?

A: Nigeria has changed and at the same time Nigeria has not changed. You find that there is a common possession in all people, a craving, a desire even in an enslaved society, slaves have always moved and propelled towards a condition of non-slavery. Now translate slavery and non-slavery into dictatorship and democracy and you find the parallels are enormous. I sometimes narrate, or try to encapsulate, the propelling motives for moving history forward as a struggle between power and freedom. If you analyse across all ideological divides, histories and so on, you will find that humanity has always been propelled by that contest between power and freedom. So it is a question of which one is triumphant at any particular time. Even in the early pre-colonial days, we have always had resistance between what we call "the masses" and the dictatorship level of society. You can translate it in terms of classes if you want to use the Marxist theory, but ultimately what you will find is a contest between power and freedom; the right to self-volition and the insistence on the right to control humanity.

That is why I say it has not changed and at the same time it has changed. It has changed in the sense that, across political divides, you now have collaboration across those lines so that those on one side are influencing those on the other. But at the same time there is that hard-core resistance that does not want to give up privilege, to give up control, which enjoys power for its own sake, even if it is power at a secondary level, tertiary level, trickle-down power. There is always a section that believes they must have others under them, always. And so they will kowtow to the people at the top, they will carry out the orders from the top, but ultimately there is a push from beneath which sometimes swallows the next layer and swallows the next layer, until there is an assault on the dictatorial level. So in many ways things have changed and not changed.

Q: That makes you a warrior of anti-establishment. When God was creating Nigeria, did he create you as its police officer?

A: Sometimes I wonder. I wrote an article recently in Nigeria in which I said that all leaders should be examined by psychiatrists from time to time. Maybe I will put myself in that rule also, because I should be psychiatrically examined. There are times when I feel I am out of sync with what is going on, that is why, after so many years, are we still involved in this same struggle? Fortunately, there are many millions of people in Nigeria who belong in the same loony bin with me, and that keeps me going.

Chapter Seventeen
KONGI! KONGI!!
Egun Oko Grammar!
'Niyi Coker Jr.

In the Fall of 1981, as third year students in Dramatic Arts at the University of Ife, (now Obafemi Awolowo University) we were all required to take the "Special Author" course, which was to be an in-depth and detailed study of a specific writer. The course required that students in the class not just acquire knowledge of the selected author's entire creative work, but the writer's biography. Essentially, what was it that made the writer function? What personal experiences and incidents combined to contribute to the 'creative fire' of the said writer? The previous class – the department's first set of students' – had studied "Bertolt Brecht" the East German writer as their 'Special Author.' We were quite certain we would be required to study the same author as well, particularly because at that time Professor Joachim Fiebach, the East German Theatre scholar was resident in the department as a Visiting Professor, so no surprises there, right? Wrong!

On the first day of class for the "Special Author" course, there we were sitting in the air-conditioned department-library-classroom space (the room served many functions) chit-chatting about the recently-ended long vacation experience. The door of the room swings open and Professor Soyinka strides in with a note-pad and sits in the teacher's chair. What was happening? We looked at each other with inquiring eyes. Where was Fiebach? Was Professor Soyinka just filling in for him? We've had him come into class to do some guest lectures over the two years we had been students in the department. But then, it was not on the first day of classes and certainly not to teach the entire course. He was Head of the Department after all and surely had more pressing business. In his typical 'WS' fashion, he got straight down into business and announced that the 'special author' we would be studying for the course would be "Jean Genet." The look we gave each other was "God help us!" Who the heck is this Genet?

We were prepared for Brecht and semi-prepared for Shakespeare, Pirandello, Beckett, Ionesco and Corneille – basically all the writers we had spent the last two years studying in Dramatic Literature and Theatre history classes. Genet, as it turned out would not be our first problem. As the class progressed, it became crystal clear to us that Professor Soyinka was not 'filling-in' or 'guest-teaching' for Fiebach. He was going to be teaching the class for the semester! I do recall there was a level of excitement in the class mixed with the anxiety of intimidation. I shall expand on the intimidation factor later on.

Professor Soyinka went on to introduce the class to Genet as we took copious notes, understanding that we had to make sojourns to the university library and to dig out every possible publication on Genet. Genet was a masochist, an ex-convict, engaged in homosexual acts. He detested society and was engaged in shocking the very society that had rejected him in every possible way. He was imprisoned a few times and published his autobiography titled, *A Thief's Journal*. His plays and writing had been banned in the United States. "So why this writer?" Needless to say, it was the best selection that could have been offered to us as budding writers and dramatists. Genet's plays, *The Balcony*, *The Maids* and *The Blacks* – were a new dimension in writing and a world that Professor Soyinka opened up for us. For one thing, Genet was not your run-of-the-mill writer. He was as unpredictable, as he was refreshing and exciting to read. Now, let us skip to Final Examinations and the preparations that went along with those examinations.

To the 'intimidation' factor: Rational study habits and normal examination preparations went out the window for this course. The majority of my classmates underwent a vigorous transformation in their study technique. There was a detailed ritual of word-cramming from the Webster's dictionary. Essentially, it was a dictionary search and quest for the 'biggest words.' Study groups were formed not in pursuit of the substance of Genet's plays or their attendant significance – No! That was now irrelevant. Most needed to *show* this Professor that they had a commanding grasp of the English language as well. Opening sentences to perceived examination questions were assembled, fabricated, constructed, deconstructed and re-convened.

The road to an "A" in this class had to be in your mastery of English with a smattering of Latin words sprinkled here and there. Each student was fully armed and crammed, with words they had never utilized, did not comprehend and would certainly never be using again – *ever*, entered the examination and prepared to take on the 'master.' After all we had tried in vain to read *Madmen and Specialists* and been confronted with Latin words such as *rem acu tetigisti*. We had also waded into *Myth, Literature and the African World* and thus were fully aware that you don't walk into a gunfight armed with a simple razor blade. So finally, the examination day arrived and *wham* we all delivered, determined not to be confined to the dungeons of illiteracy – thereby maintaining some modicum of dignity! As it would happen the grades for the class were not posted on the department notice board when the other results went up at the end of the examination period. We panicked! What could have happened? Of all the classes that semester, this one was very personal. We needed to know. The following afternoon we were at the department for an unrelated function when we developed the courage to ask Professor Soyinka, "Prof have you finished grading Special Authors finals yet?" He simply gave us that quintessential *WS* look and then he quickly switched into what we thought was an unrelated banter. He started to describe a previous incident: the arrest of a reckless driver along the Ife-Ibadan road a few days prior. (Professor Soyinka was also Road-Safety Marshall for Oyo State and commanded an army of Road-Safety Marshalls who detained reckless drivers and those exceeding the speed limits on the state highway). He said, "I was returning from a visit to Ibadan and this taxi driver was driving like a lunatic, so I had the Marshalls stop and detain him. This semi-illiterate driver started trying to explain himself in English. His explanations were so convoluted and totally incomprehensible, no one understood what he was trying to say. By the time he was done with his explanations we were completely overwhelmed and exhausted. It sounded strangely familiar listening to him, it reminded me of your papers." Silence! *We were dead*, we thought! Everyone dispersed that event in silence. No one asked again. We waited! We waited in quiet anticipation and in surrender of embracing the worst-case scenario of a repeat or resit? The results were finally posted. It did go well and I cannot recall anyone failing the class.

Come our Final year, we were privileged to have Professor Soyinka again and again and again, as he taught our required courses in *Aesthetics*, *Humanist Tradition in Drama* and the *Long Essay-Thesis* class in which he challenged us to use the *commedia dell'arte* as our comparative theme and basis in the thesis research. By this time we were quite accustomed to, and no longer intimidated by his brilliance. He did take the whole class out to *Road One* on campus, for the Aesthetics class. Just as we were appreciating the landscapes and how they influence and enrich our aesthetic perceptions and simultaneously taking copious notes, because Prof taught extemporaneously, he hurled out: "… and there is an '*Objet trouve*' staring you in the face!" All paused from note taking and we started searching each other's eyes in utter confusion. He was referring to a large piece of windshield glass, abandoned at the roadside, which had now merged into the soil and vegetation creating a new pattern – *objet trouve*!

A group of us from that class of 1983 are still in contact and recall a lot of these experiences that always induce fresh laughter during our recollections each and every time. Though we suspect it, we have not asked him if he knew how much he challenged us into being on our guard whenever he was teaching.

Aside from being his student, I was very privileged to have played lead roles in plays he wrote and directed such as *Camwood on the Leaves*, *Requiem for a Futurologist* and then to sing on his *Etika Revolution* Album. Prof always insisted on a good work ethic at rehearsals. He was always there on time and in most cases never took a break when the cast took one. I truly appreciate the 'front-seat' he had once granted me into his creative process for the *Etika Revolution Album*. This album had evolved from a guerrilla theatre performance that Prof had written and directed with the songs in 1982, on the Ife campus. Prof is an avid hunter and one afternoon after rehearsals I joked with him about sharing the antelope with us when he returned from his hunting expedition. For me it was just a joke. I was pleasantly surprised when upon return from hunting, Prof had his personal assistant named Francis, inform me the following day that I was being invited to enjoy some antelope meat at Prof's residence. I saw Prof that afternoon and thanked him in anticipation of the feast. He said, "Come with a pen and notebook." I complied that evening, arriving at Prof's campus residence with my pen, notebook and an appetite. It was a tasty meal – way better than the campus cafeteria. With the meal done, Prof said, "Okay take some notes." I grabbed my pen and notebook and he just started creating a scene for the album. It was a complete hilarious dialogue between the President and the Olympic torchbearer. I was in stitches as he spoke the dialogue and just continued dictating it with a straight face. The dictation complete, he said. 'Make a copy for Funsho (my classmate who was singing in the project as well) memorize it, and we should be set to record it in another week with Tunji (Oyelana). A week or so later, we entered the EMI studio's in Lagos at about 7am, having left Ife at about 5am that morning. We thought we were early, but there was Prof already in the studio, testing microphones in the sound booth. We got to work and did not take a break until about noon. Prof announced a break and the three of us, the late Funsho Alabi, uncle Tunji Oyelana and myself, went out for lunch while Prof stayed back to work some more. We returned and there he was, still at it! We finished at about 6pm, imbibed dinner and returned to Ife that evening. It struck us on the journey back that he had not eaten a meal that day.

Prof undoubtedly possesses a very strong physical constitution. Another case in point is a dinner party he invited six members of the cast to, during his 1981 National Theatre production of *Camwood on the Leaves*. The dinner host, Francesca Emanuel invited us over to her Ikoyi residence after an evening performance at the Iganmu theatre. It was quite a sumptuous dinner with plenty to drinks afterwards. We returned to our hotel in the wee hours of the morning, knowing we had to report for a 9am call to review and prepare for a matinee performance. Needless to say, we all reported for the production, barely able to stay awake, drowsy, bleary-eyed and worn out from the previous nights merriment Prof? There he was, looking very refreshed, rejuvenated and vitalized. This was in contrast to the chaos backstage where we were engaged in a frenzy purchasing of kolanuts from the petty traders outside the National Theatre. The last thing you wanted at a rehearsal was for Prof to zero in on your lack of preparation or tardiness. Some of those frustrations with actors have resulted in memorable phrases from Prof, such as: *"Hey, why are you walking like you have a totem pole planted down your spine?"*, or, *"Why are you suegbeing when I have not asked you to suegberize?"* That particular one was directed at a dancer named Oje. After listening to Prof's criticism of his stage performance during a rehearsal at Oduduwa hall, Oje returned to the wings backstage not comprehending. After a deep breath he uttered, *Egun oko grammar* – literally meaning, the masquerade and husband of English grammar. This man has an uncanny ability with words, just as undoubtedly as he is very quick witted!

When we were working on *Requiem for a Futurologist* in 1982, admittedly, I over-slept and arrived 10 minutes late for a Saturday 8am rehearsal. Running into the rehearsal with the urgency of being late, I announced to him, "Sorry sir, my bike refused to kick." Trying to blame the tardiness on my Kawasaki motorcycle, I stood there in front of him, trying to solicit understanding. He simply took one hard stare at me, as I tried to avoid his gaze or any eye contact and uttered, "or YOU refused to kick!" I was speechless. I had no denials and was not willing to pursue that line of defence any further. I was busted! I was thankful when he simply uttered, "get on stage!"

To know Prof is to know that he is in every sense of the word a practicing dramatist! This full awareness dawned on me in the dark Abacha years when he was again forced into exile in the United States. In those years he had to travel under heavy security and employed several disguises to get through airports and populated cities to avoid Abacha's hired assassins all clamouring to win their bosses approval as they chased their target in futility all over the Western world. In that period and during a visit to my institution in Illinois, he noted the presence of several under-cover state police and Federal security officers and the discreet manner in which they conducted their surveillance and escorted him from one venue on campus to the next. He described his experience with the Italian police which was in vast contrast to the American one. In Italy his police escorts employed sirens and would not even allow him to walk through the airports in Italy. He said they insisted on driving him straight onto the airport tarmac and right to the plane, and not stopping there, the officers escorted him unto the plane and to his seat. His fellow passengers already on the plane all watched in amazement as he took his seat, escorted by these armed officers in uniform. Having taken his seat and being a dramatist he suddenly realizes that the onlookers in the back rows watching this event unfold in front of them may not understand or properly comprehend what has transpired. It dawns on Prof that they might interpreted what they witnessed as a deportation in progress! Coming to this realization, he jumps to his feet, and commences a public display of gratitude in the full glare of the passengers. He robustly starts thanking the Italian officers for their efforts. Thanking them for a job well done. Shaking the hands of each and every one of them, conveying his familiarity with them and making it clear that he anticipates seeing them again on his very next visit to Italy. Having completed this public performance offered for the full view and consumption of the airline passengers, he settles into his seat, now completely assured that no one on the flight will mistake him for a deportee!

I laugh incessantly each time I recall his narration of that event. Only this hilarious comic genius would think and react like that. Many thanks for sharing his creative gifts with us and for making the world a better place!

Chapter Eighteen
Glimpses of "Uncle Wole"
Esi Sutherland-Addy
and Amowi Sutherland Phillips

Searching the Internet for Efua Sutherland as we both do from time to time, we were tickled to come across the work of our niece Elizabeth Efua Sutherland – the granddaughter of Efua Sutherland and a student of theatre arts, who had designed and directed *The Swamp Dwellers* by Wole Soyinka. We agreed that this was a beautiful metaphor for the continuum of mutual inspiration, spanning the generations.

We have both over the years included Soyinka's work in our literature courses with a sense of pride and with some amusement at the awe with which students learn that we have, even in this very tangential way, been a part of the world of Wole Soyinka.

Amowi, in her preface to *The Legacy of Efua Sutherland* recalls our mother's writing studio which contained 'critical archives and an extensive library of books by Pan African and world-renowned writers. The special fact for us was that quite often those same writers whose names we saw everyday on the bookshelves at home – Wole Soyinka, Chinua Achebe, Ama Ata Aidoo, amongst others – would be present in person' (Sutherland Phillips, 2007:3).[1]

In retrospect we recall that Uncle Wole also used to come to our home in the company of the effervescent Rajat Neogy, founder of the journal *Transition* and their visits often generated impassioned discussions and debate. His trademark head of standing-up-tall hair was as impressive to us then as it is to many people around the world today! We can only conjecture that being in exile in Ghana during the 1970s meant something entirely different from the visits Uncle Wole had undertaken before. Life with all its cares and joys had to be lived in Accra for this was home for now.

Wole Soyinka brought his family to our home 'Araba Mansa,' and soon, members of the family developed their own personal rapport with 'Auntie

Efua.' Amowi recalls that while Auntie Laide and Auntie Efua could, on occasion be seen in deep communion, Olaokun would play in the wonderful grassed courtyard that never failed to beckon any curious, playful child. Uncle Wole also came to 'Araba Mansa' on his own at times. He and Auntie Efua could be observed in the sort of heart to heart sharing which they both seemed to treasure as artists and friends.

Wole Soyinka appears to have sought and linked up with Efua Sutherland at different stages of his life. James Gibbs reveals in an article discussing Soyinka's early research forays into West African performance culture that Soyinka had written to Robert July about meeting Efua Sutherland. Gibbs refers to a letter dated 16/04/1960 in which Soyinka refers to a meeting with Efua Sutherland and describes the work that she was doing at the time. It would appear that he must have met her on or about 11/04/1960.

"She called her development of the convention, Anansegoro, and from the late fifties used it with projects for children. Soyinka saw something of the dramatist keen to exploit elements which he considers latent in a dance or ritual" (Gibbs, 1994:96).[2] As dramatists, Soyinka and Sutherland can be seen to have been intrigued by similar dramaturgy. They were both well-read and explored the literatures of the world which influenced different phases of their work. They undertook adaptations of Greek drama, exploring affinities and asserting the subtleties of specific African expressions. Greek tragedy held a particular fascination for both of them.[3] Perhaps it is their enchantment with the ritual, ceremonial, narrative, performance and mythological cultures of their own and other African people which made them kindred spirits.

The Ghana Drama Studio, established by Efua Sutherland was a great hub of creativity for playwrights, directors, choreographers, performers and theatre artists of every ilk. Among the challenges taken up at the studio was the production of plays by Wole Soyinka. As children, we would watch *The Trials of Brother Jero* perched on the back risers of the Studio and snatches of songs from the play became part of our stock of memorable theatre moments.

Soyinka himself spent time at the Studio. He participated in Sutherland's Children's Drama Development Programme, a multi-faceted curriculum focusing on stagecraft and cultural awareness. The group also acted as a laboratory for new scripts.

Today, this curriculum is being reiterated with freshly energized passion in the *Playtime in Africa Initiative*, a children's cultural park project in Ghana inspired by the legacy of Efua Sutherland. As we contemplate its design and use, we envisage a natural environment with reminders of our literary legacy at every turn. We imagine special places for children like Jonah, little Wole's personal rock in the parsonage in *Ake*[4] where he grew up. We hope to encourage in children the insatiable curiosity he had about everything around him, a fascination for books like Wole had with his father S. A. Soyinka's library and a better respect for flowers than he showed with that parent's roses! If we are able to accomplish this, some children in Africa will march with confidence to the beat of their own drum, as Uncle Wole always has.

Section IV
The Museum, African Art and Music

Chapter Nineteen
The Museum and Creativity
Zagba Oyortey and Malcolm McLeod

Societies need creativity. Creativity is essential for their health; without it they grow stale and rot from the inside. Creative artists, great writers like Wole Soyinka, open peoples' minds to things that were unseen and unthought, things that previously appeared to be beyond their comprehension or were simply too dangerous to express.

Do museums have a role in fostering creativity? Regrettably the relationship between museums and creativity in literature, sculpture, theatre, music and dance, has often been an uneasy, even an unproductive one, because too often museums tend to be static and divorced from contemporary concerns. Although many creative people have drawn inspiration from museum collections, the initiative has almost always been the artist's and not the museum's.

If museums are to do better they must become more than just a collection of interesting relics from which creative artists can occasionally draw – if and when they feel like doing so. How is this change to be achieved? How can museums make a greater contribution to creativity so as to give people richer and better lives? Is it time for Africa to invent new ways for museums to work?

The traditional role of museums is to show their visitors a selection of objects from other places and other times and by doing so, help them to see that their own way of life is not the sole one that is possible. Yet while many creative artists grapple with the present in order to make their art, museums too often opt for a different approach and do no more than present a simplified and static version of the past, mainly because only a limited amount of information can ever be communicated by displayed objects and their labels. In addition, much museum activity is concerned with combating change and removing objects from the flux of time by preserving them exactly as they were when they were acquired. While the world around a museum changes with increasing speed many museums tend to create a timeless, unchanging zone around themselves that is the very antithesis of creativity. By doing so they diminish the creative possibilities that lie within their collections.

What can be done to counter all this? The first step is to get more people and especially creative people, involved in the museum. A simple technique for encouraging creativity is to appoint artists-in-residence. This has been tried and tested in numerous museums and it generally works. The artist is given the run of the collections can choose the things that appeal to him or her, perhaps sketch or paint them, write about them or even put them into an exhibition with examples of his or her own work which have been influenced by the museum. Examples of this in the United Kingdom are the exhibitions at the British Museum's Ethnography Department (The Museum of Mankind) organised by Sir Eduardo Paolozzi and more recently, in the main British Museum, by the artist Grayson Perry.

Another basic step is to introduce children to the objects in museums. All good museums should have education and outreach programmes for young people so as to fire their imagination by introducing them to the objects in the collection and to the stories they tell – or might tell if they were approached in the right way. Dead objects can be brought to life by skilful storytelling. Storytelling, after all, is a crucial element in African culture and many of Africa's greatest writers have drawn on the storytelling traditions of their own people in their work. The museum should become a place of many stories.

There are of course different sorts of creativity and making and many are in danger of being lost. In Africa and elsewhere the museum can also be a place where traditional knowledge and skills, those important forms of creativity that have evolved over many centuries, can be passed on to a new generation. Here the need is to bring alive the objects in the collections by getting people who created them, or think like them, to explain how they were made and used. To do this, of course, the artefacts must be valued as embodiments of skill and knowledge and not as mere curiosities that have no direct relevance for the present. All this is about re-injecting the present into the museum and brining the museum's objects into the present. The results may be messy, even dangerous. Good.

Ideally future museums will become places where all sorts of creativity can take place. The museum must cease to be a lot of objects in cases and instead become a place where people can sing, dance, act, tell stories and make things. All this means that Africa needs to develop new sorts of museums, move away from the colonial model to something far more creative and dynamic. It will be impossible to know where this might lead but the effort will be worthwhile.

Creativity alters humankind. We need more of it.

Chapter Twenty
African Art from Past to Present
Ekpo Eyo

We need... to constantly reinforce our awareness of the primacy of Source and that source is the universal spring of culture. It is nourished by its tributaries, which sink back into the earth and thereby replenish that common source in an unending, creative cycle.

– Wole Soyinka, 1994

Art history in Africa has a long and distinguished past, one that scholars today are only just exploring. The earliest art found in Africa were the engravings and paintings done on the surfaces of rock shelters that likely served ritual foci for prehistoric peoples. Located in both the Saharan region and in southern Africa, the beginnings of these evocative works dates to roughly 10,000 years ago in the Sahara desert and 27,000 years ago in southern Africa. The artists of southern Africa were the San people, the original inhabitants of a region extending from Zimbabwe to the tip of the southern coast. Their engravings and paintings depict archaic animals from the Palaeolithic or early stone period and cattle herded in later times.

The art of ancient Egypt, while too vast a subject to deal with here, should also be considered as apart of Africa's art history. Although there was significant interchange between Egypt and the Mediterranean and Asian worlds, Egypt is also a part of the African continent, both physically and culturally. It is pointless, however to promote the arts of Africa on the back of Egypt, because within Sub Saharan Africa, there exist enough works of art that she can justly be proud of: the exquisite and sophisticated Nok terra-cottas created between the second half of the last century BC and the third century AD in what is now Nigeria; the Djenne terracotta masterpieces, made between the eleventh and fifteenth century in today's Mali. From the hoard of intricately cast and decorated bronzes excavated from Igbo Ukwu in eastern Nigeria and dated to the ninth century AD; we know that the Igbo people had a complete mastery of metalworking and a great sense of beauty. In Ile-Ife, the sacred city of the Yoruba people, which flourished between the eleventh and fifteenth centuries, were art whose serenity and reality was so impressive that the German ethnologist, Leo Frobenius, believed the city was at one time colonized by the Greeks. And when the Benin bronzes and ivories that were plundered by the British marines in 1897 reached Europe, their beauty and technical excellence so impressed the Germans scholar, Felix von Luschan, that he wrote of them: "Cellini himself could not have made better casts, not anyone else before or since to the present day." (Roth, 1903; von Luschan 1919).

These great masterpieces of antiquity are only a small part of the African cultural achievement. Yet despite this impressive history of artistic expression, there was a time not long ago when Africans were regarded by Europeans as a people without a past, with neither history not art. Europeans first learned of African art through the Greeks who established colony at Cyrenaica (today's Libya) in the seventh century BC and later, when Alexander the Great conquered Egypt. The Greeks were followed by the seafaring Phoenicians from the coast of Tyre and Siddon who established several important trading posts, including Carthage, by the ninth century BC in the Maghreb (now Tunisia), Algeria and Morocco. By the second century BC the Roman Empire had spread beyond the imperial frontiers and absorbed Carthage along with other Phoenician posts. The Roman Empire collapsed in the seventh century when North Africa was overrun by the Arabs who have remained there until today. These histories fit the northern part of Africa into the Mediterranean profile, while the rest of Africa remained a 'dark continent' to Europe.

II

Coastal Africa was explored in the fifteenth century, when the Portuguese spearheaded several voyages in search of a sea-route to the Orient. They were followed in the next century by the Dutch, the British and the French who, along with the Portuguese, established trading posts on the African coasts along the Atlantic sea-board and the Indian Ocean. The European traders were interested in the gold, ivory and spices, which they found in abundance and also sought to trade in human beings, transporting them to work on the "New World" plantations. While in Africa, European traders became interested in ivory objects carved for local use and they commissioned artists in Sierra Leone and the Benin area of Nigeria to create carvings for them. These works, now known as the Afro-Portuguese ivories, consisting of saltcellars in the form of European prototypes, Oliphants or hunting horns, spoons and forks, were displayed in the "cabinets de curiosites" of the papal collections and royal castles of southern Europe. The painter Albrecht Durer is known to have bought two of these commissioned works in 1520/21, although their origins were misattributed to India and Turkey.

African material culture was not widely known in Europe and the Americas, however, until the second half of the nineteenth century. The birth of the Industrial Revolution created the need for the importation of raw materials for the factories in Europe and also the need for external markets for the manufactured goods. The European powers were now forced to penetrate the interior of Africa to buy and sell. The scramble to secure spheres of influence led to the portioning of Africa among the western powers in 1884/5. A bye-product of this situation was that large numbers of African artifacts were collected by both traders and missionaries and exported to Europe.

The nineteenth century also witnessed the rise of anthropology as an academic discipline that treated human societies as having progressed through a series of evolutionary stages. For example, in his *Ancient Society*, the American lawyer-turned ethnologist, Lewis M. Morgan (1877), thought that human societies had progressed through three stages: savagery, barbarism and civilisation. Western societies were the civilised groups who occupied the top of this hierarchy, while the non-Western peoples were the savages at the base. With the spread of western education around the world, this classification of human societies gained a global dimension.

The taxonomic system that placed African societies at the lowest rung of human development was extended to the visual culture of the continent. Early anthropologists saw curious combinations of human and animal forms as 'proof' of the primitive nature of human development. The artefacts were never considered as art because 'primitive' people were believed to be incapable of the noble process of creativity. Such an attitude should not be surprising because the prevailing artistic taste in Europe at this time was realism, that is, the representation of forms as they actually appeared in nature. Thus, many, like the art historian Leonard Adam, believed that 'primitive" African art was not much an art, but an unsuccessful attempt to produce one (Adam 1940).

In truth, African artists often deliberately cast aside realism to relish the depiction of abstract images reflecting unknown and mythical worlds of their own. In addition, African artists employ certain conventions for the purpose of emphasis, suppressing what they believe to be unessential and exaggerating what they believe to be essential. For example, when an African artist depicts a human head out of proportion with the rest of the body, it is not because he does not know human anatomy. The deliberate exaggeration of the head reflects the artist's desire to underscore that it is the seat of reason. The African artist had this freedom to interpret the human body or object as he wished, a freedom that his European counter-part lacked. Yet, for most Europeans, the nonrepresentational nature of African sculpture was seen as 'primitive.' Consequently, African art was placed at the lowest rung of artistic development, while Western art occupied its pinnacle.

Nonetheless, despite its given low status, it was this same strange 'primitive' art that captured the imagination of European artists at the beginning of this century. Seeking an escape from their own rigid convention, French artists like

Maurice Vlaminck, Andre Derain, Pablo Picasso, Henry Matisse, Amedeo Modigliani and others, began to collect and to copy African art forms. Meanwhile in Germany, new art groups such as *Die Brucke* in Dresden and *Der Blaue Reiter* in Munich were formed, greatly influenced by conceptions of the 'primitive.' The practices of those new movements were to change the course of world art during the twentieth century.

The liberating force of African sculpture was soon felt across Europe and in the United States. Sculptors like Jacob Epstein in England, Paul Klee in Switzerland, Constantin Brancusi in Romania and Jacques Lipchitz in Lithuania, were now drawing inspiration for their creations from African art forms. In the United States, admirers of African art included Max Weber and John Graham, among others. Galleries that displayed African art in addition to modern art were opened by Robert Coady, Alfred Stieglitz and Marius de Zayas. Because of the impact made by the African art exhibition at Stieglitz's "291" gallery in New York, The World magazine section of January 24, 1915, proclaimed: "African savages: the First Futurists," a summation of the scenario of the time. Finally, there were collectors of African art like Albert Barnes and Alain Locke in the United States, who helped to popularize African art in their collections. Admirers of African art eschewed the context of African art and extolled its formal qualities. This attitude was clearly evident in Carl Einstein's *Negerplastik* of 1915, which maintained that seeking the meaning of African art was superfluous and constituted an impediment to its aesthetic appreciation.

III

The proper study of African art began when anthropologists began to conduct field research to back up their theoretical frameworks. The American Melville Herskovits, for example, conducted field research among the Fon people of Dahomey (now the Republic of Benin) in 1931, paying attention to the relationship between art and culture. Herskovits (1938) was the first anthropologist to use the concept of "culture area" in the study of African art, in which he divided the continent into ten cultural units for this purpose; the French Marcel Griaule undertook a series of field trips to the Dogon country in western Sudan in 1931, 1935 and 1937 and made an intensive study of all the religions of the Dogon that he brought to bear on the interpretation of the arts; and the Belgian Frans Olbrechts (1959) studied the people and the arts of the peoples of the then Belgian Congo (now the Democratic Republic of the Congo) noting their stylistic differences. All these men encouraged their students to carry out fieldwork by direct observation and participation in the activities of the people whom they studied, a method that has proved invaluable and is yet to be replaced. What we know and do today in African art studies follow the basic tenets that those early scholars preached and practiced.

Although Western scholarship on African art has grown immensely in the post-World War II era, the description "primitive" that is applied to non-Western art has stuck in the minds of some people, irrespective of its objectionable connotations. Some scholars still defend its use, rather paternalistically extolling the term as noble and lofty, while others have argued frivolously for its retention because changing it after its long-time usage would create problems. In 1984 the Museum of Modern Art in New York City again organised an exhibition curated by William Rubin "Primitivism in 20th Century Art," that demonstrated the affinities between twentieth-century Western art and the arts of the non-Western world. This exhibition drew much criticism because of the use of the word "primitive," a term Rubin justified as referring to a "movement" and not to African art. Yet it was freely used throughout the catalogue to refer directly to non-Western works. Susan Blier has pointed out that although the use of the term "primitive" is merely semantic, such use really lies at the heart of African art not being accepted within the field of art history. Furthermore, it was clear that the juxtaposition of some of the more aesthetically satisfying African works with their inferior European copies in Rubin's show was designed to promote superior African art, not on its own merit comparatively speaking, but on the back of the inferior European copies.

Another misnomer commonly applied to African art is the work "tribal" a term William Fagg advocated in his influential publication: *Tribes and Forms in African Art* (1982). In the book, Fagg identified a particular art style with a particular "tribe," yet the word "tribe" has yet to acquire universal definition by either anthropologists or art historians.

The tenet of "tribal art" is that each "tribe" is an artistic universe itself and that the work of one "tribe" is not understood or appreciated by another "tribe." Faced with considerable criticism, Fagg affirmed, "What is not tribal is not African." It is true, of course, that African artists worked within certain stylistic conventions that permit us to attribute their works to their groups or individuals within their group. This fact has led to the characterisation of African art as stereotyped and unchanging and this may have led Fagg to his conviction. This is incorrect however, because within these conventions, the African artist practices many innovations, so much so that no two works are ever exactly the same.

IV

That African art is static is debunked by the nature of its eclecticism. For example, where the Islamic religion had penetrated an area, its influence is reflected in certain art works. The carved wooden screens from Morocco made in the nineteenth or twentieth century were traditionally used on the windows of Muslim residences to allow women within to view the events on the street without being seen themselves. It is carved in the Islamic tradition of geometric forms without any figurative content. Another example is the marabout or holy man prayer board that includes Koranic instructional texts in Arabic and nonfigurative designs. The widespread influence of Islam on African art is eloquently documented by the noted scholar Rene A. Bravman (1973) in his book, *Open Frontiers: The Mobility of Art in Black Africa* where many more examples will be found. Western influence may be seen on the two high-backed chairs made in European fashion, one by the Asante of Ghana and the other by the Chokwe of Angola. The Asante chair or *asipim* is made of wood, leather and brass furniture tacks, probably during the nineteenth century and would be used by a chief on state occasions. The Chokwe chair was also a prestige item made after a European model to which were added ancestral images and scenes from Chokwe daily life, in this case, the birth of a child.

The fact that African art consists of a great diversity of styles is generally known, but to assume that these styles are confined to particular groups is incorrect. African art styles vary between ethnic groups and within each group. Individual artists are known to have changed their styles within their lifetime. In the last three decades scholars have devoted a good deal of attention to this subject, so much so that the authoritative *African Arts* magazine devoted one of its issues to demonstrating that styles cut across the so-called tribal boundaries. It is therefore, no longer necessary to maintain the epithet "tribal" when referring to African art and to continue to do so is to insist on dividing the arts of humankind into arbitrary and prejudiced groups. Art is universal phenomenon, a response by any creative individual to the stimulus provided by his or her environment no matter the race, colour or creed of the artist.

Unfortunately this humanistic art is dying out because of the inevitable changes that began with colonialism and Western education. These influences have worked hard to eliminate traditional African beliefs and concepts that provided the need for these works to be created. For instance, the missionaries regarded African sculptures as idols that must be consigned to the bonfire, while the educators considered them the primitive products of a savage society. Consequently, the first generation of Western-educated Africans were anxious to dissociate themselves from "idolatry" and their "primitive" past. Therefore they remained, even after the end of colonialism, oblivious or even hostile to their past thus, helping to perpetuate the colonial attitude. Happily, however, somewhere along the line, other Africans began to query the contradiction provided by the fact that these "primitive and idolatrous" objects are highly sought after in the Western world. One result of the query was the resurgence of interest in reconstructing African identity. But this task is enormous and requires a concerted effort through archaeological and ethnographic activities and the integration of culture into the educational system. The noted British archaeologist, Sir Mortimer Wheeler, once remarked on seeing the bronzes of Ife: "When the new Africa finds the moment and the mood for the discovery of its own past, here are matters which, properly understood, will provide a new chapter to world-history" (quoted in Willett 1967). The reconstruction of the African past should therefore be of concern to the entire world.

V

The future of African art is bright because many institutions are establishing new museums dedicated to its study and enjoyment. The last decade has seen the birth of the National Museum of African Art in Washington, DC, the Museum for African Art in New York City and the Dapper Museum in Paris. American universities are establishing new departments for the study and award of high degrees, up to PhD level in African art history and professional bodies like the Art Council of the African Studies Association are prompting scholarly activities. More than ever before, very exquisite publications on African art are seeing the light of day. There seems to be excitement everywhere, yet there is still a long way to go before African art takes its rightful place in the mainstream art world. If the trends observed above continue, it will not be too long before African art accomplishes its role in restoring human dignity in Africa.

We should not regret the past but should be happy that the present is witnessing a new period of artistic renaissance of the kind that takes cognizance of the past and looks to the future. Many contemporary artists are drawing upon their African cultural heritage by creating works in a range of media not seen in the traditional art of their forefathers. Bruce Onobrakpeya of the Zaria Art School in Nigeria has developed the technique of deep etching, which adds a sculptural quality to his two-dimensional prints that he employs in rendering works inspired by the culture of the Benin Kingdom and his Urhobo ancestry. The Congolese artist Kolwesi Kanyemba, using acrylic on canvass, seeks inspiration in the everyday world, as demonstrated by his depiction of carved gourds and other African cooking utensils and the fauna of his environment.

Artists such as Vuminkosi Zulu and John Ndevasia Muafangejo, both of whom were trained in the graphic arts at Rorke's Drift in South Africa, have adopted the expressive medium of woodcut to portray scenes from daily life, some of which have subtle political undertones.

Although these new artists are experiencing a different world, it is one that has not completely broken from the tradition. It is good that they wear two faces like the Roman god Janus: one looking into the past, the other toward the

151

present. In so doing they can build bridges both ways for us, so that we can preserve our identity, while participating in the present. A new gallery for African contemporary art opened at the National Museum of Africa Art in Washington, DC in October 1997, in the same place as the better-known ancient art that is on display. This is how it should be and it augurs well for the future.

It is a pity that today when the African nations yearn for development aid they generally think about technology and exclude culture or the development of the human being. Our educational system has become an unthinking routine and we are producing highly educated but depersonalised citizens. Technology should be the weft and culture the woof of the fabric of any society, for in a world troubled by fear, prejudice and bigotry, divided by wealth and poverty and torn by ideology, racism and infinite problems, we must seek anew meaningful consciousness in the sphere of culture that embraces the arts. We have to search for our roots and identify ourselves with our past achievements, convinced that we are rooted in a foundation that is solid and irrevocable, for culture, unlike technology, speaks to the soul and we should be ready for this dialogue.

Chapter Twenty-One
The Protestants from Abeokuta: Fela Kuti and His Cousin
John Collins with Ivor Agyeman-Duah

In the early 1950s, I found myself in Ghana, West Africa, where my father, Edmund, a historian was teaching at the University in Accra. Intellectual life in West Africa was as vibrant as the music of its people which had been influenced by models of colonial rule. There was a split between Francophone and Anglophone music based partly on their colonial encounters. There was Highlife in Ghana, Juju music in Nigeria and Mariga in Sierra Leone. These created on the Anglophone side, a musical hybridity as the British colonial policy of Indirect Rule accommodated experimentation as opposed to the Direct Rule of France which was rigid. Popular Francophone music developed later, in 1958 with the independence of Guinea through the established Anglophone influence.

Ghana created Highlife as far back as the 1880s in its central region of Cape Coast where it was called *Adaha* and later, *Osibisaaba*. It was after this that dance orchestras evolved with the new Ghanaian elite and the ultimate, Highlife that is, the high-class life. In Nigeria, Juju music developed from all sorts of influences. Freed slaves from Brazil who got to Lagos and Freetown in Sierra Leone, those of black soldiers coming into West Africa with the colonial army as well as Latin American music and calypso, travels of band parties all helped to create that hybridity.

By the 1940s, these had evolved strongly as musical forms. It had also been radicalized by artists or the music of the so-called veranda boys. The main types were guitar bands, the best example being E. K. Nyame of Ghana, a great fan of Kwame Nkrumah who would compose over 40 songs in his and the Convention Peoples' Party's memory. The other was the dance band of E.T. Mensah and The Tempos. E.T. Mensah had undisputed influence and ambition and for years dominated the music scene in West Africa. He took Highlife to

153

Nigeria in 1951 and Nigerian musicians adopted it in their own languages. In fact the bands in Ghana and Nigeria exchanged players and by that created the sound symbol or track for the independence movements or de-colonization of much of Africa. Though these musicians wielded a lot of influence and were very popular in their respective rights, one emerged whose personality was very captivating for all sorts of reasons – great creativity and unorthodox behaviour – Fela Anikulapo-Kuti.

II

Fela was a Highlife player and so regularly visited Ghana to update himself and to also take inspiration from its masters in the 1960s. One band that influenced him most was *Uhuru* which was also the favourite of Kwame Nkrumah. At this time, Fela was not as political as his mother, the famous Funmilayo Ransome-Kuti who had met Nkrumah on a couple of occasions and who had in 1948 organized tens of thousands of Egba market women against a British-imposed tax. This formidable woman was also the leader of the Nigeria's Women's Union and a leading member of Nnamdi Azikiwe's nationalist party. She also met with Mao Zedong and was the first Nigerian woman to visit Russia, where she received the Lenin Peace Prize and the first to drive a car.[1]

Fela's maternal grandfather was Pastor Thomas, a Yoruba slave freed in Sierra Leone. His paternal grandfather was the Revered Josiah Ransome-Kuti, a musically inclined preacher who spread Christianity to many parts of Yorubaland. He was also one of the first Africans to record vernacular hymns when, in 1929, he released 44 sacred Yoruba pieces for piano and voice on the Zonophone label. It would seem that Fela inherited his musical gifts from his grandfather, his radicalism from his mother and his rebelliousness from his adolescent reaction against both his grandfather's and father's stern Victorian attitudes.

These illustrious antecedents are more than matched by the achievements of Fela's siblings. His older brother, Olikoye, went on to become a doctor and at one point, Nigeria's Minister of Health. His older sister, Oludulope, went into nursing. His younger brother, Beko, became a doctor and then a lawyer-activist in the 1990s in Nigeria's human rights struggle. Africa's first Nobel Prize laureate, Wole Soyinka is his cousin.

Fela would get closer to Soyinka when in 1958 his parents sent him to study Law or Medicine in England. Against their wishes he switched to music, which he studied at Trinity College, London. It was also in London that Fela met his wife, Remi, who had Nigerian, British and Native American ancestry. Fela shared a flat with Soyinka in the White City area of West London. It was however not England that would radicalize him but America ten years later through the soul music of James Brown and the Black Panther Movement. This was through an African American singer, Sandra Iszidore (Smith) at a Black Panther Movement meeting that Stokley Carmichael attended. She was the one who also introduced Fela to *The Autobiography of Malcolm X* adding a new perspective to Fela's little understanding of African history. He stayed in America for nine months and his music changed from Highlife to Afro-soul; he particularized it and gave it the name Afro-beat. His lyrics became more controversial from 1969.[2]

III

I first met Fela in 1974 when he came to Ghana under the Supreme Military Council government of General Ignatius Kutu Acheampong and later in the same year went to visit him in Nigeria. Fela was detested by the Governments in both Accra and Lagos because of his anti-military music against General Olusegun Obasanjo's government which had ripple effects on Ghanaians' view of their own. On that visit and later in 1977, I visited The Kalakuta Republic to participate in the production of *The Black President*. I arrived there and met his Lebanese friend Victor (a chef) and the Ghana Film crew. Fela was in his usual pants. All were happy to see me. Then Fela dramatically told me that I had to do my part well or my children would not be allowed to stay in Africa. I was surprised by this bit of melodrama as the two parts in the film for whites, me as Inspector Reynolds and Albert (another Lebanese friend of Faisal Helwani, Fela's friend and producer) as the governor of the Elmina slave castle had been picked by Faisal and Fela.

Except for the small swimming pool, things remain much the same at The Kalakuta as before. The monkey at the gate, the donkey in the yard and his big shaggy Alsatian dog, *Wokolo* ("go and find prick") still around. It was in fact during these two visits that I got closest to understanding the man, his disposition and sometimes strange ideas including his anti-western values. My visit to The Kalakuta was paid for by him and as a gesture I thought I should use my free time to teach his children. He got home one afternoon furious that I was teaching them science. When I asked what was wrong with that, he said, "science is colonialism." We exchanged arguments and his mother, who was in the house simply ordered Fela to get out of her sight and instructed that I teach the children. It did not matter that I was his visitor. The result of Fela's attitude to education was the effect on his eldest son who never had a good one and would blame the father later for that. At The Kalakuta Republic he told me that one of the things he wanted to accomplish before his death was to undo what his grandfather Reverend Josiah Ransome-Kuti did with the spread of Christianity in Yorubaland including the vernacular hymns and the sacred Yoruba pieces for piano and others. In fact one of Fela's heroes was General Idi

155

Amin of Uganda. He insisted that Amin was only settling scores with the Indian traders in his country.

Fela was a musical warrior. People think that music should be used for leisure but he used it for confrontation through many innovations over the years – a combination of Highlife, Soul, Jazz, Yoruba drumming and Latin influences. All his songs – over 100 were born out of actual events and social problems. He did not like the education system and so he wrote the song, "Teacher Don't Teach Me Nonsense," "Yellow Fever" was against bleaching by women, "Gentleman" – pretences and western influence in dress by African men, "Shakara" – a bully, or pompous person, "Expensive Shit" – on police indiscretion and corruption. Though these social commentaries shifted to political ones when his mother died after being thrown out through the window by the police, Fela could also make poignant statements and acts such as placing the coffin outside Obasanjo's residence. Either he ordered the murder or it was under his regime that it was carried out. A song, "Coffin for Head of State" was produced. By this time in 1978, Fela's anti-militarism had become such a thorn in the side of the Ghanaian government that, as Faisal Helwani later made known, he was banned from entering Ghana. But a year later in 1979, Jerry John Rawlings who would continue with military governance of the country lifted the ban. In fact Rawlings shared some of Fela's ideological positions in respect of Africa's colonial past and had been in touch with him, according to Helwani before his popular 1979 Uprising. He invited Fela to Ghana.[3]

IV

Fela obviously is not Wole Soyinka notwithstanding bloodlines and common faith in basic fundamental rights of people – free speech and association. Ideological positions were different, Soyinka respects civilizations, African and western and they show in his works including technical details whether in theatre or poetry. The same exposure to cosmopolitan ideas did not work for Fela. Some of the people who influenced his career were not Africans yet he was adaptable totheir ideas to suit his perceived African orientation. Fela in his career also did something few musicians in the world ever did – he mentioned the names of leading politicians and important leaders in his songs. Most protest singers use innuendoes or metaphors like Bob Bylan, the archetypical white rock protest singer who sang, "The Times They Are A-changing" or closer home to, Bob Marley who used "Babylon" as a metaphor for western civilization or governments. Fela was far from these. He was the bravest person I have ever met, an internal rebel, a dare devil, a confrontationist who drew musical energy from social misplacements. Though he would be arrested more than 50 times for this, it did not stop him and Amnesty

International had to continuously come to the rescue. Soyinka on the other hand uses metaphors to criticize kings and ruling classes in traditional stories as a dramatist; sitting behind a desk reflecting for hours, days and years whilst Fela would rather have direct political meetings within his shows, what he called, *Yabbis*.

Fela's poetic song contrasts with another, "Lady" which pokes fun at refined Nigerian women. It was popular across West Africa especially with chauvinistic groups uncomfortable with women's transitional roles from hewers of wood and water to professional positions. Fela who ironically enjoyed women and lived with over a dozen wives and engaged in extra-marital affairs in The Kalakuta Republic thought they had a traditionally defined role. Beyond that frontier would be opportunism.

Lady:
If you call am woman
African woman no go gree
She go say I be lady-o
She go say I no be woman
She go say market woman na [is] woman
I want to tell you about lady-o
She go say she equal to man
She go say she get power like man
She go say anything man do she self fit [can] do
I never tell you finish
She go take cigar before anybody
She go make the man open door for am
She go make man wash plate for her kitchen
She want sit down for table before anybody
She want take piece of meat before anybody
Call her for dance she go dance lady dance
[But] when African woman go dance she go dance fire dance
She know man na master
She go work for am, she do anything he say
But lady na be so, lady na master.[4]

Soyinka contrasts this with his belief in the fundamental respect for womanhood beyond the traditional expectation. Women or female characters are fearless and self-respecting whether in romantic situations as in *The Lion and the Jewel* or political uncertainties in *Kongi's Harvest*. Unfair traditional arrangements in Soyinka's view sometimes suppress their talents in all aspects of human endeavour. In his contrasting poem, "Night," though not originally intended and only incidental to Fela's above are the comforts that women could provide in the storms of life sometimes represented by evil doings at night.[5]

"Night"
Your hand is heavy, Night, upon my brow,
I bear no heart mercuric like the cloud, to dare
Exacerbation from your subtle plough.
Woman as calm, on the sea's crescent
I saw your jealous eye quench the sea's
Fluorescence, dance on the pulse incessant
Of the waves. And I stood, drained
Submitting like the sands, blood and brine
Coursing to the roots. Night, you rained
Serrated shadows through dank leaves
Till, bathed in warm suffusion of your dappled cells
Sensations pained me, faceless, silent as night thieves.
Hide me now, when night children haunt the earth
I must hear none! These misted calls will yet Undo me; naked, unbidden,
at Night's birth.[6]

It is in their political poetics that the differences show clearly: the street language of Fela when allowed and often it did, could send people unto the streets to protest against national leadership, violence and destruction. In 1979 he composed and sang in Nigeria and abroad, "Vagabonds in Power." It was direct criticism of military interventions in politics, corruption and stealing from the treasury. Few lines of the song: why! why ! incapable of understanding the minds of people he called vagabonds.

…Man get power
Him talk nonsense
Ha, ha, why?
I don't know!
Man get power
Him take am
Cheat person
Ha, ha, why?
I don't know!
Man get power
Him take am
Steal money

Ha, ha, why?
I don't know!
You don't know anything at all...[7]

These sent him frequently to jail. Soyinka would indict as well but with subtleties. When he criticised Obasanjo years later for bringing more troubles to Nigeria than whatever good, it was:

Our contributory option to the corrective social mechanism is known by that already named dread phrase – A Sovereign, or National Constitutional Conference, the genuine article, not the fake, self-serving, manipulative tinkering as the nation underwent during, the tenure of the Great Hypocrite of Otta Farm.[8]

You may need some footnotes to know the accuser. You have to know that Obasanjo is a big time farmer and that he mostly lives in his farmhouse in Otta.

If Fela were to write about the lawlessness of Boko Haram, it would have been in the vein of, *Mr Who Are You?* Or *Beasts of No Nation* and not Soyinka's, *The Unappeasable Price of Appeasement*:

We, economists of human assets, insist on the primacy of the sanctity of life and the value of that irreplaceable asset, but also of its quality, irrespective of gender, culture or religion...while castigating the conduct of one individual and bringing him to justice, we fail to emphasise the fact that in many other parts of Nigeria, hundreds of thousands to millions of our own investment in the future are subjected to... devaluation and curtailment of potential returns to the nation.[9]

Sometimes the accusers in such dense paragraphs may not even know they are the subject of abuse. The middle and upper class readers will agree with him and praise his prose, bravery and adore him but they would not take to the streets as easily as Fela could get his followers and patrons to.

Artists, especially musicians and writers mirror events and do drafts of history of their times. The strategies and technical approaches maybe different but truth and fundamental socio-cultural protocols and freedoms are universal. Today, there are inevitably new forms of music using a lot of technology. Time changes and globalization is upon us but the mission of the musician or writer should be the same. Rebellion is not always a negative undertaking to its adherents. Fela was a serial rebel and in some ways, Nigerians benefitted. His funeral (he died of AIDS) was one of the biggest

Nigeria has ever seen. The unofficial funeral song was one of his best, "Zombie." It was extensively covered by the global media including correspondents of *The Financial Times* and the *Wall Street Journal.* A parent's anticipation of a lawyer or doctor of a son's career turned into one of the greatest musicians had ended on both a sad and happy note. But Soyinka lives and still writes about Nigeria, Africa and the world addressing the remaining issues and sometimes the same as his cousin did: me and my cousin against the injustices of the State.

Section V
Poetry for the Threshold

Chapter Twenty-Two
Poetic Prelude for the Loyal Son
Derek Walcott

2005 – I don't know that any writer deliberately separates politics and writing. Nobody wants to be a martyr, but if you go through that experience, you often find a strength that astonishes you. The quality of human endurance is an astonishing thing.

1997 – While we speak today for a brother writer, we know that he is in danger because of his work for all Nigerians. And so we stand, with him, in solidarity with the Nigerian people whose deprivation of the rights of democratic citizenship Wole Soyinka and many of those accused with him have made theirs. The Nigerian government has charged him with treason against Nigeria, a man who is surely one of that country's most loyal sons.

Chapter Twenty-Three

The Lord Has Entered the House
Abena P. A. Busia

Akinwande Oluwole Soyinka, *
And so it is.
It is a myth that there is no literature in the African world,
Your art impresses that
After all the dialogue and still more outrage,
The burden of memory must give way
To the muse of forgiveness.

Born to play among the giants,
Essay knew when he declared
A brave one has come
That The Lord had entered the house,
A house encircled by wizards
Who bear your name.

Only the years of childhood
Followed by those years of journeying,
Ake, Ibadan, Samarkand,
And all the other markets you have known,
Make one wonder about those encircling wizards:
Who whether encircling to guard
Or surrounding to guide
Always bear your name.

They have walked with you
Through the contradictions of eight decades

Of Harmattan hazes on African Springs
With Ogun battling to heal
The open sores of a continent
In a climate of fear -
With you as Interpreter.
There have been seasons of anomy
With the dread of roaring lions
And seasons of harvest
When, brave one among imprisoned prophets
Your jewels of words a weaving shuttle in the crypt of time:
Became an intervention so men do not die.

Such it has ever been, in the nature of the trials
Brother Jero, Kongi, Baabu and all the tricksters
Madmen, specialists and oh so vengeful gods or wizards
Require forceful interventions:
So the strong breed, swamp dwellers all
Who stride this Mandela's earth
Assembled at your command,
to dance the dance of the forests
First as operatic interlude for a hope filled past
and then as requiem for a disappointed future,
In the unending dramatic rituals of poetic words and dance.

No, the dance for justice is not over.
The Lord entered the house
And whatever wizards rule,
The kings and all their eternal horsemen
In a kaleidoscope of death and beauty
Follow the imperative of the brave one come
That with enduring strength and resolution
We must still set forth at dawn.

[*Poem based on the meaning of Soyinka's full name in first line. Akinwande-the brave one has come. Oluwole – the Lord has entered his house. Soyinka-surrounded by wizards].

Chapter Twenty-Four
The Lion and the Jewel of Ogun Abibiman Literature
Aderonke Adesola Adesanya and Toyin Falola

I. Of Genealogy and Genius

Wole Soyinka:
Eminent songster of Ake,
Abiku! An herbalist's nemesis
Extraordinary entity and in-betweener
The narrator that splits the four-lobe kolanut
A pact with Ogun for an assured pathway
The pilgrim's homage and thoroughfare
On a prodigious journey

In *Ake: The Years of Childhood*
The personal connects the political
The writer's craft, a chronicled past:
Muses, nuances and testaments
Family, friends, foes, and [a tale of] a city;
Of roots and reminiscences,
The ruler and the ruled,
The elite and the commoner,
Jostling for space in a personal recall
Knowledge rides horses of memory in private and public episodes
Ethos endure in vintage lore
Reality courts parodies
In the master storyteller's script

Ake[the city and its nuances], is etched in stone

The boulders bring forth
An avalanche of lore
Stories straddle generations
Time skips like lambs
Distance is abridged
Tradition collides with modernity

The private meets the public

In the writer's orbit
Power reveals and conceals
Religious orders multiply
In stiff competition for prominence and converts
A society is stunned and confused.
Transformed…yet tenaciously retentive,
The lens and pen of the writer
Archived the ups and downs,
Reel to reel, twined time
A magnificent tapestry
A harvest of creativity,
The drama and panorama,
Even a comedy of errors,
The foibles of youth,
The innocence of a child;
Requesting that his blood
Shed from a head gashed
Be restored!
And many idiosyncratic details
All are not elided
In the spectacles of the era

II: Local and Global Politics

WS is a gem of global appeal;
A precious jewel mined from Abeokuta.
The city which grew from many huge boulders,
A city known for her illustrious outspoken indigenes,
From ancient to modern warlords and formidable entities
From Sodeke to Soyinka
The city of the restless in pursuit of justice,
The waters of the city,

The truth seekers 'Dee-N-Ay
The social crusaders gene
Inextricably locked within WS
Stirs his blood and spurs him
To whip recalcitrant broods in his path.

III: 'Ogunic' Lore

Many are the parts;
The persona and proficiency
Of he who replicates Ogun
Yoruba god of iron and warfare
Deity and master craftsman
The divinity around whose mythology
WS framed his wealth of creativity
Ogun and WS are fecund
As Ogun's ore bursts forth in creative energy
So does the inkwell of WS
Resonate in creative synergy

IV: War and Artistry

WS runs with Ogun
As Ogun straddles continents and time
He reverberates across continents
Illustrious at home and famous abroad
His work ties tradition
In manifold cords and chords
A force to endure across time
Ogun has supplied abundant metal
And opened his ore
For unbridled creativity
WS is energized
He forges relentlessly
Prodigy of African literature
Phenomenal playwright, prolific poet
Novelist and dramatist
Though he pours in torrents
His gourd remains pregnant
The vintage hourglass drum
Releases melody from its double-edged ends

The lore of Ogun stokes WS's fire
Like Ogun and his metallurgy, WS is versatile
Shaping the world and shaming the wicked
As Ogun's machete severs the head of the treacherous
WS cuts through tyrannical bodies with words
His satires and naked truth
Seer through abject bodies
Contaminated cadavers seeping stench and abominable fluids
Bodies of shame in Africa's polity
Of military juntas and civilians alike

Similar to Ogun, an aggressive entity
WS is ever at war
As he combats tyranny
He is impatient with ineptitude
Cross with corrupt entities
When you seek the social crusader
Look beyond *The Interpreter*
To comprehend the root and depth of his wrath
His repudiation of a contaminated social body
His disgust with incompetence

V: 'Po'-ettiquettes

Wedded to reformation
A conjugal frenzy
Fecund and furious
Like a possessed being
WS writes and writhes
In rituals of birthing and purgation
Satires rival critical works
In distinguished repertory
Unmistakable hallmarks of a social crusader
Menace of inept and corrupt leaders
Arbiter of the oppressed
Critic of repressive regimes
A lion in Africa's riotous jungle

WS, a gem hewed from rare genre
A gift from Soyinka's clan to the world
A pearl from Abeokuta, sparkle from Nigeria

A treasure from the West African literary space
A beacon of hope from Africa
East to West, North and South
His laurel adds a luminous luster
To mother Africa's crown

A persona of uncommon pedigree
Creative prowess evident in brilliant legacies
Plays, poems and speeches
Six Plays
Dozen dramas
Repertoire of speeches
Countless essays
Endless list of creativity

VI: Percusor

If I were a stone sculptor
I would select porphyry, the purple stone
Used for the statues of Roman emperors
To cut the image of WS
The literary guru
A stunning piece
Mounted on spectacular pedestal
To daze the senses and jade the eyes
Of friends and foes

If I were a portraitist,
I would paint WS in strong hues,
In colors that dazzle;
I would paint his form
As a puzzle,
An ambivalent subject;
Smiling and frowning
To illustrate his ambivalence

VII: Portraits and Power

In my study
Of the one that holds the mace,
I would scrutinize this player with the ace,

My gaze transfixed by his face,
I would tease out the part of him,
That leaders love to hate
And the other part
His peers peer at with masked rage,
To produce a masterpiece.

I would also dare to confront the fiercest stare
Of the lion's ravenous glare
My canvas would reveal
The characteristic gape at preys
Those that strayed into the lion's den,
And those afar yet trapped by the jungle king's penetrating gaze
My brush would speak the bloody truth;

The image would send jitters
Down the spine of detractors
I would cause my white paint to lavishly drip
To define the mane that crowns his head
My titanium white soaked brush would illuminate
His lush beard,
The mark of wisdom,
Of his physical and intellectual maturity
And not of a terrorist.

The image would be the 'holy grail' of WS's portrait
An eloquent testimony of my sitter
WS would bleed transparent at each stroke.
My palette knife would cut the image
On thick paste of colours,
The outlines of his form
Would dance on my canvas
In the form, I would hide visual codes and metaphors
To complicate the tasks of symbologists
And future art historians
I would dare to compete with Da Vinci
And pitch my WS portrait against Mona Lisa

VIII: Nature's Treasure

The writer's image frozen in time

The uncommon thoroughbred
Fixed on my canvas
Would be my prized treasure
In years to come.
I would bid my time
A collector's item
A potential prized auction piece
At Sotheby's
Or other auction houses,
The bait is worth the wait
Long after the sage is gone

If I were a nature poet
I would derive inspiration from *angelica*
I would craft metaphors of flowers and landscapes
Of hills and valleys, of order and disorder in nature
Of nature's endearing, effusive and eruptive moods
To symbolize the difference of WS to personas and situations
Lilies, roses, and orchids to peacemakers
Allspice to the downtrodden
Spines, prickles and thorns for tyrants
Hurricanes, thunderstorm and tornados for despots
Aloe to evildoers
In whirlwinds, WS would confront despotic rulers
He would loom large like a colossus
Ride the storm like Sango
The ultimate karma of *King Baabu,*
I would make WS a garland of *Bird of Paradise.*

If I were a songster,
I would script lyrics
In Fela Anikulapo-Kuti's style,
In praise of Kongi, and his harvest
And in recall of his admonitions
His remedies force-fed to ailing bodies

Eh! Hen…Hen
Oh yes!
Right now!
Before the blackout
Kongi did a number

The lion roared
Rrrrrrrrrrrrr! A loud frightening growl
Animal kingdom scatter, scatter
Monkeys began to hop upside down
Men and women ran helter-skelter
An apocalypse
People danced upside down
Everybody kept going inside out
This number remains an odd rhumba
A Dance of the Forests
A classic riotous beat
For a jungle nation

Aye! Aye! Aye!
Everybody run left and right
In pursuit of truth and equity
The citizen and the state
Locked in battle
Eddy and headlong
Suddenly! Suddenly!
King Kong appear from nowhere
He wants to challenge Mr. Lion
What will ensue?
Hmmm… hmmmmm!
Long! Long! Long! Battle Royale
Long! Long! Long! Fight to finish

IX: Suture

If I were an historian
I would string the works of WS
Like choreographed beads
Starting with two classic works:
Death and the King's Horseman
An adaptation of tradition at Old Oyo
Then *King Baabu*
A satire about the idiotic modern Nigeria military ruler
A despot ousted without bloodshed
Shamed by an inglorious death from 'applecide'
For their classic satire,
Apocalyptic tenor,

Poignant topicality
A stab at the heart of tyranny and power drunkenness
I would string both set of beads
To precede *A Season of Anomy*
Trailed by *The Trials of Brother Jero*
And its sequel, *Jero's Metamorphosis*
Mockeries of the sores at the heart of a society
Consumed by religious bigotry

The Detainee
Would form the beaded wristlets
For the prisoner who wrote us
Poems from Prison
Idanre and Other Poems
And pricked us with
Ogun Abibiman
For the eager ears, WS etched
Mandela's Earth and Other Poems
To stab at the stony hearts
Of modern imperialists
And predators alike
Lest they forget
The essence of humanity

X: A Last Straw for a Drowning Continent?

As a poet
Persuaded by WS artistry
Enamoured by his repertoire
I would develop a creative response
To *The Interpreters*
And *Madmen and Specialists*
I would seek wisdom from *Kongi's Harvest*
I would avoid the rotten apples in the vineyard
And separate foul onions
From contaminating a promising cuisine
My ears will stand upright as the hare's
Alert to the narratorvoice
And the lessons embedded in
The Open Sore of a Continent: A Personal Narrative of the Nigerian Crisis.
With calculated steps

I would navigate my course carefully
Lest I get lost on *The Road*
And my remains shuffled in *A Shuttle in the Crypt*

Did I forget *The Man Died*?
There are wisdom nuggets from the sage
And lengthy homilies,
Let eagerears be droned
By necessary dins,
Let those who care to listen
The Swamp Dwellers
In the Niger Delta,
The greedy pigs
With noses mired in the Lagos lagoon
Sucking the wealth and waste of a city
Or the city rogues
Who live in glass houses in Abuja
A fake safe haven
Unlimited Liability Company
Establishments of prodigals
Let it be known to them
Even the beggars and the sultry prostitutes
Learn lessons from *Opera Wonyosi.*

Those who eat salt with relish
Slices and spices their innards
For the worms of the earth
Eager to devour their remains
In the not too distant future
Sodium is opium
Best left on the podium
At the blares of a health scare

Be bemused by
An intriguing parody;
The Beatification of Area Boy

The broth of the master chef is not finished:
Art, Dialogue and Outrage,
Requiem for a Futurologist,
Trapped in a labyrinth

A Play of Giants,
Is performed in the land of Lilliputians
A messy affair ensue in *Ibadan: The Penkelemes Years,*
In spectacles of comedies and debacles
Abiku returns
To dance on the herbalist's grave

The art of WS
Birthed in consummate style
Incessant in seasons,
The writer purred and poured
From conversations to monologues
In *Telephone Conversation*
From the classic knell for *King Baabu,*
His terse letters to fellow countrymen,
Samarkand and Other Markets, I have Known
To his rebel broadcast on *Radio Kudirat*
Testaments of an unrepentant political activist.

WS is whimsical and resolute
His craft waxes strong
As he approaches his twilight
The Sage reminds
In tales by moonlight
You Must Set Forth at Dawn.

Africa
To where does the odyssey lead?
Grovelling giant
Is this another aimless rigmarole?
A wasted generation in endless peregrinations
Moving towards a hazy horizon?
Despots and prodigals digressing headlong
Down a blind alley
Alley cats regard the knell of the muse
The decades the lion had rumbled
To tame a bewildering jungle
Are shorter than doomsday
The lion had roared hoarse,
Far too long for the desired change,
In the tumultuous wilderness

In the flickering light
The poet's eyes scan the Lion's den
The quizzical gaze on the dais
Meets a barren vista
Where is the pride?
Where are the broods?
Show me a Lion's pride without its cubs
The planter seeks the seeds
For the next planting season.

Chapter Twenty-Five
"A Tomboucktouyan Anti-Palanquinity"
Atukwei Okai

I

THE HORIZON,

Like an unhurried cassava leaves-
    reading Custodian
Of the Solitary and Almighty Sky,

Whose Kangarooyan flywhisk arms
    serenadingly encircle
The baobab waist of history
Seven times,

FLINGS

Eighty white kolanuts across
    the surface of the waters
Of the patient soothsayer pond,

And the ripples,
Like flamingoes in majestic flight,
    and in concentric unison,

RESPOND:

When the dirges drown

the daylight-extinguishing
   drums of the drones,
When his images demystify
   the pillars of earthy thrones,
When toppling taboos
   release
Wild wailings and grievious groans,
Remind Abeokuta not to falter,
   but obey the commandment
   of Ogun
That continues to hold our dreams
   at bay:

"… *if they take you*
   in the morning,
They will come for us in
   that night."

II

Our Abeokuta love wished you
   into human existence;
My womb walled and willed into
   you the spirit of ancestral
   resistance

Against

Whatever seeks to sink the soul
   of man
Into the sewage tunnels of dread
   and despair
Where
   we breathe the fart-fattened
   fumes
Of the psyche-disenfranchising
Air.

III

We sent you forth with amulets
    and bows and arrows,
With an assegai, catapult
    and prayers...
We have watched you navigate
    the Victoria Island waters ...
We watched you dive into
    the ocean depths ...
We watched you scale
    the Kilimanjaro of courage ...

Do not be in a hurry to rush home
    to us ...

More souls are languishing
    behind political prison bars,
More citizens are hustling
    to cope with a few kobos
    a day
In a gritty subsistence
    that gravely jars.

IV

When the fireball of fate danced
    around the ocean of destiny,
The drummers of Oshogbo land
Chronicled in shrill and eloquent
    tones

The birth of a leap-year seer-scribe
    whose anointed nib, nibbling
    at the lungs
    of the manufactured fib,
Would break and crush many
    sacred and kingly bones.
We monitored your strides
    into the Sundiatayan sunset
Where you threw down

your Guadelopean gauntlet:

With anti-palanquinity as your
*   scepter,*
Of conditions and persons,
*   you are no servile respecter.*

V

Your soul carries the Pharaonic
    totem pole of Tutankhamen !
Your word controls the caravans
    of Mansa Kankam Musa !
Your spirit scrolls the chronicles
    of Kumbi Saleh !
Your tongue congregates
    the griots of Songhai and Mali !

Your psyche's memory feeds upon
    the legendary tablets of ancient
    Tomboucktou !

VI

You
Commandeer the parade of the pages
    who bear the paraphernalia
    and insignia of the sages !
Avalanchise now their wisdom unto
    the parchment pages
Till they overflow the intellectual
    banks
    of even the borderless Ganges,
Till they overwhelm the covenant-
    carrying crucible of the ages.

VII

It pleases the elements that
*   in you shall "all fullness dwell."*

Onto the eardrums of harmful
  hamlets, drunk and drowning,
  you shall toll the knell !

Where dread dehydrates
  the adrenalin
  dripping in the bold,
The tongue of your conscience
  shall stretch out,
  all the truth to yell !
You shall not crane your neck
  to ascertain where the unfaithful
  fell,

You shall daily count your blessings,
  and be prepared
  the whole household to tell.

Iniquities and unfairness your
  words shall ever seek to quell !
It does please the ancestors
  that in you goodness
  shall always dutifully
Rebel !

Chapter Twenty-Six
The Aparos Are Wary,
So the Antelopes!
Ogochukwu Promise

As I remember it, there he goes, with practiced steps
Angular, plainly clad in faded brown trousers
Pastel shaded long sleeved top, sun hat and boots
Making swift incursion into the wild, wild bush.
His mien, genteel, puzzling, oyinbo-ijegba!

The aparos* are wary, so the antelopes!

I, the bush-beater, could see the slight bow of his legs
Could follow his uncanny steps, see him squat, take a studied gaze
A bird whirrs past, the eyes of the master squint, deft fingers grip the gun
The day is closing in, still no shot is heard, could the bush-beater be the jinx?
Aparos may feast on the wavering sight that will claim them upon its return!

Still the aparos are wary, so the antelopes
As their meat soon saturates the refrigerator of the master!

Next hunting expedition. A peep into the distance
Range of hills rise on the left, so do birds and blasts
In the glimpse of sky's lights the bush-beater stands exonerated
As her sack-bag swells with feathered friends from master's precision
But there is no glamour of sunshine yet in the eyes of the master.

The aparos are wary, so the antelopes
Squirming now in the silences of their unknowing
Their little faces, a scrapyard of pain.

But I have not seen through the night –
Quadruped had the reins until the musk of sweat from master's brows
Soaks into their splendid dusk with a dialect of grief.

Like pellets in the empty eyes of the antelope, dislodging them
From any other sight as they ride home in the game-bag of the master…

Indeed, the aparos are wary, so are the antelopes
Looking at dwellings for groans as the wind soaks up
Courage which once captured their dreams
With a furtive promise of the privacy of slumber

I wonder what lies at the root of master's white fluffy hair
As he aims at a fleeing bird, a creeping creature –
Downing a Riesling afterwards, I see his laughter tinge
When a dictator's teasing fat face fills the TV screen. Master unsheathes
A ballpoint pen, out of which pellets flow in the bouts of our foolish fright!

Yes, the aparos are wary, so the antelopes, even now as I look out the window,
Life has aged, I with it. Across the table, master's ageless wit, having risen
Into startling eminence, drives me into the habit of remembering how a bite
Of aparo provokes tolerant smiles from critics glutted with pleasure
While a boiling pen, beholding a laughing beast, scalds everything in-between.

[*Aparo is Guinea Fowl].

Chapter Twenty-Seven
Legacy
Francesca Yetunde Emanuel (Nee Pereira)

A stairway; imposing
Lined in living livery,
Waiting hearts beating a cadence
To history in its making.

Then, an ecstatic ambience
An unambiguous wafting folk tune
Announcing the victor; simply clad
Stepping confidently
Ushered by royal grandeur.
Pomp and pageantry
Delightful to behold, to cherish.

My thoughts wander from this glorious instant
That declares recognition of effort and growth,
To symptoms and beginnings;
A tapestry, unweaving
Noting thoughts, words and deeds
Formed in colour, defined in shape.

Childhood pranks and formative years
The gathering of knowledge
Discernment of truths
Dreaming –
The choosing of paths to follow

Ways parted; fresh exposures

Hurdles surmounted, yet stumbling
Rising again towards accomplishments
Only to find purpose anew,
Feats past, merely a vehicle
For higher tasks.
Rightness to uphold, to honour
Man's dignity to uplift
Harmonious existence to establish
The cost uncounted

Sporadic encounters on divergent paths
Common vision silently confirmed
Resolve yet unbroken.

Often I wander the maze of my mind
Trying to grasp the essence of this strange link,
Yet always emerging mystified, perplexed,
Yet always knowing, I am not alone

A curious ENTREAT pries and questions;
WHAT forges this bond?
WHO devised its link?

Spiteful manipulations entrap, INQUIRE:
HOW did this start?
WHEN shall it end?

Intrusive promoters AFFIRM as partisan;
WHY should this not stand?
HERE lies its celebration.

Needless contention …
For this bond; unconstrained by time and space
Is unconditional, assured, gratifying
And endless.

We forge ahead
Feet weary perhaps,
Hearts mayhap despairing
Yet we forge ahead
Shedding fear, passing milestones
A torch to pass along
To a greater tomorrow.

Section VI

Tradition and Modernity of Governance

Chapter Twenty-Eight
Traditional Leadership in Africa's Democratic Transition
Otumfuo Osei Tutu II

What does the continent known as Africa possess that the rest or a greater part of the globe does not have already in superabundance? Such, obviously, cannot be limited to material or inert possessions-such as mineral resources, touristic landscapes, strategic locations-not forgetting the continent's centuries-old designation as human hatcheries for the supply of cheap labour to other societies, East and West. There also exist dynamic possessions-ways of perceiving, responding, adapting or simply doing that vary from people to people, including structures of human relationship. These all constitute potential commodities of exchange not as negotiable as timber, petroleum or uranium perhaps but – nonetheless recognizable as defining the human worth of any people and many actually contribute to the resolution of the existential dilemma of distant communities, or indeed to global survival, if only they were known about or permitted their proper valuation.

– Wole Soyinka, *Of Africa*, 2012.

The bulk of Africa's close to a billion population is in rural areas. For them, as for many more in urban Africa, there is an unbroken link with their heritage symbolized by their traditional rulers. These constitute the primary pillars of governance in much of the continent. Contrary to what some may think, African kings and chiefs are no relics of a bygone era. They remain not just the custodians of our tradition and culture, but the very embodiment of the hopes and aspirations of our rural people. Chieftaincy in Ghana and parts of Africa is one of the major components in the architecture of good governance, and the stability which those with them enjoy today is owed greatly to our success in integrating our traditional governance into the new democratic structure.

Apart from our role as the custodians of the land, we are the primary arbiters in the resolution of conflict on daily basis and helping to maintain peace and order at all levels. Presidents and governments look up to us for advice and counsel from the perspective of non-partisanship, in the pursuit of their constitutional mandate. Our traditional system of arbitration is now a source of considerable study among international legal authorities. And it is becoming clear that much of the conflicts in Africa arise in areas and under conditions of breakdown of traditional authority. Inevitably therefore, our traditional rulers have to be key players in the development agenda of the continent. That is why it is impossible to contemplate the realistic wholesome development of Africa without listening to the voice that brings to the forum the true aspirations and hopes of rural Africa.

Africa like all continents has problems with natural resources management and here chieftaincy's role in outreach programmes and confronting challenges cannot be underestimated. Norway and its Nordic neighbours for instance, present critical lessons in the management of natural resources, which no African country can ignore if the continent is to avert climatic and environmental catastrophe. One of the greatest dangers facing Africa is the creeping desertification and rapid deforestation of the land. In Ghana alone, close to 70% of the country's forest reserves suffered one form of degradation or another from only three short decades of the exploitation of forest resources. Contrast this with Norway which has been felling and exporting timber since the 1600s – yes, for five hundred years, and additionally, they have exploited forest resource for energy, for construction and to feed its massive paper and pulp industries and yet the forest cover has actually increased. Indeed, in the last hundred years, despite intensive exploitation of her forest resources, the standing volume of forest has more than doubled. They did not have to resort to rocket science to achieve this. The sound, sustainable management practices that have allowed them to continue to reap the benefit without losing its cover completely and leaving the land in a degraded state is possible to replicate in Africa.

Fortunately there is a welcome departure from the erstwhile portrayal of the continent as an irredeemable basket case, condemned to endure harrowing famine and the horrors of civil wars, endemic corruption and bad governance. This portrayal of Africa as a burden to be placated with charity may still persist in some media but it is heartening to see that institutions including the World Bank, have come to bear the counter message that Africa is not a burden to mankind, only a challenge to our creativity and enterprise which means that the continent can partner with others in natural resources management as it can with other bodies within the European Union and outside of it.

Africa's development has certainly taken a new turn. Fortunately we have seen lately the emergence of a new consensus, with the establishment of the African Union (AU) and the commitment of our political leaders to a New Partnership for Africa's Development (NEPAD). The birth of the African Union and NEPAD had given fresh hope to the people of Africa that at long last our dreams for development may be on the horizon. While this new hope may have been well-founded, many in Africa may already be worrying about the slow pace of progress and the dangers that our African Union may not yet suffer the fate of the Organization of African Unity.

No one disputes that 54 disparate states, the majority of them desperately poor, but resourceful, can never muster the voice to be taken seriously in the affairs of the world. The marginalization of Africa is a painful reality and whether we like it or not, it will continue until the continent is able to unite and speak with one voice. Equally, the economic case has been well made. A United Africa, providing a market of over 800 million people, is the spur needed for growth and development. So what is holding back our progress? There is a cultural dimension that is acting as a psychological block on African development. I believe that at the root of the African condition today is the lack of confidence in ourselves. We have separated ourselves from the initial thrust of inspiration from our forefathers that sought to instill in us the spirit of self-belief and the capacity to achieve the best. This lack of confidence springs from the fact that we have allowed ourselves to be persuaded that there is nothing useful in our culture worth preserving and building upon. We have acted almost in the belief that there is nothing in our genes and we are simply fated to failure. As a consequence, we have almost jettisoned our culture and traditions and surrendered to everything foreign.

I am the occupant of a sacred stool that embodies the heritage of a great and proud people. The history of the Golden Stool and the Asante Kingdom spans over four centuries over which a system of governance evolved that stood the test of time in peace as in battle. We had a developed administrative, legislative and judicial systems on which our kingdom was run before our encounter with the West. Nobody can suggest to me that there was nothing of value in our system and in our values. There are traditional Kingdoms in other parts of Africa with a history and civilization going back to antiquity. Is Africa not the cradle of world civilization? So how come we have suddenly lost confidence in ourselves and abandoned our heritage?

To understand how crucial this is, is to understand the works of Wole Soyinka. He criticizes African military dictatorships and other bye-products of it a lot. He does so from a mastery of his Yoruba culture – in drama, poetry, journalism and human rights crusades showing us there is nothing in ourselves that detests freedom of the individual and democratic political succession. He has managed to use Yoruba and for that matter African social settings, values and philosophies and turned them into universal values and made a strong case for their relevance using a Western tool – the English Language.

We can do a contrast of Africa with Asia's models of development and we will find that there are vital cultural statistics to their growth. The Great Economic Miracles of the past century has not been in Europe or America. The miracle has been in Asia and particularly South East Asia. The miracle of post-war Japan has been followed by the miracle of the Asian Tiger Economies. Now China stands on the verge of becoming the world's Economic Super power.

Neither Japan or China nor any of the so-called Asian Tigers have achieved their status by abandoning their heritage. Yes the free market has been the driving force but I will draw attention to the fact, even if less publicized that underpinning the phenomenon is the absolute self-confidence of the people derived from their culture and history.

I do not imply that we need a complete return to our past. That will be rejecting the very valid case for democracy and the right of people to choose their leaders and governments. But I strongly suggest that in this pursuit we should not be seen to throw the baby out with the bathwater. For there are institutional structures developed over centuries that can be fused into the new democratic structures to make them more meaningful.

Ghana for example, was conceived in the proposition that the African has the capacity and the resources to be a full member of the global economic community when Kwame Nkrumah declared Independence in 1957. We have gone through periods of trials and tribulations, but through it all, we have emerged stronger, fitter and better able to pursue our goals. That is not just the story of Ghana. In a nutshell, it is the new African story.

Trials and tribulations there have been, and there will be. But the right lessons have been learnt and Africa is moving forward, if not at the speed of Usain Bolt, at least with the persistence and perseverance of Mo Farah. Today, the world is suffering one of the worst economic crises in history. The United States is still struggling and few economists will dare predict when and how it will emerge from its economic downturn. Even fewer still will dare predict how Europe emerges from the intense Eurozone crisis. The economic tigers of Asia are no longer immune from the global financial shocks and now even the economy of China, expected to drive the world out of recession, is slowing. Amidst all the gloom, it is comforting to note that Africa is more than holding its own.

Three years ago, Ghana recorded the fastest rate of growth in the world, albeit on the back of its newfound oil. But even before oil came on-stream, our rate of growth had remained remarkably impressive. Again, in the face of all the external financial shocks, the economy continues to show great resilience, recording a growth rate well above its peers despite a massive 20% drop in foreign remittance and a further sharp drop in foreign direct investments. The strong performance of our two key commodities of gold and cocoa were important but no less important must be the improvement in the fiscal and monetary policy environment.

What lies behind this relatively satisfying picture? It is the combination of the quiet emergence of a remarkable consensus within the country's political establishment and civil society alike over the general shape and direction of the economy as well as the continuous improvement in the process of policymaking. The years of sharp ideological cleavages, which created uncertainties about fundamental policy directions appears to be dead and buried.

This is not the story of Ghana alone. Most African countries are set on the same path of sound economic policy-making and management. The demons of the past may not be killed completely but they are being gradually exorcised, opening the way for the vast opportunities in the continent to be fully explored for development.

It is time to ask that the African poor may not be looked upon as the burden of humanity but as the missing consumers from the global market place. Yes, Africa is sitting on more than half a billion consumers who are missing from the market place because of poverty and illiteracy. As we give them the tools of education, we will soon have the components of another engine capable of driving the world economy forward.

Only a few decades ago, China was seen as some economic wilderness. Today it is the engine that is driving the world economy as Europe and America grapple with recession. Africa, I suggest, is the last wilderness, waiting to be explored. Maybe we have dwelt for too long on poverty alleviation and now need the courage to reach out for wealth creation, to effectively harness our resources for economic growth and development.

Chapter Twenty-Nine
Achebe, Soyinka and Africa's Twenty-First Century Optimism
John Dramani Mahama

In May 2013, African leaders across the continent gathered again in Addis Ababa, Ethiopia, to celebrate the founding 50 years ago of the Organization of African Unity (OAU) now the African Union (AU). It was one of renewal and reaffirmation of what was left to be done on the vision slate of the forefathers – from 1963 and what the current generation needed to do with their own dreams. But just days earlier, some of us were at Ogidi, in eastern Nigeria to bid farewell to one of the greatest writers we ever had – Chinua Achebe who in 1963 had already risen to global heights. He was given all the honours a nation and a continent can to a son and a father. But yet there is another anticipation of a literary and cultural celebration from the other side of Nigeria – Abeokuta, the 80th birthday of the iconic playwright and poet, Wole Soyinka. There are no greater rallying moments for reflections than these three.

Achebe had such influence on the African political landscape such that in 2010 he started convening an annual colloquium at Brown University in the United States where he was a Professor. It brought leaders, scholars and artists to discuss "strengthening democracy and peace on the African continent."

When I was introduced to his writing in the 1970s, during secondary school, there seemed to be no discernible separation in Africa between politics and the arts. We attended demonstrations against political and school authorities almost as frequently as we attended discos. The music that we listened to, from Fela Kuti to James Brown, was filled with racial pride and political protest.

It was, however, the literature of Achebe, namely his classic novel, *Things Fall Apart* that provided me with a larger context for the various maladies that were taking place on the continent. Reading that book was like a rite of passage. The books that I'd been reading previously were peopled with foreigners whose lives and concerns, though fascinating, bore no resemblance to mine. I read about Okonkwo and his story resonated because it was rooted in a culture that felt familiar.

"Storytelling has to do with power," said Achebe. "If you do not like someone's story, write your own." I read his other novels and then those of Ngugi wa Thiong'o, Ayi Kwei Armah, Ama Ata Aidoo, Kofi Awoonor and Wole Soyinka.

Of Soyinka's many plays, the ones I enjoyed most and which still resonate within me because of the issues they address are the Jero plays – *The Trials of Brother Jero* and *Jero's Metamorphosis*. Though written in the mid – 1960s as comedy, it is amazing if not prophetic how the charlatan preachers of the 1960s who "use Christian superstition for their salvation" have multiplied or how the profit-minded "prophet' thwarts a government attempt to cleanse the beach of all the dubious brethren who ply their trade there…"

These social and religious issues still plague not only Nigeria but most of Africa. Soyinka forces us to sometimes see our own unpleasant images in the mirror. It is this type of literature that empowered me and others to believe in our ability to create change. They urged us to see the value of our cultural inheritance and the potential of our continent and its people. It was this vision that challenged many of us to pave the paths upon which we now find ourselves. In my case, activism was and remains a natural bridge between politics and the arts.

During a recent discussion about Achebe, a political contemporary asked me if I felt as though I had somehow become part of the system that we so bitterly decried in our youth? "No," I replied without hesitation. "I entered politics because I wanted to be part of changing the system." One of the things I learned from Achebe and the others is that "the system" is nothing more than a collection of people, their values and their behaviours. We are all a part of a system; and all systems are subject to change.

Change can be difficult, even for those who claim to want it. Nostalgia is a powerful force. It can keep us locked into the status quo.

Africa is constantly amending its story and adding new chapters. We have experienced political, cultural and digital revolutions. Those who stay beholden to only the story of colonialism, apartheid and ethnic warfare will never allow themselves to know the Africa that now also tells a story of equality, democracy and capital cities that are as crowded and cosmopolitan as those of any other continent.

Likewise, those who still talk of African leadership using only words like corrupt, dictator or despot will miss the opportunity to take part in creating a new vocabulary – be it one of praise or criticism – for the men and women who are now working with the citizens of their countries to craft new styles and processes of leadership.

Missing out will truly be a shame because just as we all play a part in nation-building, we must also play a part in the writing of our stories. This is the new Africa we are creating.

We will also do this through mechanisms and institutions. Pivotal in this enterprise will be the AU. But the priorities of the organization could only mirror the priorities of its member nations. There were years when some nations were being devastated by war, famine, ethnic strife and crippling poverty. The continent was fragmented. Many nations were too busy struggling for their own survival to take on the additional burden of being another country's keeper. And, not surprisingly, the despots and coup-makers who were looting their country's coffers balked at the idea of accountability.

During those years, which are often referred to as "the lost decades," the OAU seemed to exist in name only; many referred to it as a toothless bulldog. Nevertheless, everyone still recognized the need for its existence.

In 2002, the OAU was dissolved and replaced with the AU. It was more than a superficial makeover. The postcolonial growing pains that had resulted in chaos and poor governance for many nations were now giving way to peace, democracy and the rule of law. And once again, we recognized the strength and power in unity. The AU is a well-structured organization with precise goals, a primary one of which is "to accelerate the political and socio-economic integration of the continent." In order to hasten this integration, eight regional economic communities were created: the Economic Community of West African States (ECOWAS) and the East African Community (EAC), being two of them.

It is without a doubt that these sub regional bodies have played a significant role in bringing economic stability. So much so that the majority of the nations listed as the world's fastest growing economies are on the African continent. Now that the majority of African nations are committed to the development of their democracies, the AU is also better able to define its role when there is a need for conflict resolution. And because the challenges facing our nations are increasingly becoming ones that have no regard for national boundaries, challenges such as effectively enforcing laws to end the trafficking of drugs and human beings, addressing the impact of climate change, deforestation, desertification and land degradation, the AU's member states will come to an agreement on how to grant the organization full legislative powers, while at the same time enabling nations to maintain their sovereignty.

Just like the continent that it oversees, the AU is a work in progress. As a student of history, I know that 50 years is a relatively short span of time, amounting to nothing more than a page in a history textbook. When considered in that context, the AU has come a very long way since its inception – three whole decades before the inception of the European Union – and given the limitations that it has faced over the years, AU has achieved a great deal.

At that first African summit in Addis Ababa, Emperor Haile Selassie said, "May this convention of union last 1,000 years." With renewed sense of potential on the African continent, indeed it shall.

Chapter Thirty

Africa's Renaissance and New Partnership for Development

Thabo Mbeki

Africa – concept or reality – is an acknowledged continent of extremes and by the same token, it is hardly surprising that it draws extreme reactions. Africans themselves are just as divided in their responses or strategies of accommodation – acquiescing, protective, resigned or fiercely defensive, identifying with, justifying or dissociating themselves from what is apparent or presumed to lie beneath the surface. The increasingly accepted common ground, both for the negatives and optimists, is the admission that the African continent is an intimate part of the histories of others, both cause and consequence, a complex organism formed of its own internal pulsation and external interventions, one that continues to be part of, yet is often denied, the triumphs and advances of the rest of the world.

– *Wole Soyinka,* Harmattan Haze on an African Spring, *2012*

Thirteen years ago, in the year 2000 marking the close of the 20th century, the World Bank published a Report provocatively entitled, *Can Africa Claim the 21st Century?*
Seeking to answer this question, the Report said:

The question of whether Sub Saharan African can claim the 21st Century is complex and provocative. Our central message is Yes, Africa can claim the next century. But this is a qualified yes, conditional on Africa's ability – aided by its development partners – to overcome the development traps that kept it confined to a vicious cycle of underdevelopment, conflict and untold human suffering for most of the 20th Century.

In their preface the authors said: "This report proposes strategies for ushering in self-reinforcing processes of economic, political and social development. Progress is crucial on four fronts:

Improving governance and resolving conflict b) Investing in people c) Increasing competitiveness and diversifying economies d) Reducing aid dependence and strengthening partnerships.

They went on to say:

Claiming the future involves enormous challenges – not least of which is resolving the problems of the past. Much of Africa's recent economic history can be seen as a process of marginalisation – first of the people, then of governments. Reversing this process requires better accountability, balanced by economic empowerment of civic society – including women and the poor – and firms relative to governments and of aid recipients relative to donors. Without this shift in power and accountability, it will be difficult to offer the incentives Africa needs to accelerate development and break free of poverty.

It is probably true that all these World Bank observations are in themselves correct and unexceptionable.

However, notable by its absence in these observations is an element I consider to be of vital importance if Africa is to claim the 21st century – the need for Africa to recapture the intellectual space to define its future and therefore the imperative to develop its intellectual capacities.

This is the first point I would like to make concerning what we need to do to ensure that we claim the 21st century. The tasks we continue to confront in this regard were identified even as the Organisation of African Unity (OAU) was established in 1963. In this context, this is what Emperor Haile Selassie of Ethiopia said when he opened the Conference which established the OAU:

We stand today on the stage of world affairs, before the audience of world opinion. We have come together to assert our role in the direction of world affairs and to discharge our duty to the great continent whose two hundred and fifty million people we lead. The task on which we have embarked, the making of Africa will not wait. We must act, to shape and mould the future and leave our imprint on events as they pass into history.

And he said:

We seek, at this meeting, to determine whether we are going to chart the course of our destiny. It is no less important that we know whence we came.

An awareness of our past is essential to the establishment of our responsibility and our identity as Africans.

He further said:

Thousands of years ago, civilisations flourished in Africa which suffer not at all by comparison with those of other continents. In those centuries, Africans were politically free and economically independent. Their social patterns were their own and their cultures truly indigenous.

The obscurity which enshrouds the centuries which elapsed between those earliest days and the rediscovery of Africa are being gradually dispersed. What is certain is that during those long years Africans were born, lived and died. Men on other parts of this earth occupied themselves with their own concerns and, in their conceit, proclaimed that the world began and ended at their horizons. All unknown to them, Africa developed in its own pattern, growing in its own life and in the Nineteenth Century re-emerged into the world's consciousness.

Reading the world today, there can be no doubt about the answer those who had gathered in Addis Ababa in 1963 would have given if they had been asked the question, Can Africa Claim the 21st Century?

The critical importance of the awareness of our past and its relevance to the establishment of our personality and our identity as Africans was identified by the very earliest among our own modern intelligentsia, a hundred years before.

In August 1862, the Rev Tiyo Soga, educated at the Lovedale Institution in the Eastern Cape and the University of Glasgow in Scotland, where he trained in theology, started publishing what I believe was the first African newspaper in South Africa, managed and edited by Africans, called *Indaba* (News).

In his editorial comment in the first edition of the paper, he wrote:

I see this newspaper as a secure container that will preserve our history, our stories, our wisdom. The deeds of the nation are worth more than our cattle herds, money and even food. Let the elderly pour their knowledge into this container. Let all our stories, folk and fairlytales, traditional views and everything that was ever seen, heard, done and all customs, let them be reported and kept in the national container.

Did we not form nations in the past? Did we not have our traditional leaders? What happened to the wisdom of these leaders? Did we not have poets? Where is their poetry? Was there no witchcraft in the past? Did we not fight wars? Who were the heroes? Where is the distinctive regalia of the royal regiment?

200

Did we not hunt? Why was the meat of the chest of the rhino and the buffalo reserved for royalty? Where are the people to teach us our history, our knowledge and our wisdom? Let even the spirit of the departed return to bless us with the great gift of our heritage, which we must preserve!

Tiyo Soga wrote these words sixteen years before the end of the last colonial war to subjugate the indigenous people in the Cape Province. He had seen that despite the continuing fierce resistance of the Africans, colonialism was bound to emerge victorious. To guarantee its victory it had started and was determined to wipe out the history, the customs, the self-worth, the identity and dignity of the African oppressed.

Soga knew that if this was allowed to happen, it would break the will of the colonised to continue the struggle to achieve their liberation, hence his call:

Let even the spirit of the departed return to bless us with the great gift of our heritage, which we must preserve!

Confirming that what he had in mind was the ultimate liberation of Africa, in a May 11 1865 article in the King William's Town Gazette and Kaffrarian Banner, entitled "What is the Destiny of the Kaffir Race," Tiyo Soga wrote:

Africa was of God given to the race of Ham. I find the Negro from the days of the old Assyrians downwards, keeping his 'individuality' and 'distinctness,' amid the wreck of empires and the revolution of ages... I find him enslaved and find him in this condition for many a day – in the West Indian Islands, in Northern and Southern America and in the South American colonies of Spain and Portugal. Until the Negro is doomed against all history and experience – until his God – given inheritance of Africa has been taken finally from him, I shall never believe in the total extinction of his breathen along the southern limits of the land of Ham.

Important contemporary members of the African intelligentsia have also understood the challenges Tiyo Soga posed and their responsibility in this regard. For example the Ghanaian novelist and thinker, Ayi Kwei Armah, has said:

We need to regain knowledge of ourselves, the something that we are. To do that we have first of all to end the addition to the poisons that put us to sleep. Secondly, we need to cultivate healing values that will help us remake ourselves and then remake the universe.

What is our history? (Cheik Anta Diop) spent a lot of time answering the question because there was a time, not long ago, when the idea itself of Africans having a history was considered unsound, academically wrong. Now his answer was, "Not only do we have a history, we are all the root of humanity, we were there at the beginning. That is to say that all human beings are kin to us, whether they recognise that or not.

He also said that we are at the root of civilisation. This is another area from which we had been pushed. He learned to read the records of ancient Egypt before he was able to assert: "No, you people are dying."

Now for centuries, we have been organised according to principles that are completely alien to us, principles of profit and advantage. The greatest African values are principles of justice, reciprocity, which the ancient Egyptians called Maat. You will not find these principles at work in the great institutions of the modern world.

"We are people who have suffered from the search for profit. People have come to Africa to buy people, human beings. There are certain resources that should never be sold. Africans values were on top of our existence, we would never sell land, we would never sell water, we wouldn't sell the air, the sun and we wouldn't sell human beings. But we did, and in order to recover our values we have to go back and know what they are and find ways of affirming them against all the power of the destroyers."

Another celebrated African intellectual, Ngũgĩ wa Thiong'o, drew attention to the responsibility of the African intelligentsia to play its role in 'the making of Africa.' When he spoke in 2003 at a conference to mark the 30th anniversary of the establishment of CODESRIA, the Council for the Development of Social Science Research in Africa, he said:

Despite her vast natural and human resources, indeed despite the fact that Africa has always provided, albeit unwillingly, resources that have fuelled capitalist modernity to its current stage of globalisation, Africa gets the rawest deal. This is obvious in the areas of economic and political power. But this is also reflected in the production and consumption of information and knowledge. As in the political and economic fields, Africa has been a player in the production of knowledge.

The increase in universities and research centres, though with often shrinking resources, have produced great African producers of knowledge in all fields such that brilliant sons and daughters are to be found in all universities in the world.

CODESRIA is reflective of the vitality of intellectual production in Africa and by Africans all over the world.

Has this vitality resulted in the enhancement of a scientific and democratic intellectual culture? Are African intellectuals and their production really connected to the continent? Even from a cursory glance at the situation it is clear that there is a discrepancy between the quality of this production of knowledge and the quality of its consumption by the general populace. Ours has been a case of trickle down knowledge, a variation of the theory of trickledown economics, a character of capitalist modernity, reflected more particularly in its colonial manifestation, which of course is the root base of modern education in Africa. And here I am talking of social production and consumption of knowledge and information in the whole realm of thought, from the literary to the scientific. Since our very mandate as African producers of knowledge is to connect with the continent, it behoves us to continually re-examine our entire colonial heritage, which includes the theory and practice of trickle down knowledge. This means in effect our having to continually examine our relationships to European memory in the organisation of knowledge.

Thus did Ngugi, as did Armah and Tiyo Soga before them, challenge the African intelligentsia to understand that their very mandate as African producers of knowledge is to connect with the continent, precisely to act as a motive force for the renaissance of Africa.

From this surely it must follow that one of the tasks of this renaissance, which would enable us to give a positive reply to the question Can Africa Claim the 21st century? must be the cultivation and nurturing of an African intelligentsia which understands its mandate in the same way that Ngugi understands the mandate of the African producers of knowledge.

I believe that in this regard the African intelligentsia has to understand that it has to carry out a veritable revolution along the entirety of what we might call the knowledge value chain. It must therefore address in a revolutionary manner the integrated continuum described by:

Analysis of African reality and the global context within which our Continent exists and pursues its objectives.

The policies relevant to the renaissance of Africa that would seek to transform the reality discovered through analysis,

The politics of Africa that needs to translate these policies into the required transformative programmes, and

The institutions that must be put in place to drive the process towards the renaissance of Africa.

I am certain that when it proceeds in this manner, seeking both to understand our reality and to change it, our intelligentsia will rediscover its mission as a vital agent of change, obliged critically to re-examine the plethora of ideas emanating from elsewhere about our condition and our future, including what have become standard prescriptions about such matters as the democratic construct, the role of the state and civil society, good governance, the market economy and Africa's relations with the rest of the world.

Thus should we depend on our intelligentsia as our educators and no longer mere conveyor belts of knowledge generated by others outside our Continent about ourselves and what we need to do to change our reality?

One of the urgent contemporary tasks that confronts these African producers of knowledge is to understand the meaning of the global economic crisis to the African continent and what the continent needs to do to overcome the development traps that kept it confined to a vicious cycle of underdevelopment, conflict and untold human suffering for most of the 20th century, as the World Bank had said in 2000.

The second major point I would like to make with regard to Africa's challenge to claim the 21st century is that the Continent has to take the necessary steps to ensure that it occupies its rightful place within the global community of nations, bearing in mind the ineluctable process of globalisation. This means that Africa must, practically, regain its right to determine its destiny and use this right to achieve the objective of the all-round upliftment of the African masses.

In June 2000 we attended the meeting of the European Council, the EU Summit Meeting held in Feira in Portugal. The central objective of our mission at this meeting was to mobilise the EU to support what ultimately became the New Partnership for Africa's Development, NEPAD.

Immediately prior to our interaction with the EU Heads of State and Government we held discussions with the leadership of the European Commission. The leaders of the EU Commission surprised us with an unexpected message about the attitudes of the EU towards Africa. In essence they warned us that the EU did not have any strategic perspective relating to Africa, as it did with other areas of the world such as East and Central Europe, the Middle East, Asia and the United States.

In short, in their view the EU did not consider Africa to be of such importance to its future that it was compelled to place the continent within a conscious and deliberate strategic framework. The EU knew that willingly, that is, whether it liked it or otherwise, Africa would continue to provide Europe with raw materials and serve as a market for its products. Beyond this, the Continent had no possibility to act in a manner that would threaten Europe's interests.

We therefore understood that in terms of the advice we received, the prevalent view among important sections of the European leadership, even sub-consciously, was that contrary to the situation with regard to other regions in the world, the relationship between Africa and Europe did not merit any purposeful strategic reflection on the part of the EU.

This communicated the very short message to us that for Africa to assume its rightful place among the community of nations, especially in relationship to the developed countries, she had to demonstrate in theory and practice that she was a strategic player in the ordering of human affairs, globally.

Thus would we defeat the pernicious view that Africa was but a hapless appendage to the rest of humanity, condemned to survival as an object of pity and benevolent charity and contempt and the actions that derive from this perspective.

We took this important advice into account when we engaged the EU Heads of State and Government, determined to convince them that we had not come to them as supplicants but as partners they needed in their own interest. In the result, the Final Communiqué of the European Council said:

> The European Council, agreeing that the challenges facing the African continent require extraordinary and sustained efforts by the countries of Africa helped by strong international engagement and cooperation, reaffirmed its willingness to continue to support measures aimed at rapid economic growth and sustainable development. This will only be possible in a proper environment of peace, democracy, respect for human rights and the rule of law.

Understanding the strategic imperative facing the EU, the President of the European Commission, Romano Prodi, said in 2003:

> The Africans are not asking Europe or the US for charity. What I hear from my African colleagues is a clear appeal to the rich countries to put policies in place that will allow Africa's people to take their destiny in their own hands.

In this regard, in a March 31 2001 Address at the Third African Renaissance Festival in Durban, I said:

> (The) response (of the EU) to the imperatives Africa faces as part of the global hinterland, are driven by considerations of conscience and guilt rather than fundamental necessities to which it must respond, in its own strategic interest.

I then said that to respond to this,

It is necessary that the peoples of Africa gain the conviction that they are not, and must not be wards of benevolent guardians, but instruments of their own sustained upliftment. Critical to this is the knowledge by the people that they have a unique and valuable contribution to make to the advancement of human civilisation, that Africa has a strategic place in the global community.

In this regard, the Founding Framework Document of NEPAD said:

Africa's place in the global community is defined by the fact that the continent is an indispensable resource base that has served all humanity for so many centuries. These resources can be broken down into the following components:

Component I: The rich complex of mineral, oil and gas deposits, the flora and fauna and the wide unspoiled natural habitat, which provide the basis for mining, agriculture, tourism and industrial development;

Component II: The ecological lung provided by the continent's rainforests and the minimal presence of emissions and effluents that are harmful to the environment, a global public that benefits all humankind;

Component III: The paleontological and archaeological sites containing evidence of the origins of the earth, life and the human race and the natural habitats containing a wide variety of flora and fauna, unique animal species and the uninhabited spaces that are a feature of the continent; and

Component IV: The richness of Africa's culture and its contribution to the variety of the cultures of the global community.

The first component is the one with which the world is most familiar. The second component has only come to the fore recently, as humanity came to understand the critical importance of environmental issues. The third component is also now coming into its own, emerging as a matter of concern not only to a narrow field of science or of interest only to museums and their curators. The forth component represents the creativity of African people, which in many important ways remains underexploited and underdeveloped.

There are at least two other elements we can add to the four components mentioned by NEPAD.

One of these is that over the years Africa has exported significant numbers of qualified professionals to the developed world, who have and are contributing in important ways to the further socio-economic development of these countries.

The second relates to that which certainly the Europeans consider to be a threat, illegal migration from Africa and elsewhere. The fact of the matter is that as long as our Continent remains mired in poverty, so long will many of our people leave and try to enter and stay in Europe regardless of steps that might be taken to stop this human flow.

This makes the point that even if some Europeans sustain the view that they do not need a strategic perspective relating to Africa, the illegal African migration they consider to be a threat obliges them to treat Africa as a partner of one kind or another. For half-a-millennium Africa had been treated especially by many in the white world as part of their patrimony which they could exploit and dispose of as they wished. Even during the period after the independence of the majority of African countries, the Continent has had to live with the reality of the system of neo-colonialism which perpetuated Africa's dependence.

Inter alia, it was this history that made it possible for some Europeans to convince themselves that they had no need to define a strategic relationship between themselves and our Continent.

The end of the Cold War created the possibility for our Continent finally to claim its right to determine its destiny and, among other things, define its relations with the rest of the world.

NEPAD was adopted at the last Assembly of the OAU Heads of State and Government which was held in Lusaka, Zambia in 2001. The partnerships we visualised as we worked on NEPAD were:

A mutually beneficial partnership among ourselves as Africans; a mutually beneficial partnership between Africa and the rest of the world.

I am convinced that one of the greatest achievements of the African Continent and its organisations, the OAU and the AU, during the first decade of this century, was the acceptance of NEPAD and its partner African Peer Review Mechanism, the APRM, by the rest of the world as the defining programme which should inform the relations of the Continent with the rest of the international community.

In this regard:

In September and December 2002, speaking for the world community of nations, the UN General Assembly adopted a Declaration and Resolution which said respectively:

We affirm that international support for the implementation of the New Partnership for Africa's Development is essential (We urged) the international community and the United Nations system to organise support for African countries in accordance with the principles, objectives and priorities of the New Partnership in the new spirit of partnership.

The Declaration adopted at the first African-EU Summit Meeting after the birth of NEPAD, held in Lisbon in 2007, said:

In recognition of our ambitions and of all that we salute today and have shared in the past, we are resolved to build a new (EU-Africa) strategic political partnership for the future, overcoming the traditional donor-recipient relationship and building on common values and goals in our pursuit of peace and stability, democracy and rule of law, progress and development. We will develop this partnership of equals, based on the effective engagement of our societies.

Earlier, in 2002, in their Africa Action Plan the G8 had said:

We, the Heads of State and Government of eight major industrialised democracies and the Representatives of the European Union, meeting with African Leaders at Kananaskis, welcome the initiative taken by African states in adopting the New Partnership for Africa's Development (NEPAD)... We accept the invitation in the NEPAD, to build a new partnership between the countries of Africa and our own, based on mutual responsibility and respect.

Addressing the Summit Meeting of the Forum for China-Africa Cooperation in 2006, Chinese President Hu Sintao said:

China values its friendship with Africa. To strengthen unity and cooperation with Africa is a key principle guiding China's Foreign Policy. China will continue to support Africa in implementing the New Partnership for Africa's Development and in its effort to strengthen itself through unity, achieve peace and stability and economic revitalisation in the region and raise its international standing.

When he spoke in South Africa on January 9, 2001, the then Prime Minister of Japan, Yoshiro Mori, conveyed his clear understanding of Africa's strategic place in the world when he said:

In this age of globalisation, as the world becomes increasingly unified, it would be unthinkable to talk about "the world of tomorrow" without considering how Sub Saharan Africa can overcome the difficulties it faces and open the way towards a bright future. Africa will probably become the driving force behind vibrant development of human society in the 21st century.

On the other hand, if the problems of Africa are neglected and one fourth of the world's nations remain alienated, there is no reason that the world community should be able to prosper and maintain stability. Indeed, there will be no stability and prosperity in the world in the 21st century unless the problems of Africa are resolved.

I believe that we should agree with Yoshiro Mori that "there will be no stability and prosperity in the world in the 21st Century unless problems of Africa are resolved." The current global economic and financial crisis has thrown into very sharp relief the important question how should the international community act to respond to the challenge posed by Yoshiro Mori. In this context it had seemed to be self-evident that because they are poor, Africans would be among those who would suffer most from the effects of this crisis and therefore that any meaningful response to the crisis would pay particular attention to Africa.

Our hopes were raised when the April 2, 2009 London G20 Summit Meeting Communiqué said:

We recognise that the current crisis has a disproportionate impact on the vulnerable in the poorest countries and recognise our collective responsibility to mitigate the social impact of the crisis to minimise long-lasting damage to global potential.

Earlier we spoke about the adoption by the G8 of the Africa Action Plan in 2002, which constituted a detailed response to support the objectives contained in the NEPAD programme. The reality is that the G8 Africa Action Plan constitutes the only extant and comprehensive framework defining an equitable partnership between Africa and the developed world. The tragedy is that in practical terms this Action Plan has fallen by the wayside. The G20 has now replaced the G8, which, despite its obvious limitations, signifies an important step forward towards the democratisation of the system of global economic governance.

Despite taking some welcome measures to assist Africa and the developing world to mitigate the effects of the global economic crisis, the G20 has not adopted the African Plan. It therefore does not have an integrated programme to respond to Africa's development challenges.

In their communiqué issued after their meeting in Washington, DC, in 2010 the G20 Finance Ministers and Central Bank Governors said:

We will ask the World Bank to advise us on progress in promoting development and poverty reduction as part of rebalancing of global growth." What all this means is that in its programmes relating to the global economic crisis, the developed world has not treated the response to the challenges of Africa's development as one of its strategic tasks.

In a March 2009 paper on Africa and the Global Financial Crisis the United Nations Economic Commission for Africa discussed the importance of the stimulus packages put in place by the developed countries to mitigate the impact of the crisis by increasing aggregate demand. In this regard it said:

How does Africa feature in the discussion on the global increase in aggregate demand? The answer is that Africa has not featured in this discussion except in asides that refer to the limited ability of emerging and developing countries to undertake fiscal stimulus programmes.

The reality is that once more Africa has drifted to the periphery, contrary to what we sought to achieve, that is to place the challenge of Africa's development at the centre of the global agenda arguing, as Yoshiro Mori did, that "there will be no stability and prosperity in the world in the C21st century unless the problems of Africa are resolved."

The situation emphasizes the vitally important imperative that among the things we must reenergise our programmes focused on:

Relying on our resources to achieve Africa's development, inspired by the objective to encourage self-reliance;
Promoting our regional and continental integration, including building trans-boundary infrastructures; and,
Building the international solidarity movement to help ensure the necessary resource transfer and access to market which Africa needs to achiever her development.

In this context, the question that remains to be answered is what is to be done! In this regard I would like to propose Six (6) steps forward.
First of all we should recall what Haile Selassie said 50 years ago that:

The task on which we have embarked, the making of Africa will not wait. We must act, to shape and mould the future and have our imprint on events as they pass into history. We seek… to determine whether we are going and to chart the course of our destiny.

During the 50 years since the founding of the Organisation of African Unity, our Continent has taken many collective decisions that answer the question, whither are we going? And therefore chart the course of our destiny.

Accordingly and fortunately, we are not faced with the task to elaborate the fundamental policies that will result in the renaissance of Africa. This work has been done. The work that has been done has taken into account our many painful experiences since we freed ourselves from the shackles of imperialism, colonialism and apartheid. This includes the lessons from our journey to achieve Africa's rebirth in a situation in which we were constrained by a global political geometry defined by the Cold War and institutions dominated by Africa's erstwhile colonial masters, by violent conflicts among ourselves, including the horrendous Genocide in Rwanda, constrained by domination by leaders who were nothing less than rapacious monsters, failures to implement such far-sighted programmes as the Lagos Plan of Action for the socio-economic transformation of Africa, by the prevalence among our ruling elites of a culture of self-enrichment through theft and corruption and by the demobilisation of the masses of the people, turning them away from the task to engage in continuing struggle as their own liberators.

The challenge we confront is to answer the question practically what shall we do to translate the policies and programmes our Continent has adopted to achieve Africa's renewal into reality?

We must therefore identify the practical steps we must take to achieve this objective.

One of these is to build and nurture an intellectual cadre committed to the transformation of Africa as visualised by leading African patriots and thinkers for 150 years, from Tiyo Soga, to Uhadi waseluhlangeni, and Haile Selassie, and onward to Cheik Anta Diop, Ayi Kwei Armah and Ngugi wa Thiong o', among others.

An urgent task in this regard is to rebuild and sustain our universities and other centres of learning, attract back to Africa the intelligentsia that has migrated to the developed North, build strong links with the intelligentsia in the African Diaspora, and give the space to these the time and space they need to help determine the future of the Africans.

Another is to develop the capacity in our state, government, business and civil society institutions to implement the already agreed Continental programmes, which visualise a renewed Africa of peace, democracy, development, unity and pride in its place as 'the driving force behind vibrant development of human society in the 21st century" of which Japanese Prime Minister Yoshiro Mori spoke.

What this surely means, among other things, is that we should resurrect the African Renaissance Movement which many African patriots in many African countries launched at the beginning of the 21st century, which sought to mobilise and unite the African masses so that, once more, as we did in the struggle against colonialism and apartheid, we act our own liberators.

When I spoke at an occasion in August to launch the South Africa chapter of this Movement, I said that, "To be a true African is to be a real force in the cause of the African renaissance, whose success in the new century and millennium is one of the great historic challenges of our time."

Further, we quoted the Senegalese, Cheik Anta Diop when he said, "the African who has understood us is the one who, after reading our works, would have felt a birth in himself, of another person, impelled by an historical conscience, a true creator, a Promethean carrier of a new civilisation and perfectly aware of what the whole earth owes to his ancestral genius in all domains of science, culture and religion."

The African Renaissance Movement of which l speak should indeed seek to inspire the millions of the African masses to 'feel a birth in themselves, of another person, a true creator, a Promethean carrier of a new civilisation." Together we must be the organisers of this Movement.

Yet another practical step we must take is to increase the momentum in terms of which the development and transformation of Africa came to take its rightful and prominent place in the global agenda, binding the rest of the world to interact with our Continent according to principles, objectives and programmes Africa itself has set, which include the critically important objective of the eradication of poverty and underdevelopment.

In this context our international partners agreed to join us in creating the necessary institutional mechanisms to give practical effect to the kind of partnership spelt out in NEPAD and effectively address the challenges of 'mutual accountability."

In this regard we must engage in struggle to ensure that the global agenda addresses such imperatives as capital and other resource transfers to Africa, the conclusion of the Doha Development Round, as a development round and the democratisation of the international system of governance, which must not be delayed any further.

Another matter on which we must act is to achieve African cohesion in terms both of what the Continent says to itself and what it says to the rest of the world.

The objective to achieve the unity of our Continent, perhaps as a federation or confederation of states, will take time to achieve. However this does not mean that Africa cannot speak with one voice on matters of common interest.

Of critical importance in this regard is that we should do everything possible to strengthen both the regional organisations, the regional Economic Communities, such as SADC and ECOWAS and the African Union and its institutions, including the Pan African Parliament and others.

There is no gainsaying the fact that all these institutions are relatively weak, which militates against the capacity of our Continent to act collectively to advance the interest of the African masses as a whole, and which is a fundamental condition for the success of each of our countries, as was the unity of the oppressed in our country with regard to the struggle for our liberation.

The last point we would like to make in the context of what we need to do to help ensure that Africa claims the 21st Century relates to what Tiyo Soga said almost 150 years ago that we must develop the media and the means to communicate correctly about who we are, what we are, what we are doing to change our condition and where we seek to be tomorrow and theday after.

Thus should we, on the objective and the subjective planes, act to determine our destiny to 'keep our' 'individuality' and 'distinctiveness,' amid the wreck of empires and the revolution of ages,' as Tiyo Soga put it.

Unfortunately during its third year Soga's paper, *Indaba* ceased publication. However, it was replaced by Isigidimi sama Xhosa, which became a platform for vigorous debate among the emerging African intelligentsia. One of its most active contributors was Jonas Ntsiko, who also wrote under the pen-name, Uhadi waselulangeni, "the Harp of the Nation."

In 1883 Uhadi wrote an article that sought to alert Africans about the threat posed to all of them by the system of imperialism and colonialism, regardless of their specific nationality. Specifically the article mentioned how the kings of the baSotho and Xhosa and the communities they led had fallen victim to colonialism, having engaged in separate struggles to oppose this eventuality.

Uhadi therefore urged that the Africans should start an open debate among themselves to determine how they should respond to this threat, suggesting that only their unity would guarantee their independence.

This sentiment was repeated 30 years later when the African National Congress was established in 1912, with the task, among others, "to bury the demon of tribalism."

Uhadi wrote:

Therefore create in the newspaper the arena for those who have this view or the other, to talk about things that serve the welfare of the black people and theirs, so that we come to know what should be done. On that arena will appear orators and poets who will sing our praises and others who will hail the Other. What harm will it do if a MoSotho who speak in what you consider a contrary voice says:

> Arise offspring
> Of the Thaba Bosuin,
> The Wild dog howls
> The white wild dog,
> Hungry for the bones
> The bones of the Moshoeshoe
> Moshoeshoe who sleeps
> On the mountain top.
> Weighed down by its bloated stomach
> Bulging with the bones of kings,
> Its mouth is bright red
> Red with the blood of sandile

In the article we have just cited, Uhadi said:

> It would seem to me that during these days, when the nation has been subjugated, when it is victim to protracted wars and a short period of peace, the patriots call on their leaders both to give them the time and space they need to determine the future of the nation and to give due importance to the history the oppressed are making.

In concluding this essay we would do well to remember that as Uhadi said almost 130 years ago "Arise offspring of Thaba Bosuni, the wild dog howls, still, hungry for the bones of the children of Africa."

In this situation we should give ourselves the time and the space the African masses need to determine the future of our contin   al a times conscious of the glorious history that Africans have m   through the ages and the history they continue to make to this day as they strive to claim the 21st Century.

Notes, References and Works Cited

Introduction

1. Wilks, Ivor, *One Nation, Many Histories-Ghana Past and Present* (Accra: Anansesem Publications, 1996).
2. Ibid.
3. Obituary statement "On the Passing of Chinua Achebe" jointly issued by Wole Soyinka and J.P. Clark on March 23 2013.

Chapter Four – Fragments from a Chest of Memories

1. Professor Martin Banham, Critical Responses to African Theatre. Wole Soyinka's *The Lion and the Jewel.* Royal Court Theatre, London, December 1966, April 2012 National Theatre, Black Plays Archive. The correspondence Banham quotes is held in Special Collections, Brotherton Library, University of Leeds.
2. The National Archives, Kew, PREM 13/2826.
3. Wole Soyinka, "Bangs big and small," *The Weekend Guardian: Africa – Voices of protest and pride*, 21–22 October 1989, pp. 21, 23.

Chapter Eight – Being, the Will, and the Semantics of Death: Wole Soyinka's *Death and the King's Horseman*

1. Penelope Gilliat, "A Nigerian Original," *Observer*, 19 Sept. 1965, p.25.
2. Personal Interview with Wole Soyinka by Henry Louis Gates Jr., 7 Oct. 1979.
3. John Mortimer, "Nigeria-Land of Law and Disorder," *Sunday Times*, London, 28 Nov.1965, p.5.
4. John Povey, "West African Drama in English," *Comparative Drama*, 1, No.2 (1967), 110.

5. Wole Soyinka, "The Writer in a Modern African State," in *The Writer in Modern Africa,* ed.Per Wasberg (New York : Africana Publishing, 1969), p.15.
6. Wole Soyinka, "Live Burial," in his *A Shuttle in the Crypt* (London: Rex Collings/Eyre Methuen, 1972), p.60.
7. Wole Soyinka, *The Man Died: Prison Notes of Wole* Soyinka (London: Rex Collings, 1972), p.13.
8. Soyinka, *The Man Died*, p.1.
9. Angus Calder, rev. of *The Man Died, New Statesman*, 8 Dec.1972, p.866.
10. Soyinka, The Man Died, p.13.
11. Wole Soyinka, *Madmen and Specialists* (London: Eypre Methuen, 1971).
12. Mel Gussow, "Psychological Play from Nigeria," *New York Times*, 3 Aug. 1979, p.38.
13. Wole Soyinka, "The Fourth Stage: Through the Mysteries of Ogun to the Origin of Yoruba Tragedy" in *Myth, Literature and the African World* (Cambridge, Eng. Cambridge Univ. Press, 1976).
14. Soyinka, "The Fourth Stage," p.150
15. Soyinka, "The Fourth Stage, "p.150.
16. Soyinka, *The Man Died*, p.88.
17. Soyinka, "The Fourth Stage," p.158.
18. Duro Ladipo, *Oba Waja* in *The Nigerian Plays*, ed. and trans. Ulli Beier (London: Longmans, 1967). Beier's translation captures almost nothing of the lyricism of the Yoruba.
19. Soyinka, "The Fourth Stage," p.142.
20. Chicago, Goodman Theatre, 1979.
21. Samuel Johnson, *A History of the Yorubas: From the Earliest Times to the Beginning of the British Protectorate*, ed. O. Johnson (London: Routledge & Kegan Paul, 1969).
22. William Shakespeare, *Hamlet*, Act III, Scene 1.
23. The Traditional Yoruba read, "Owe l'esin oro, bi oro ba sonu owe ni a fi n wa a."
24. Personal interview with Soyinka by Henry Louis Gates Jr., 5 Oct. 1979.
25. Wole Soyinka, "Drama and the Revolutionary Ideal," in *In Person: Achebe, Awoonor and Soyinka*, ed. Karen Morell (Seattle: Institute for Comparative and Foreign Area Stud. 1975), pp. 68–69.
26. Personal interview with Wole Soyinka by Nancy Marder, July 1979.

Chapter Sixteen – There Is Always Somewhere We Call Home

1. Anyidoho, Kofi, *The Place We Call Home and Other Poems* (Oxfordshire: Ayebia Clarke Publishers, 2011).
2. Mazrui, Ali, *The Trial of Christopher Okigbo* (London: Heinemann, 1975).

3. Achebe,Chinua, *There Was A Country : A Personal History of Biafra* (New York: Penguin, 2012).
4. Olguibe, Olu, Okigbo, Obiageli, "The Return of Christopher Okigbo" in *Fathers and Daughters, An Anthology of Exploration,* ed. Ato Quayson (Oxfordshire: Ayebia Publishers, 2008).
5. Soyinka, Wole, *Harmattan Haze on an African Spring* (Ibadan: Bookcraft, 2012).
6. Soyinka, Wole, *You Must Set Forth at Dawn* (Methuen/Bookcraft, 2006).

Chapter Eighteen – Glimpses of "Uncle Wole"

1. Adams A., Sutherland-Addy E., (Eds.) *The Legacy of Efua Sutherland*: *Pan African Cultural Activism* (Oxfordshire: Ayebia Clarke Publishing Limited, 2008).
2. Gibbs, J., "Marshall of African Culture" or Heir to the Tradition?" Wole Soyinka's Position on His Return to Nigeria in 1960" in V. Mihailovida-Dickman (Ed). Cross Culture 12 "Return" in Post-Colonial Writing: A Cultural Labyrinth. Amsterdam, Rodopi.
3. Efua Sutherland wrote *Edufa* (1967) inspired by Euripides' *Alcestis* while Soyinka has a number of adaptations including *Euripides' Bacchae* which he entitled *The Bacchae of Euripides: A Communion Rite* (1973).
4. Soyinka, Wole, *Ake: The Years of Childhood* (New York: Vintage, 1989).

Chapter Twenty – African Art from Past to Present (Works Cited)

1. Adam, L., *Primitive.* (London: Pelican, 1940).
2. Bravamann, R.A., *Open Frontiers: The Mobility of Art in Black Africa* (London: Cambridge University, 1973).
3. Einstein, C., *Negerplastik* (Leipzig: Verlag der Weissen Bucher, 1915).
4. Fagg, W.B., *Tribes and Forms in African Art* (New York and London: Tudor, 1965).
5. Herskovits, M., *Dahomey: An Ancient West African Kingdom* (New York: J. J. Augustin, 1938).
6. Morgan, L.M. "*Ancient Society*" in White, L.A., ed. (Boston: Harvard University Press, 1877).
7. Olbrechts, F.M., *Congolese Sculpture* (New Haven: Human Relations Area Files, 1982).
8. Roth, H.L., *Great Benin, Its Customs, Art and Horrors* (Halifax: F. King, 1903).
9. Willet, F., *Ife in the History of West African Sculpture* (London and New York: Thames and Hudson, 1967).

Chapter Twenty-One – The Protestants From Abeokuta: Fela Antikulapo-Kuti and His Cousin

1. Collins, John, *Fela-Kalakuta Notes* (Amsterdam: KIT Publishers, 2009).
2. Ibid.
3. Ibid.
4. Ibid.
5. Agyeman-Duah, Ivor, *Wole Soyinka – Author, Playwright, Activist* (Paris, London: The Africa Report, October 2008, pp106–109).
6. Soyinka, Wole, "Night" in *A Selection of African Poetry*, edited by K.E. Senanu and T. Vincent (London: Longman, 1976).
7. Collins, John, *Fela-Kalakuta Notes* (Amsterdam: KIT Publishers, 2009).
8. Soyinka, Wole, *The Unappeasable Price of Appeasement* (Ibadan: Bookcraft, 2011).
9. Ibid.

Chapter Twenty – Five "A Tomboucktonyan Anti-Palanquinity"

Tombouckton (from Tomboucktou or Timbuktoo) a city in Mali, a key centre of learning for the Islamic World. It had great libraries and higher educational institutions from medieval times. The Ahmed Baba Institute holds 30,000 manuscripts. It is a UNESCO World Heritage Site; a symbol of enlightenment.

Anti-Palanquinity denotes a readiness to question sacred cows, as well as question and subvert a negative or unjust status quo.

A palanquin is a covered litter, bearing a high personage, carried by four or more people. Rulers in many West African countries are carried in palanquins during festive occasions.

Ogun, a Yoruba divinity, is the classical warrior and is seen as a powerful deity of metal work. In the syncretic traditions of contemporary Brazil, Ogun is mighty, powerful and triumphal "yet is also known to exhibit the rage and destructiveness of the warrior whose strength and violence must not turn against the community he serves." Linked to this theme is the new face he has taken on in Haiti, that of a powerful political leader who gives strength through prophecy and magic. It is Ogun who is said to have planted the idea in the heads of, led and given power to the slaves for the Haitian Revolution of 1804.

"... *if they take you... in that night*." This is the last line of James Baldwin's "Open Letter to My Sister Angela Y. Davis" of 19th November 1970. Angela Davis is an intellectual and a Pan Africanist activist.

Oshogbo, The Ogun-Osogbo Sacred Grove is a sacred forest along the banks of the Oshun River just outside the city of Osogbo, Ogun State, Nigeria. It is among the last of the sacred forests which usually adjoined the edges of most Yoruba cities before extensive urbanisation. In recognition of its global significance and its cultural value, the sacred Grove was inscribed as a UNESCO World Heritage Site in 2005.

"…*all fullness dwell*" is taken from the Bible, Colossians 1: 19

Notes on Contributors

Chief Emeka Anyaoku is the third Secretary-General of the Commonwealth of Nations who served from 1990–2000 and afterwards as President of the Royal Commonwealth Society in London (2000–2007) and also of The Royal African Society, London (2000–2007). Chief Anyaoku served as the International President of the Swiss based World Wide Fund from 2002–2009, Chairman of the Presidential Council on Foreign Affairs, Nigeria and a Trustee of the British Museum. He also previously served in Nigeria's diplomatic service and was the country's Foreign Minister in 1983. Chief Anyaoku has received decorations from Nigeria and the highest national civilian honours of Cameroun, Lesotho, Madagascar, Namibia, Republic of South Africa and Trinidad and Tobago's Trinity Cross and a Knight of the Grand Cross of The Royal Victorian Order from Queen Elizabeth II. He served as a Distinguished Visiting Fellow at the Centre for the Study of Global Governance at the London School of Economics from 2000–2002. In 2003 the Institute of Commonwealth Studies, University of London Professorial Chair was established in his name. He is a holder of 32 honorary doctorate degrees from universities around the world. His publications include: *The Racial Factor in International Politics* (1977); *The Missing Headlines* (1997); *The Inside Story of the Modern Commonwealth* (2004) among others. Chief Anyaoku studied Classics at the University College of Ibadan graduating with a University of London Honours degree in 1959.

Ngũgĩ wa Thiong'o is the Director of the International Centre for Writing and Translation, University of California Irvine, where he is also a Distinguished Professor of English. Before then, he was Visiting Professor at New York University (1989–92), Yale University (1988) and at Amherst, Mount

Holyoke, New Hampshire, Smith and East Massachusetts, Northwestern University and earlier in his career, a Fellow in Creative Writing at Makerere University in Uganda and Lecturer at the University of Nairobi. A social activist and critic, he suffered detention in Kenya for his writings and especially the peasants and workers staged play, *Ngaahike Ndeenda*. Ngugi's famous and award-winning publications include, *Weep Not, Child* (1964); *A Grain of Wheat* (1967); *Petals of Blood* (1977); *Devil on the Cross* (1980); *I Will Marry When I Want*; *Matigari* (1986); *Wizard of the Crow* (2006); *Something Torn and New: An African Renaissance* (2009); *Dreams in a Time of War: A Childhood Memoir* (2010) which the *Washington Post* says has a "startling similarity with Barack Obama's *Dreams From My Father*."

A campaigner of African languages preservation he has travelled and lectured extensively around the world. Ngugi has beenthe1984 Robb Lecturer at Auckland University in New Zealand. He has also delivered the 1996 Clarendon Lectures in English at Oxford University, the 1999 Ashby Lecture at Cambridge, and the 2006 MacMillan Stewart Lectures at Harvard University. He has received seven honorary doctorates and many other honours including the 2001 Nonino International Prize for Literature.

Nadine Gordimer is a South African novelist, founder of the Congress of South African Writers, and an African National Congress activist during the anti-Apartheid era, won the Nobel Prize for Literature in 1991. Among her 15 novels are: *A Guest of Honour* (1970); *Burger's Daughter* (1979); *July's People* (1981); *My Son's Story* and *None to Accompany Me* (1994). Gordimer received in 1961 the W.H. Smith Commonwealth Literary Award and won the Booker Prize in 1974 for *The Conservationist*. Her non-fiction works include *The Essential Gesture*; *On The Mines* and *The Black Interpreters*.

She has received over 15 honorary degrees. The include some from: Yale, Harvard, Columbia, York and Cambridge Universities and the Cape Town University. For her writings and also political and social activism, she was made a Member of Order of the Southern Cross, South Africa, has received the Order of Friendship, Republic of Cuba and holds a Presidential Medal of Honour of the Republic of Chile. She has lived in South Africa for almost all the 89 years of her life.

Sefi Atta is the author of *Everything Good Will Come*; *Swallow*; *News from Home* and *A Bit of Difference* is the winner of the 2006 Wole Soyinka Prize for Literature in Africa and the 2009 NOMA Award for Publishing in Africa. Also a playwright, her radio plays have been broadcast by the BBC and her stage plays have been produced internationally.

Margaret Busby is a publisher, writer and broadcaster of Afro-Caribbean parentage. After graduating from Royal Holloway, University of London, Busby became in the 1960s, the youngest and first black woman publisher in the United Kingdom. She co-founded Allison and Busby Limited and for over twenty years served as its Editorial Director publishing the works of C.L.R. James, Buchi Emecheta, Sam Greenlee, George Lamming, Ishmael Reed, John Edgar, Nuruddin Farah and several others. She also became the Editorial Director of Earthscan and published Frantz Fanon and Carolina Maria de Jesus. Busby edited the well-known, *Daughters of Africa: An International Anthology of Words and Writing by Women of African Descent* (1992); radio work and dramatizations include the Radio 4 award-winning play, *Minty Alley*, works of C.L.R. James, Wole Soyinka, Walter Mosley and Henry Louis Gates Jr. Stage productions include, *Sankofa* (1999); *Yaa Asantewaa – Warrior Queen* (2001–2002). Busby has also written extensively for *The Guardian, Independent, Observer, New Statesman* and *The Times Literary Supplement*. She was awarded the Order of British Empire (OBE) and is currently Chair of the Soroptimist International of Leeds Literary Prize, and was previously Chair of The Caine Prize for African Writing, The Orange Prize, The Independent Prize for Foreign Fiction and The OCM Bocas Prize for Caribbean Literature.

Nicholas Westcott is The European Union's (EU) Managing Director and most senior diplomat for Africa based in Brussels since 2011. Westcott, who was awarded The Most Distinguished Companion of the Order of St. Michael and St. George and served at one time as the British High Commissioner to Ghana and Ambassador to Cote d'Ivoire, Burkina Faso, Niger and Togo. He had also previously served as Deputy High Commissioner to Dar es Salaam in Tanzania from 1993–1996 where earlier in his career he was a Research Associate at the University of Dar es Salaam. Westcott was also Head of Economic Relations at the Foreign and Commonwealth Office responsible for managing the Birmingham G8 Summit in 1998, was Representation Member to the EU in Brussels and has s served at one time as Minister Counsellor of the British Embassy in Washington, DC. A Fellow of The Royal Geographical Society, Westcott's PhD in African Studies is from the University of Cambridge. He has publications on Tanzania and African economic history.

Toni Morrison is an African American novelist, literary critic, editor and currently Robert F. Goheen Professor in the Humanities at the Lewis Centre for the Arts at Princeton University. She previously taught at Yale and Howard Universities. Morrison won the Nobel Prize for Literature in 1993 and both the Pulitzer Prize for Fiction and Anisfield-Wolf Book Award in 1988 for her novel, *Beloved* (1987), which has also been produced as a film starring Oprah

Winfrey and Danny Glover. In 2012 she received the US Presidential Medal of Freedom, the highest civilian honour in America. Her other novels include: *Song of Solomon* (1977), which received the National Book Critics Circle Award, *Tar Baby* (1981); *Jazz* (1992); *Paradise* (1997) and *Home* (2012). She has also received an honorary Doctor of Letters from Oxford University (2005), the Commander of Arts and Letters, Paris (1993) and the Robert F. Kennedy Award (1988).

Like Soyinka, Morrison believes in the blending of the arts and created in 1994 the *Princeton Atelier* an arts curriculum project of composers, musicians, poets and writers. Morrison's works with *Atelier* have included the lyrics, *Honey and Rue* commissioned by Carnegie Hall, and *Four Songs* and *Sweet Talk*. She wrote the libretto for the opera *Margaret Garner*. She was in 2006, Guest Curator at the Musee du Louvre where she curated *The Foreigner's Home*.

Ama Ata Aidoo is the founder of Mbaasem, a literary organisation that supports women writers, is best known as an international award-winning playwright, poet and university Professor. Until recently from 2004– 2010, she was a Professor in Africana Studies at Brown University and before then – from 1993–1999 served as Visiting Professor, Department of English, Hamilton College, Distinguished Visiting Professor, Department of English, Oberlin College, The Madeleine Haas Russell Visiting Professor of Non-Western and Comparative Studies, Brandeis University, Visiting Professor, English and Theatre Departments, Smith College and others. She has also taught at the University of Cape Coast and started her teaching career at the University of Ghana where she had earlier graduated from. Famous works of hers include *The Dilemma of a Ghost* (1965); *Anowa* (1970); *No Sweetness Here* (1970); *Our Sister Killjoy* (1977); *Someone Talking to Sometime* (1985) which won the Nelson Mandela Prize for Poetry; *Changes: A Love Story* (1991) winner of the Commonwealth Writers Prize for Africa; *An Angry Letter in January* (1992); *The Girl Who Can and Other Stories* (1997); *Diplomatic Pounds and other Stories* (2012). She has also edited *African Love Stories – An Anthology* (2006). Aidoo has served as a Minister of Education in Ghana and has before been on the boards of The Ghana Broadcasting Corporation, The Medical Council and The Arts Council of Ghana. Among others, she is a Member of the Order of Volta of the Republic of Ghana.

Henry Louis Gates Jr. is The Alphonse Fletcher University Professor and Director of the W.E.B. Du Bois Institute for African and African American Research at Harvard University. He previously taught at Duke, Cornell and Yale universities and is the author of over twenty books including, *The*

Signifying Money (1989); *Loose Canons: Notes on the Culture Wars* (1992); *Figures in Black* (1989); *Colored People* (1994); *Thirteen Ways of Looking at the Black Man* (1995). He is also the General Editor of *The Schomburg Library of Nineteenth Century Black Women Writers* (in 30 volumes); and is co-author with Cornel West of *The Future of the Race* (1996). He has co-edited with Kwame Anthony Appiah, *A Dictionary of Global Culture* (1997); and *Africana: The Encyclopaedia of the African and African American Experience* (1999). He has written and produced twelve documentaries including the BBC and PBS series, *Into Africa* and *Wonders of the African World*, *African American Lives*, a genealogical investigation and DNA analysis of famous African Americans and *Black in Latin America*. Some few years ago, he made the headlines with his wrongful arrest by the Cambridge police sparking a Race debate that drew into the fury the President of the United States, Barack Obama. He is the recipient of fifty-one honorary degrees and awards, including the MacArthur Fellowship. Gates graduated from Yale University and worked on his PhD in English Literature with Soyinka at Cambridge University.

Ato Quayson is the Director of the Centre for Diaspora and Transnational Studies at the University of Toronto since 2005 is also Professor of English. He was previously a Fellow at Pembroke College, Cambridge University and a Member of the Faculty of English where he eventually became a Reader in Commonwealth and Postcolonial Studies. He was Director of the African Studies Centre at Cambridge from 1998–2005 and is General Editor of the *Cambridge Journal of Postcolonial Literary Inquiry* and Editor of *The Cambridge History of Postcolonial Literature* (2 Volumes). Quayson was a Cambridge Commonwealth Scholar from 1991–1994, a Fellow of the Cambridge Commonwealth Society, Research Fellow at the University of Oxford, Research Fellow at the W.E.B. Du Bois Institute for African and African American Research at Harvard University, Visiting Professor at the University of California, Berkeley and has lectured extensively in Europe, Africa, North America and the Middle East. He is also a Fellow of the Ghana Academy of Arts and Sciences. Quayson's publications include: *Strategic Transformations in Nigerian Writing* (1997); *Postcolonialism: Theory, Practice or Process?* (2000); *Relocating Postcolonialism* (with David Theo Goldberg, 2000). He wrote the Introduction and Notes to Nelson Mandela's *No Easy Walk to Freedom*, Penguin Classics edition, 2002 and is the editor of *Fathers and Daughters-An Anthology of Exploration* (2008). Quayson graduated from the University of Ghana and had his PhD from Cambridge University.

Femi Johnson is Wole Soyinka's trusted and best friend. Soyinka has remarked of Johnson in *You Must Set Forth at Dawn as* "..Perhaps what drew me to him was part recognition of that road not taken, the suppressed artist within a nattily suited businessman." A successful businessman and insurance broker, Johnson was until his death, Managing Director of Femi Johnson and Company and a devotee of theatre and opera. He was also an actor who played lead roles in some of Soyinka's plays including: *Kongi's Harvest* and *Madmen and Specialists*.

Yemi Ogunbiyi is a university lecturer, media executive and dramatist. Ogunbiyi is described as Soyinka's younger and bosom friend and a former student of his who later worked with him at the Drama and Literature Department of the University of Ife together with Biodun Jeyifo and Kole Omotoso. Ogunbiyi later taught at Brooklyn College in New York. He was once Managing Director of *Daily Times*, Executive Director of *The Guardian* Newspapers in charge of Public Affairs and Marketing and currently serves as Chairman of Tanus Communications and member of Global Advisory Board at Repro India Limited.

Cameron Duodu is a Journalist and African Affairs specialist in the last half century who has lived in London since 1983 and written for *The Observer, The Sunday Times, The Times, The Financial Times, The Independent, The Guardian* and the *New African* all of London, De Volkskrant (Amsterdam), *The Mail and Guardian, City Press* (Johannesburg) and *Ghanaian Times*, Accra. He is also a creative writer of short stories, poems and plays. In 1960 he was made editor of the Ghana edition of *Drum* magazine and worked with *New Nation* magazine earlier from which he moved to Ghana Broadcasting Service. By this time, "Tough Guy in Town" his first short story had not only been read on Radio Ghana but made him more interested in radio drama. The Service produced one of his plays, *The Powers That Be* and his novel *The Gab Boys* published initially by Andre Deutsch in London was translated into German as *Flucht nach Akkra*. Three other plays, *Mammy Water's Lover; Poison Pen;* and *Mango Blood* have been performed as have several other poems on the BBC. Born in 1937 and without formal education in any of these genres, Duodu is self-educated largely through classes that were organised by the People's Educational Association with lecturers from the then Extra Mural Studies Department of the University of Ghana where he studied for his Ordinary and Advanced Level certificates.

Kwame Anthony Appiah Before he left for New York University in early 2014, he was the Lawrence S. Rockefeller University Professor of Philosophy at the University Center for Human Values at Princeton University. For years he was the Charles H. Carswell Professor of Afro-American Studies and Philosophy at Harvard University and was previously Professor at Yale, Cornell, Duke and Cambridge universities. A world renowned philosopher and according to *Forbes* magazine one of the seven best thinkers in the world, one of 100 for *Foreign Policy*, he was given the National Humanities Medal by President Obama in 2012. He is the Herskovits award-winning author of *In My Father's House: Africa in the Philosophy of Culture* (1992); *The Ethics of Identity* (2005); *Ethics in a World of Strangers* (2008); *The Honor Code: How Moral Revolutions Happen* (2010), some of which have been translated into Chinese, Dutch, French, German, Hebrew, Indonesian, Italian, Korean, Portuguese and Spanish. He is also general editor of Amnesty International's *Global Ethics Series*. With Henry Louis Gates Jr., he co-edited *Africana: The Encyclopaedia of the African, African American Experience* (1999) with Wole Soyinka as Chair of the Advisory Board and of *Transition* of which the two are publishers with Soyinka as Advisory Chair. Anthony Appiah is also a detective novelist of *Avenging Angel* (1990); *Nobody Likes Letitia* (1994); *Another Death in Venice* (1995). He studied Philosophy at Cambridge earning a First Class and a PhD.

Ali A. Mazrui is Director of the Institute of Global Cultural Studies at the State University of New York, Binghamton, an Albert Schweitzer Professor-at-Large in the Humanities and Development Studies at the University of Jos in Nigeria; Andrew D. White Professor-at-Large Emeritus and Senior Scholar in Africana Studies at Cornell University, New York; Walter Rodney Distinguished Professor at the University of Guyana and the BBC Reith Lecturer in 1979. Mazrui has also been Visiting Professor at Stanford and at National University of Singapore. He is currently the Chancellor of the Jomo Kenyatta University of Agriculture and Technology in his home country Kenya. A distinguished political scientist, Mazrui was selected by both *Prospects* and *Foreign Policy* magazines as one of 100 World Intellectuals. An essayist, polemist, editor, novelist and documentary filmmaker most famous for the BBC's *The Africans: A Triple Heritage* his published books include: *The Trial of Christopher Okigbo* (1971); *A World Federation of Cultures: An African Perspective* (1976); *The Titan: Julius N. Nyerere's Legacy* (2012); *Africanity Redefined: Collected Essays of Ali Mazrui* (2002). Mazrui studied at Manchester and Columbia Universities and the University of Oxford where he was awarded a Doctor of Philosophy degree.

Maya Jaggi is one of Britain's most influential arts and culture journalists and writer. The international award-winning Jaggi has been a profile-writer and critic for the *Guardian Review* in London since 2000. She has written on literary affairs from five continents and for such publications as *The Guardian, Financial Times, The Independent, The Economist and Newsweek* and done profile writings on over a dozen Nobel laureates in Literature including: Wole Soyinka, Gunter Grass, Mario Vargas, Jose Saramago, Toni Morrison and Orhan Pamuk. She has also written on other great writers such as Chinua Achebe, Umberto Eco, Tom Stoppard, Eric Hobsbawn, Noam Chomsky and Salman Rushdie. The late Palestinian poet and literary scholar, Edward Said once described Jaggi as being in a class of her own. She is also a radio presenter contributing to the BBC and Radio 4's Any Questions? She wrote and presented, for BBC TV, the documentary, *Isabel Allende: The Art of Reinvention*. Jaggi's work has been published in anthologies including: *Lives and Works* (2002) and *Writing Across Worlds* (2004). She was Chair of The Man Asian Literary Prize in 2012 and previously a Judge of the Caine Prize, the Orange Prize, Commonwealth Writers Prize, the Banipal and David Cohen Prizes among others. She studied at Oxford University and the London School of Economics and Political Science.

'Niyi Coker Jr. is the E. Desmond Lee Distinguished Professor in African and African American Studies, Theatre and Media Studies at the University of Missouri, Saint Louis. He has served as Artistic Director of several theatre companies including K3 in Malmo, Sweden and Black Box Theatre in Bermuda. He is founding Artistic Director of the African Arts Ensemble in New York City. Coker Jr.'s staged plays include, *Quary*, on the Southern Ute Indians of Colorado in 1992; *Endangered Species* (1995) British Council Commissioned; *Preemptive*, Shaw Theatre (London) 2010. Directed Off-Broadway plays in New York include, *Booth!* a musical on the life of Edwin Booth, New York University Skirball Theatre. His work in documentary film writing and directing include, *Black Studies USA* which won the best short documentary at the Berlin Black Film Festival in Germany in 2005, the Silver Remi Award Winner at the Houston International Film Festival in 2007 and Finalist at the Hollywood Black Film Festival in 2007. Coker Jr. is also a recipient of the Washington DC Kennedy Center Merit Award. His latest feature *Pennies for the Boatman* was winner of Best Screenplay 2012 at the Madrid International Film Festival. Published books include *A Study of Music and Social Criticism of African Musician Fela Kuti* and *Ola Rotimi's African Theatre: The Development of an Indigenous Aesthetic*.

Esi Sutherland-Addy is Professor of African Literary and Cultural Studies at the University of Ghana where she has also been the Head of Language, Literature and Drama Section at the Institute of African Studies. She is the eldest daughter of the late distinguished Ghanaian playwright and cultural activist, Efua Sutherland. Prof Sutherland-Addy has for years played a leading role in the work of the Pan African Theatre Festival of Arts and Culture and is

Chairperson and Convenor of Ghana Culture Forum. She runs the *Mmofra* Foundation, a children's literary organisation in Accra. Her publications include co-editorship of: *Women Writing Africa, West Africa and the Sahel, (with Aminata Diaw, 2005); The Legacy of Efua Sutherland: Pan African Cultural Activism* (with Anne V. Adams, 2007); *Where the Beads Speaks,* (2011) a coffee-table photo/poetry/essay book with Ama Ata Aidoo.

Amowi Sutherland Phillips is Adjunct Lecturer in African Literature and Contemporary Culture at Whitworth University in the United States. Her background is in legal practice and advocacy for women and children. She serves as the international representative for the literary and cultural organisation, *Mmofra* Foundation (in memory of her mother the playwright and dramatist, Efua Sutherland) and is President of its US-based partner, Friends of *Mmofra*. She is also a developer of African cultural content for children in audio-books, electronic media and most recently, in child-centred urban spaces through her leading role in the *Playtime in Africa* children's park initiative of the *Mmofra* Foundation.

Zagba Oyortey is the Director of the Museums and Monuments Board in Ghana since 2013, Oyortey spent over twenty years working in the arts in Europe. He managed cultural groups and projects and the training of personnel in management and policy. This includes: Methodologies for Enhancing the Contemporary Use of African Artefacts: British Museum, 2006; Rethinking the Adaptation of African Stories from Television: South Africa Broadcasting Corporation, 2006; African Creative Industries in the Context of the International Centre for Creative Industries: Bahia, 2005; Arts Organisation in Acton, London and their role within the cultural economy of Ealing Borough, London, 2003; Best Value Review of Creative Industries in Greenwich: London, 2003. Oyortey had also served as consultant to the British Museum on its Africa's programme. He was a member of the Brazilian government's initiative to launch the International Centre for Creative Industries in Salvador de Bahia and of the UNESCO supported Maputo based Observatory for Cultural Policies in Africa and is a contributor to its publication, *Cultural Indicators of Development: An African Perspective* presented at The World Congress on Cultural Rights in Barcelona in 2004. Oyortey also worked as advisor to The Arts Council of England as well as Arts Officer for Greenwich Council and was Executive Directive of Adzido then the largest culturally diverse performing group in Europe that also produced the epic musical *Yaa Asantewaa Warrior Queen*. Oyortey who has written extensively on cultural issues, history and administration obtained has a PhD from Goldsmiths, University of London.

Malcolm D. McLeod was a Pro-Vice Chancellor of the University of Glasgow, Scotland and also professor of African studies. He started his career as a Research Associate at the Institute of Social Anthropology at Oxford University. He was a curator at the Museum of Archaeology and Ethnology at Cambridge University and later lecturer and Director of Studies of Magdalene and Girton Colleges, Cambridge before becoming a Fellow of Magdalene between 1972–1974. He was Keeper of Ethnography of the British Museum and in charge of The Museum of Mankind prior to Directorship of the Hunterian Museum and Art Gallery, Scotland. McLeod has been chairman of the Scottish Museums Council and was also curator, The Royal Society of Edinburgh from 1999–2002 and chairman of the Caledonian Foundation Inc. USA since 2003. In the 1960s and 70s he researched and taught in West Africa and was curator of the American Museum of Natural History's *Asante: Kingdom of Gold* (1984). He was an advisor to the setting up of The Manhyia Palace Museum. Awarded the Commander of the British Empire (CBE), McLeod's publications include: *The Asante* (1981); *Treasures of African Art* (1981); *Ethnic Sculpture* (co-author), 1985; *Joseph Epstein Collector* (co-author), 1989. McLeod read History and Social Anthropology at Hertford and Exeter Colleges at the University of Oxford graduating with an MA and BLitt.

Ekpo Eyo is deceased – he was previously Professor of African Arts and Archaeology at the University of Maryland, College Park and the first Director-General of the National Commission for Museums and Monuments in Nigeria from 1979–1986. Other public policy work included Vice-President of the Advisory Council of the International Council of Museums and of the UNESCO Committee on the Convention of the Illicit Transfer of Cultural Property. In 1980 he was awarded an Officer of the Federal Republic of Nigeria and in 1984 won the Smithsonian Regency Fellowship and the Arts Council of African Studies Association Leadership Award at Harvard University. Among his publications are, *From Shrines to Showcases: Masterpieces of Nigerian Art*; *Two Thousand Years of Nigerian Art*; co-author of *Treasures of Ancient Nigeria: A Legacy of Two Thousand years.*

John Collins is a British music professor, musicologist and World Bank Consultant, Collins has since 1952 when he came to Ghana worked on the West Africa music industry with Nigerian and Ghanaian bands and groups including, the Jaguar Jokers, Black Berets and also individuals such as Fela Kuti, E.T. Mensah, Koo Nimo, Bob Pinodo and many more. Collins has also been a film consultant for international film companies such as *Brass Unbound* for the IDTV of Amsterdam, *Highlife* for German Huschert Realfilm, *African Cross Rhythms* or *Listen to Silence* for Humanities & Sciences, New Jersey, *When the*

Moment Sings for Norwegian Visions Company. He played the role of British colonial officer in Fela Kuti's, *The Black President* and also the harmonica on Faisal Helwani and Fela's *Onukpa Shwapo* and *Yeah Yeah Ku Yeah* later labelled as *Makola Special* and *Volta Suite* recorded in Apapa, Lagos. The results of these collaborations led to over 100 journalistic and academic publications including seven books – a biography, *Fela-Kalakuta Notes* (2009); *Highlife Time* (1996); *West African Pop Roots* (1992); *Music Makers of West Africa* (1985) and others on African popular and neo-traditional music. He also did over 40 broadcasts on African music for the BBC including the series, *In The African Groove*. Collins who had his Doctorate in Ethnomusicology at the State University of New York, Buffalo has given lectures and led workshops on African music in Canada, the US, the Caribbean, the United Kingdom, Scandinavia, Holland, Germany and France among others.

Derek Walcott is an 83 year-old Saint Lucian poet who won the Nobel Prize for Literature in 1992, was one of three other laureates (including Nadine Gordimer, Toni Morrison and Wole Soyinka) who celebrated the latter's 70th birthday at Harvard University under the auspices of one of this anthology's contributors, Henry Louis Gates Jr. Well known for his epic book-length poem, *Omeros* (1990) and *The Prodigal* (2004), he is also a playwright and has published over twenty plays including *Wine of the Country* (1953) and *The Seat Damphin: A Play in One Act*. Walcott was awarded the Order of British Empire (1972); Queen's Gold Medal for Poetry (1988) and received the T.S. Eliot Prize for Poetry in 2011 as well as the OCM Bocas Prize for Caribbean Literature also in 2011.

Abena P.A. Busia is Associate Professor and Chair of Women's and Gender Studies, Rutgers School of Arts and Sciences, The State University of New Jersey where she has taught for over 30 years. She has been Senior Research Fellow and Visiting Professor at the Universities of Ghana and Cape Coast and earlier in her career, a Visiting Lecturer at the Department of African and Afro-American Studies, Yale University and an External Tutor, Ruskin College, Oxford. Her teachings have been influenced by being a black woman in the diverse migrant exile communities of Africa, Europe and America. She became President of the African Literature Association of the United States between 1993–94; a Member of the Board of Directors of the African Studies Association of United States (1992–93) and Executive Committee Chair, Modern Languages Association (Division on African Literature). Busia has received many international academic honours, awards and grants. Publications include: *Testimonies of Exile* (1990); co-editor of *Theorizing Black Feminisms: The Visionary Pragmatism of Black Women* (1993); *Song in a Strange*

230

Land; Narrative and Rituals of Remembrance in the Novels of Black Women of Africa and the African Diaspora (forthcoming) and *Traces of a Life: A Collection of Elegies and Praise Poems* (2008). Born in Ghana, she lived in Holland and Mexico before her family settled in England where she studied English at St. Anne's College, Oxford. She has DPhil in Social Anthropology (Race Relations) from Oxford University.

Adérónké Adésolá Adésànyà is an Art historian, poet, artist and cartoonist, is a Faculty Member in the School of Art, Design and Art History, James Madison University, Harrisonburg, Virginia. She is the co-author of *Migrations and Creative Expressions in Africa and the African Diasporas* (2008); *Etches of Fresh Waters* (2009) and *Carving Wood, Making History* (2011). Her essays have been published in several edited volumes and peer reviewed journals, and her cartoons featured in more than three Nigerian tabloids.

Toyin Falola is the Jacob and Frances Sanger Mossiker Chair in the Humanities and University Distinguished Teaching Professor at the University of Texas, Austin where he had previously been a Distinguished Teaching Professor and the Frances Higginbotham Nalle Centennial Professor in History. He is also the Vice-President of the African Studies Association (ASA) of the United States. Falola has published over 100 books including his award winning, *A Mouth Sweeter Than Salt* (2004). Falola is the Series Editor of the Rochester Studies in African History and the Diaspora, the Culture and Customs series of Africa by Greenwood Press and the Classic Authors and Texts on Africa series by the Africa World Press among others. He was the recipient of the Distinguished Africanist Award of the ASA and currently serves as Chair of its Herskovits Prize as well as being a Member of The M. Klein Book Prize committee for the American Historical Association and The Joel Gregory Prize committee for the Canadian ASA.

Atukwei Okai has been the Secretary-General of the Pan African Writers Association (PAWA) since it's founding in 1989. A poet and professor in African and Literary Studies, he was from 1971 to1991, President of the Ghana Association of Writers and for decades, a Research Fellow, who also taught at the University of Ghana, Legon and the University of Education, Winneba. He has written seven volumes of poetry including, *Oath of Frontonfrom* (1971); *Lorgorligi Logarithms* (1974) and has published in numerous anthologies and journals including: *The New African, Okyeame, New American Review, The Atlantic Monthly, Black World* and *Literary Cavalcade*. He has also published for children such titles as: *Slim Queen in Palanquin* (2011); *The Anthill in the Seas* (2011); *Pawpaw on a Mango Tree* (2011). Atukwei Okai is the recipient of many international awards and honours including: The Iqbal Centenary Commemorative Gold Medal by the Government of Pakistan (1979), the International Lotus Prize and Gold Medal award in 1980 by the National Council for Research in Italy and the Entertainment and Critics and Reviewers Association of Ghana, highest award, Flagstar in 1991. He has been elected a Fellow of the Royal Society of Arts, United Kingdom. He studied at the University of London in 1971 and earlier at the Gorky Literary Institute in Moscow in 1967.

Francesca Yetunde Emanuel (Nee Pereira) is referred to as 'singer and life-long collaborator' in Soyinka's *You Must Set Forth at Dawn*. She in turn says: "Yet we forge ahead shedding fear, passing milestones… to a greater tomorrow." Pereira retired from the Nigerian Civil Service where she spent over three decades as its first female administrator in 1959 and later as the first Permanent Secretary or Chief Director. She has been Commissioner of the United Nations International Civil Service Commission, New York (1987–1992), Member of the Governing Council of Abubakar Tafawa Balewa University (1989–1993); a Foundation Member of the Nigerian Environmental Forum (1986). She is also a Member of the Nigerian Institute for International Affairs (1980); a Member of the National Institute for Policy and Strategy Studies (1985); a Fellow of the Nigerian Institute of Management and currently chairperson of The Lumina Foundation. She has accomplishments in Drama, Singing, Poetry, Gardening and Dressmaking, among others. She has served as a Grand Patron of the Association of Nigerian Authors and a Trustee of the National Association of Theatre Art Practitioners. She has received international awards in all these areas. Pereira graduated from the University College of Ibadan and University College London in 1959.

Otumfuo Osei Tutu II is the 16th King of the Asantes of Ghana, an ancient African Kingdom known for the Anglo-Asante wars from the 1800s. He is also the Chancellor of the Kwame Nkrumah University of Science and Technology in Kumasi. Otumfuo's Education Fund for needy but brilliant students together with other foundations on Health-HIV/AIDS have received international acknowledgement. Together with the then President of the World Bank, James Wolfensohn they designed the Promoting Partnership with Traditional Authorities Project which looked at primary education, preventive health, cultural heritage preservation and capacity building, a novel model of development by the Bank in 2000 for the Asanteman Council. He has received several international awards including honorary doctorate degrees from the University of Glasgow, the London Metropolitan University, the Georgia State University in Atlanta, the Kwame Nkrumah University of Science and

Technology, the University of Professional Studies, Ghana and has been one of 100 influential Africans in the reckoning of the *New African* magazine. He previously lived in Britain and worked with Oxfam and the Manpower Services Commission of the London Borough of Brent in deprived communities in Harlesden, Stonebridge and Wembley during the Brixton Riots and later also worked in Canada with the Ontario Mutual Insurance Group in Toronto.

Osei Tutu II studied at the University of Professional Studies before further studies in Accounting, Human Resource Development and Public Administration at the University of North London.

John Dramani Mahama has been President of the Republic of Ghana since 2013. He previously served as Interim President after the untimely death of President John Evans Atta Mills in 2012 and before then as Vice-President. He has been a Member of Parliament from 1996 to 2008 from where he was elected to the Pan African Parliament to chair the West African Caucus. He also served as Minister of Communication and earlier as Deputy Minister in 1998 and 1999 respectively. President Mahama worked at the Embassy of Japan in Accra as Information, Culture and Research Officer and later as the International Relations, Sponsorship, Communication and Grants Manager at the Ghana Office of PLAN International, an international development charity that has committed itself to alleviating child poverty around the world. An avid reader of particularly literary works and history, he has also written extensively for both local and international media. His best-selling memoir, *My First Coup D'etat* (2012) has a background of the first military coup in 1966 that overthrew the Kwame Nkrumah Government of which his father served as minister and was subsequently arrested after the coup. He is currently writing his second book. Educated at the University of Ghana, he read History and later postgraduate studies in Mass Communication at the same university. He also studied Psychology at graduate level at the Institute of Social Sciences in Moscow.

Thabo Mbeki was President of South Africa from 1999 to 2008 and previously as Deputy President to Nelson Mandela. He was credited with many public policy initiatives, including the Black Empowerment Movement to enlarge the black middle-class and making South Africa, through the attraction of Foreign Direct Investment, Africa's engine of growth. He would however be remembered most as a Foreign Affairs President who travelled the world particularly situating Africa in its affairs and helping with the setup of the India-Brazil-South Africa Dialogue as well as leading the arguments for African leadership to participate in the G-8 and G20 meetings. He was one of the architects (with Olusegun Obasanjo of Nigeria and Abelaziz Bouteflika of

Algeria) of the New Partnership for Africa's Development and negotiated whilst still President of South Africa, the complex crisis in Burundi, the Democratic Republic of Congo, Cote d' Ivoire and Zimbabwe. After his presidency he was chief negotiator for the Sudan crisis which led to the independence of South Sudan; he has set up the Thabo Mbeki Foundation which is dedicated to Africa's Renaissance and the Thabo Mbeki African Leadership Institute affiliated to the University of South Africa. Son of Mandela's prison contemporary, Govan Mbeki, Mbeki lived in Botswana, Swaziland, Nigeria and Zambia before his presidency, has received many international honours and awards for leadership in Africa. He studied economics at the University of Sussex in Britain.

The Editors

Ivor Agyeman-Duah is the Director of the Centre for Intellectual Renewal in Ghana and currently an Advisor to The Lumina Foundation, Administrators of the Wole Soyinka Prize for Literature in Africa, an award-winning author on development and international cooperation as well as on literary issues, he is co-author and editor of *Pilgrims of the Night: Development Challenges and Opportunities in Africa* (2010) and *Africa – A Miner's Canary Into the Twenty-First Century: Essays on Economic Governance* (2013). He was part of the production team for the BBC and PBS-*Into Africa* and *Wonders of the African World* presented by Henry Louis Gates Jr. He wrote and produced the acclaimed TV series, *Yaa Asantewaa: Heroism of an African Queen*; he was chief advisor to the Arts Council of England and Ford Foundation and supported the theatrical production of *Yaa Asantewaa – Warrior Queen* performed at West Yorkshire Playhouse, Leeds, Alexandra Theatre in Birmingham and Edinburgh Festival among others; editor of the anthology, *Some African Voices of Our Time* (1995) and co-edited, with Peggy Appiah and Kwame Anthony Appiah, *Bu Me Be: Proverbs of the Akans* (2007). Agyeman-Duah received the Distinguished Friend of Oxford award from the University of Oxford (2012); Member of the Order of Volta, Republic of Ghana (2007) and won the Commonwealth's Thomson Foundation award in 1994 among others. He has held fellowships at the W.E.B. Du Bois Institute for African and African American Research at Harvard University and a Hilary and Trinity resident scholar at Exeter College, Oxford. He holds graduate degrees from the London School of Economics and Political Science (LSE) and the School of Oriental and African Studies (SOAS), London.

Ogochukwu Promise is the Founder and Chief Executive of The Lumina Foundation, Administrators of the Wole Soyinka Prize for Literature in Africa. She received the 1999 Cadbury Prize for poetry with her collection, *My*

Mother's Eye Speak Volumes, while her novel, *Surveyor of Dreams* was awarded the 1999 Spectrum Prize for prose, also in the same year. In 2000, she was awarded the Okigbo Poetry Prize for *Canals in Paradox* and again won the Spectrum Prize for prose in 2000 for her novel, *Deep Blue Woman*. In 2002, she earned the maiden ANA/NDDC Prize with *Half of Memories* as well as The Matatu Prize for children's literature the same year with *The Street Beggars*. In November 2003, she won the Flora Nwapa Prize for prose with *Fumes and Cymbals* whilst her 2004 *In the Middle of the Night* book won the first Pat Utomi Book Prize. Again, *Swollen and Rotten Spaces* and *Naked Among These Hills* were selected for the Flora Nwapa Prize for Literature as one of the best three poetry books in Nigeria respectively. Promise is an Azikiwe Fellow in Communication as well as a Fellow of Stiftung Kulturfonds and the Iowa International Writing Program. She has enjoyed fellowships in the US, Italy and Germany and travelled extensively in Europe, Africa and Asia as a scholar, playwright and poet. She is also an essayist and has written, *Creative Writing and the Muse*, *The Writer as God*, *Dreams, Shadows and Reality* and *Wild Letters in Harmattan*. She also does abstract paintings and has exhibited in Nigeria. She holds a PhD in Communication and Language Arts from the University of Ibadan.

Index